Situations and Individuals

Situations and Individuals   Paul D. Elbourne

The MIT Press
Cambridge, Massachusetts
London, England

MIT Press books may be purchased at special quantity discounts for business or sales promotional use. For information, please e-mail special_sales@mitpress.mit .edu or write to Special Sales Department, The MIT Press, 55 Hayward St., Cambridge, MA 02142.

This book was set in Times New Roman on 3B2 by Asco Typesetters, Hong Kong. Printed and bound in the United States of America.

Library of Congress Cataloging-in-Publication Data

Elbourne, Paul D.
Situations and individuals / Paul D. Elbourne.
    p.   cm. — (Current studies in linguistics ; 41)
Includes bibliographical references and index.
ISBN 0-262-05080-3 (alk. paper) — ISBN 0-262-55061-X (pbk. : alk. paper)
1. Semantics. 2. Grammar, Comparative and general—Syntax. 3. Grammar, Comparative and general—Pronoun. 4. Grammar, Comparative and general—Article. 5. Names. I. Title. II. Current studies in linguistics series ; 41.
P325.E38   2005
401'.43—dc22   2005043897

10   9   8   7   6   5   4   3   2   1

To my father
To the memory of my mother

Contents

Preface   xi

Chapter 1

Introduction   1

1.1   Overview of the Book   1

1.2   Accounting for Covariation   3

1.3   The Description-Theoretic Approach   5

1.4   Dynamic Theories   12

1.5   A Variable-Free Theory of Donkey Anaphora   34

1.6   Conclusion   39

Chapter 2

D-Type Pronouns   41

2.1   Introduction   41

2.2   Semantics   48

2.3   The Truth Conditions of Donkey Sentences   51

2.4   The Problem of the Formal Link   64

2.5   Donkey Sentences and Strict/ Sloppy Identity   68

2.6   The Other Uses for D-Type
Pronouns   79

2.7   Some Objections   83

2.8   Conclusion   91

Chapter 3

**On the Semantics of Pronouns and
Definite Articles**   93

3.1   Introduction   93

3.2   Bound and Referential Pronouns
93

3.3   The Semantics of the Definite
Article   98

3.4   Pronoun Plus Relative Clause
120

3.5   Pronouns Revisited   122

3.6   Conclusion   135

Chapter 4

Indistinguishable Participants   137

4.1   The Nature of the Problem
137

4.2   Previous D-Type Solutions
138

4.3   The Problem of Coordinate
Subjects   145

4.4   A New D-Type Solution   146

4.5   Conclusion   156

Chapter 5

Japanese *kare* and *kanozyo*   159

5.1   Introduction   159

5.2   The Basic Data   159

5.3   Previous Accounts   161

5.4   A New Account   163

5.5   Consequences for Other Theories
165

5.6   A Residual Problem   166

5.7   Conclusion   168

Chapter 6
Proper Names   169

6.1   Introduction   169

6.2   Kripke's Objections to
Descriptive Theories   173

6.3   Further Evidence in Favor of
Burge's Theory   178

6.4   Conclusion   184

Chapter 7
Conclusion   185

7.1   Expressions of Type e   185

7.2   Accounting for Donkey
Anaphora   185

7.3   Situations   186

Appendix A
DPL Calculations   189

A.1   A Conditional Donkey Sentence
in DPL   189

A.2   A Relative-Clause Donkey
Sentence in DPL   190

Appendix B
Situation Semantics Calculations
193

B.1   A Conditional Donkey Sentence
193

B.2   A Relative-Clause Donkey
Sentence   196

Notes   201

References   221

Index   231

Preface

This book deals with the semantics of the natural language expressions that have been taken to refer to individuals: pronouns, definite descriptions, and proper names. It claims, contrary to previous theorizing, that they have a common syntax and semantics, roughly that which is currently associated by philosophers and linguists with definite descriptions as construed in the tradition of Frege.

Besides advancing this proposal, I hope to achieve at least one other aim, that of urging linguists and philosophers dealing with pronoun interpretation, in particular donkey anaphora, to consider a wider range of theories at all times than is sometimes done at present. I am thinking particularly of the gulf that seems to have emerged between those who practice some version of dynamic semantics (including DRT) and those who eschew this approach and claim that the semantics of donkey pronouns crucially involves definite descriptions (if they consider donkey anaphora at all). In my opinion there is too little work directly comparing the claims of these two schools (for that is what they amount to) and testing them against the data in the way that any two rival theories might be tested. (Irene Heim's 1990 article in *Linguistics and Philosophy* does this, and largely inspired my own project, but I know of no other attempts.) I have tried to remedy that in this book. I ultimately come down on the side of definite descriptions and against dynamic semantics, but that preference is really of secondary importance beside the attempt at a systematic comparative project.

I owe a great intellectual debt to Irene Heim, whose writings and comments have inspired and improved this work at all stages of its production. This book is a revised version of my 2002 MIT PhD dissertation by the same title, for which Heim served as committee chair. I also owe a great deal to the other members of that committee, Kai von Fintel, Danny Fox, and Michael Glanzberg, for the many hours they have spent insightfully discussing this material with me. For detailed comments on drafts of various chapters, often in the form of earlier papers, I am very grateful to Daniel Büring, Noam Chomsky, Kai von Fintel, Danny Fox, Michael Glanzberg, Dan Hardt, Irene Heim, Sabine Iatridou, Stephen Neale, Uli Sauerland, Bernhard Schwarz and an anonymous *Natural Language Semantics* reviewer. I am especially grateful to Stephen Neale, who kindly acted as reviewer for the MIT Press and provided thought-clarifying comments in a very short space of time. For other valuable discussion and comments I thank Klaus Abels, Karlos Arregi, Mark Baltin, Chris Barker, Abbas Benmamoun, Lina Choueiri, Kit Fine, Lila Gleitman, Jim Higginbotham, Hajime Hoji, Polly Jacobson, David Kaplan, Richard Kayne, Ed Keenan, Richard Larson, Julie Legate, Lauren Macioce, Alec Marantz, Luisa Marti, Lisa Matthewson, Jason Merchant, Shigeru Miyagawa, Barbara Partee, Christopher Peacocke, David Peset-'sky, Colin Phillips, Paul Postal, Liina Pylkkänen, Tanya Reinhart, Mats Rooth, Barry Schein, Stephen Schiffer, Yael Sharvit, Michal Starke, Anna Szabolcsi, Satoshi Tomioka, Karina Wilkinson, Alexander Williams, Ruth Yudkin, two anonymous SALT reviewers, and five anonymous WCCFL reviewers. Special thanks to Ken Hiraiwa, Shinichiro Ishihara, Shigeru Miyagawa, Shogo Suzuki, and an anonymous FAJL 3 reviewer for giving me Japanese judgments and helping me construct examples for chapters 1 and 5.

Chapter 2 of the present work is a revised version of Elbourne 2001a, which appeared in *Natural Language Semantics*. Material from this article is reprinted here with the kind permission of Kluwer Academic Publishers.

I am extraordinarily thankful to my friends for keeping me surprisingly relaxed and happy over the last few years. Invidious as it may be to single out a proper subset thereof, I cannot neglect to thank Lee Jackson and Joanne Dixon, for much hospitality and good cheer, and my academic, avocational, and moral advisers Síofra Pierse and Liina Pylkkänen. Síofra, vivamus, mea Hibernica, atque amemus.

With gratitude for everything, this book is dedicated to my father, David Elbourne, and to the memory of my mother, Jacqueline Elbourne.

Chapter 1

Introduction

1.1 Overview of the Book

This book argues that those natural language expressions that semanticists take to refer to individuals—pronouns, proper names, and definite descriptions[1]—share more than just their semantic type. In fact, the syntax and semantics of all these expressions is based around one common structure: a definite article (or other definite determiner) that takes two arguments: an index and an NP predicate. In the course of the argumentation, it is shown that proper names have previously undetected donkey anaphoric readings. This fact has deleterious consequences for what philosophers call the direct-reference theory, which holds that the sole contribution of proper names (and maybe other items) to the truth conditions of sentences in which they occur is an individual. Further examples create difficulties for the well-known related doctrine that proper names are rigid designators (Kripke 1972). Meanwhile, from the point of view of contemporary generative grammar, the idea that pronouns, proper names, and definite descriptions have the same syntax and semantics is welcome, given the further assumption, natural within this framework, that this structure is part of Universal Grammar and is thus innately known: once a child learning its native language figures out that a certain expression is used to refer to an individual, it will thereby have access to the basic syntax and semantics of that expression, even if these are not obvious from the audible surface forms. Thus the language-acquisition task is facilitated.

I must immediately acknowledge one complication that besets my assumption that pronouns, proper names, and definite descriptions are all of type e. To account for certain phenomena, such as the ability of these expressions to be conjoined with quantifier phrases, it seems to be necessary to view them as being of type $\langle et, t \rangle$, or an intensionalized variant thereof. One could of course suppose that this is always their type, as Montague (1973) did. Alternatively, one could suppose that they are basically of type e but can have their denotations raised where necessary to the corresponding generalized quantifiers. So an expression α of type e, with normal semantic value α', could also have the semantic value $\lambda P. P(\alpha')$. See Partee and Rooth 1983 for one influential treatment of this idea. I am inclined to follow these latter authors, but even if Montague's position were correct, the argumentation in this book would still have consequences for the syntax and semantics of these expressions. I will henceforth ignore this complication and regard pronouns, proper names, and definite descriptions as straightforwardly being of type e.

To look ahead briefly, I begin by addressing the problem of donkey anaphora, concentrating mainly on pronouns, with the idea of finding out what is needed to account for this notorious problem and then bringing the other things we want to say about pronouns into line with that. In chapter 2, then, I argue that donkey pronouns should be regarded as definite articles followed by NPs that have been deleted in the phonology by NP-deletion. In chapter 3, I set out my view of the syntax and semantics of normal definite descriptions like *the table* and *the King of France*; the chapter then returns to pronouns and expands on chapter 2, showing how we can also deal with referential and bound uses of pronouns if we think that they are a kind of definite article. It thus provides a unified semantics for the donkey anaphoric, bound and referential uses of pronouns, which is surely desirable, since no language makes any lexical or morphological distinction between pronouns used with these allegedly different meanings. The prospect is discussed of unifying the syntax and semantics of pronouns thus arrived at with the syntax and semantics of normal definite descriptions. Chapter 4 fills in a gap left in the previous chapters and analyzes the problem of indistinguishable participants (to be introduced in section 1.3), which is posed by both pronouns and definite descriptions when they occur in donkey sentences. Chapter 5 analyzes the behavior of the Japanese pronouns *kare* 'he' and *kanozyo* 'she', which are shown to have interesting implications for the correct analysis of donkey anaphora and the existence and formulation of Reinhart's Rule I. In chapter 6, I argue that proper names are also to be regarded as syntactic and semantic definite descriptions, and set out the problems that this causes for the theories of direct reference and rigid designation. Finally, chapter 7 summarizes the conclusions reached, and examines the consequences of the preceding argumentation for the rivalry between description-theoretic and dynamic theories of covariation without c-command, an issue I now introduce at greater length.

1.2 Accounting for Covariation

If some linguistic item displays a covarying interpretation, the logical resource used to model this is variable binding.[2]

Empirical work on natural language has shown that for a pronoun to have the semantics of a bound individual variable, a quantifier phrase (QP) or other operator must c-command it (Reinhart 1983). Any demonstration along these lines is complicated, of course, by the possibility raised by Chomsky (1976) and May (1977), and incorporated into much subsequent work, that QPs can raise at LF (quantifier raising) and thereby c-command positions that they did not c-command on the surface. We can obviate this difficulty, however, by examining QPs inside islands for syntactic movement, in the sense of Ross 1967. The examples in (1)–(3) involve the prohibitions on extraction from relative clauses, subjects, and *if*-clauses, respectively.

(1) a. *Which boy$_2$ did the woman who met t$_2$ not like him$_2$?
     b. The woman who met every boy didn't like him.

(2) a. *Which boy$_2$ did the rumor about t$_2$ not affect him$_2$?
     b. The rumor about every boy didn't affect him.

(3) a. *Which boy$_2$ does Mary, if she meets t$_2$, ignore him$_2$?
     b. Mary, if she meets every boy, ignores him.

Note that the QP *every boy*, when embedded inside these islands, cannot bind *him* in any of the (b) examples—that is, there can be no interpretation where *every boy...him* is interpreted as "for every boy *x...x*." It seems, then, that when there is no way for a QP to occupy a position c-commanding a pronoun, it cannot give it the semantics of a bound individual variable.

On the syntactic and semantic details of variable binding in natural language, I basically follow Heim 1993 and Heim and Kratzer 1998 in supposing that what actually does the work in these cases is a λ-operator in the syntax, which creates a λ-abstract in the semantics by means of a syncategorematic rule and binds any coindexed pronouns or traces in its scope. Thus the denotation of the constituent α in (4a) is (4b), and the sentence will be true if and only if every individual that is a man satisfies this predicate.

(4) a. [every man][$_\alpha$ λ_1 t$_1$ beats his$_1$ donkey]
    b. $\lambda x.\, x$ beats x's donkey

In the system of Heim and Kratzer 1998, these λ-operators are inserted immediately below phrases that have moved and are obligatorily coindexed with the trace. In chapter 3, I will suggest some alterations to the conception of traces and indices implicit here, but the basic picture of pronouns and traces being bound by a c-commanding λ-operator will remain the same.

It is also evident, however, that pronouns sometimes display covarying readings, suggestive of binding, without being c-commanded by any obvious potential binder. The best-known cases are the so-called donkey sentences, which were discussed by the medieval logicians and came to the attention of modern philosophers and linguists through the work of Geach (1962). In Geach's classic example (5a),[3] *it* has a covarying reading, so that the sentence means, roughly, what we would express in first-order logic by (5b).

(5) a. Every man who owns a donkey beats it.
    b. $\forall x \forall y ((\text{man}(x) \wedge \text{donkey}(y) \wedge \text{owns}(x, y)) \rightarrow \text{beats}(x, y))$

We cannot maintain that the covarying reading comes about by the apparent antecedent *a donkey* raising by quantifier raising (QR) and adjoining to the root, so that it c-commands *it*. For one thing, this constituent is inside a relative clause, which, as we have seen, is an island for movement. For another thing, even if it did raise in this manner the sentence would not thereby obtain the reading that in fact it has: it would mean, "There is a donkey such that everyone who owns it beats it." We are faced with a problem, therefore.

There have been two major approaches to this problem, namely, description-theoretic solutions and dynamic binding solutions. It is a matter of considerable theoretical interest which of these approaches is right, and semanticists are currently split into opposing camps along these lines. In the next two sections, I outline the basic assumptions of each theory, as they stand at the moment, and describe the problems that each theory currently seems to face. After that, I do the same for a relatively recent but very interesting account of donkey anaphora suggested by Pauline Jacobson (2000a) within the framework of categorial grammar and variable-free semantics. One aim of this book is to show that the description-theoretic approach need not suffer from some problems with which it currently seems to be afflicted. I will tentatively suggest at the end of this work that the empirical balance may have tilted against the dynamic binding theory and the variable-free account and in favor of the description-theoretic approach.

1.3   The Description-Theoretic Approach

1.3.1   Outline of the Description-Theoretic Approach

The description-theoretic approach[4] claims that definite descriptions play a crucial role in the semantics of donkey pronouns. This admittedly vague formulation is designed to accommodate two subtypes, which, following Sommers 1982 and Neale 1990, I will call the *E-type* and *D-type* theories.

The E-Type Analysis   According to the E-type analysis of Gareth Evans (1977, 1980), donkey pronouns and certain other pronouns that he took to be anaphoric to non-c-commanding quantificational antecedents are rigidly referring expressions (in the sense of Kripke 1972—see below) that have their references fixed by description, where the description is extracted (largely) from the linguistic environment. Take (6) for example:

(6) John owns some$_i$ sheep and Harry vaccinates them$_i$.

In this example, according to Evans, *them* is an E-type pronoun and refers rigidly to the sheep that John owns.

Why was Evans insistent that these pronouns be rigid designators? According to Kripke,[5] "a designator d of an object x is rigid, if it designates x with respect to all possible worlds where x exists, and never designates an object other than x with respect to any possible world." Evans thought that this was a desirable characteristic of E-type pronouns, because of examples like (7a) and (7b).

(7) a. A man murdered Smith, but John does not believe that he murdered Smith.

   b. A man murdered Smith, but John does not believe that the man who murdered Smith murdered Smith.

Example (7a) has no reading on which it attributes to John a contradictory belief; John is simply said to believe of the murderer that he is not the murderer. But (7b), on the other hand, has a reading, perhaps the most prominent one, according to which John irrationally thinks something like, "The man who murdered Smith did not murder Smith." But how can this difference between the two sentences exist if *he* in the first sentence is interpreted as a description "the man who murdered Smith"?

The answer, says Evans, is to suppose that the pronoun does not have the interpretation of a description but instead rigidly designates a certain individual, who is determined on the basis of the descriptive content "unique man who murdered Smith (in the actual world)." So all that is contributed to the proposition expressed by *he* is an individual, and John is implicated in no contradiction if he merely believes of this individual that he did not murder Smith. On the other hand, given the possibility of *de dicto* readings of descriptions in attitude contexts, the presence of *the man who murdered Smith* in (7b) opens up the way for the reading on which John has contradictory beliefs.

How does Evans use this semantics for E-type pronouns to achieve the right results in donkey sentences?

(8) Every man owns a donkey and beats it.

The answer lies in his semantics for quantifiers. According to Evans, (8) is evaluated as follows: it is true if and only if every sentence of the form "β beats it" is true, where β is a constant naming a man who owns a donkey and *it* has as reference (in each sentence) the donkey β owns. Thus in each "β beats it" sentence, *it* is in fact referential. Evans admits that an E-type pronoun in a donkey sentence can no longer be regarded as having a reference. But he maintains that no new explanation of its role is called for.

There are, however, some serious objections to the above argument that E-type pronouns are needed.[6] It seems, in spite of the impressiveness of (7), that the requirement that the pronouns in question be rigid designators is in fact far too strict, as we see from examples like the following:

(9)   A man murdered Smith. The police have reason to think he injured himself in the process.

(10) Hob thinks that a witch killed Trigger. He also suspects that she blighted Mathilda.

As Davies (1981) and others have pointed out, these examples have the same form as (7), but they have readings that would result from the pronouns being interpreted as definite descriptions interpreted *de dicto*. The most plausible reading of (9), for example, does not require there to be any particular man such that the police believe of him that he injured himself in the process of murdering Smith. That is, the police do not need to think that they have solved the case in order for us to truthfully say (9). They just need to think that *whoever* murdered Smith injured himself in the process, perhaps because there is blood at the crime scene that does not belong to the victim. If *he* was a rigid designator referring to a particular man, or even a definite description that obligatorily scoped over the attitude verb, there would be no way to obtain this reading. This is a grave problem for the E-type analysis.

We are left, of course, with the question of how to distinguish (7a) from (7b). Neale (1990, 186) suggests that we might argue that the *de dicto* reading of (7a) is technically available but so unlikely that it is not seriously entertained. But this does not deal with the problem as reported by Evans (1977): (7a) is unambiguous, attributing only a noncontradictory belief, whereas (7b) is ambiguous, with a clearly available reading that attributes contradictory beliefs to John. If *he* really were interpreted as a definite description, the objection goes, we would expect (7a) to be ambiguous too. We cannot just appeal to the absurdity of the missing *de dicto* reading, then, since the absurd reading is clearly available when the definite description is overt. The answer, I think, lies in distinguishing between different definite descriptions that could be the interpretation of the pronoun. It is true that (7b) is ambiguous. But (11) is not:

(11) A man murdered Smith, but John does not believe that the man murdered Smith.

This, like (7a), only has a *de re* reading. That is, John is being said to believe of a particular man that he did not murder Smith. So we can say that *he* in (7a) is interpreted as a definite description after all; it is just not interpreted as "the man who murdered Smith," but instead as "the man." It seems, then, that we will need a theory that will restrict the descriptive content of pronouns of this kind to being rather minimal. I provide a theory that meets this requirement in chapter 2.[7]

The D-Type Analysis The D-type analysis of donkey anaphora and related phenomena (Cooper 1979; Heim 1990; Neale 1990; Heim and Kratzer 1998) claims that pronouns are actually interpreted as definite descriptions. It is useful to distinguish two kinds of D-type theory: those that have pronouns merely be interpreted as definite descriptions, without their having the syntax of definite descriptions too; and those that also say that pronouns spell out syntactic material that is of the form expected for a definite description. Let us call these *semantic* and *syntactic* D-type theories respectively, without overlooking the fact that both types of theories end up making claims about the semantics.

For expository purposes, it is convenient to begin with a recent syntactic D-type theory. (An earlier one is found in the latter part of Heim

1990.) Heim and Kratzer (1998, 290–293) propose that pronouns can spell out LF fragments of the kind in (12).

(12) [the [$R_{\langle 7, \langle e, et \rangle \rangle}$ pro$_{\langle 1, e \rangle}$]]

(They suppose that there is a rule stipulating that DPs consisting of a definite article followed by nothing but unpronounced items are spelled out as pronouns.) Let us consider Geach's example (13) under this analysis.

(13) [every man who owns a donkey] [λ_1 [t$_1$ beats [the [$R_{\langle 7, \langle e, et \rangle \rangle}$ pro$_{\langle 1, e \rangle}$]]]]

The relation variable $R_{\langle 7, \langle e, et \rangle \rangle}$ will be assigned the salient relation *donkey-owned-by* by the variable assignment. The individual variable *pro*$_{\langle 1, e \rangle}$ will be bound by the λ-operator below the subject, and the whole sentence turns out to be true if and only if every individual x such that x is a man who owns a donkey beats the donkey owned by x. Where appropriate, we could have simply a variable over functions of type $\langle e, t \rangle$ as the complement of the definite article here, or alternatively a variable with greater adicity than $\langle e, et \rangle$ plus the requisite number of arguments.

The same truth conditions are obtained by semantic D-type theories, such as those that view pronouns as able to be interpreted in the semantics as the value of a contextually salient function f applied to an argument x, perhaps by having semantic interpretation proceed by means of translation of natural language items into a formal language that is then subject to model-theoretic interpretation, as in Montague 1973. So pronouns would be translated as function-argument groups like "$f(x)$" (Cooper 1979; Heim 1990). In such an approach, x will be bound by the subject, and, in the standard example, f would be the function that maps each individual x in the domain to the unique donkey owned by x.

Thus the distinction between syntactic and semantic D-type theories. There is another useful distinction that crosscuts this one, between theories according to which the descriptive content can be any contextually salient function or relation and theories that give an explicit algorithm for constructing the descriptive content on the basis of the linguistic environment. Let us call these theories *contextual* and *linguistic* respectively, without overlooking the fact that the linguistic environment is part of the overall context. We arrive at the following four-way division and exemplification of D-type theories: syntactic contextual (Heim and Kratzer 1998), syntactic linguistic (the latter parts of Heim 1990), semantic contextual (Cooper 1979), and semantic linguistic (Neale 1990). (See section 2.4.2 for more details of Heim's second 1990 theory and the theory of Neale 1990.) The theory that I will present in chapter 2 falls basically into the syntactic linguistic slot, but will not fit entirely comfortably there for reasons that will become clear.

The D-type analysis might appear to suffer from a problem that arises directly from the semantics of definite descriptions. In particular, Heim (1982, 81–102) argued that the uniqueness presuppositions inherent in the semantics of these expressions[8] are not in fact met in some cases where the D-type analysis analyzed pronouns as definite descriptions. Let us first note that, in addition to the examples with a quantifier and relative clause to which we have largely restricted our attention so far, the donkey problem also arises in conditionals. So (14a) also seems to mean something like (14b), even though *he* and *it* cannot be bound by their apparent antecedents *a man* and *a donkey*.

(14) a. If a man owns a donkey, he always beats it.
      b. $\forall x \forall y ((man(x) \land donkey(y) \land owns(x, y)) \rightarrow beats(x, y))$

Now let us consider (15a) (Heim 1982, 93), which means something like (15b).

(15) a. If a man is from Athens, he always likes ouzo.
      b. $\forall x (man\text{-}from\text{-}Athens(x) \rightarrow likes\text{-}ouzo(x))$

Again, we have what is plausibly a covarying interpretation for a pronoun without the pronoun being able to be bound by its apparent antecedent. This seems to call for a D-type pronoun. But a straightforward application of the D-type strategy here, making *he* have the meaning of a definite description whose descriptive content is recoverable from the context, would have the sentence meaning the same as (16).

(16) If a man is from Athens, the unique man from Athens always likes ouzo.

That is, we end up presupposing that there is only one man from Athens, presumably an unwelcome result. On the basis of problems like these, Heim (1982) abandoned the D-type theory and went on to invent one of the ancestors of today's dynamic binding theories.

As Heim herself later pointed out, however, it is not clear that this type of example really is problematic for the D-type analysis (Heim 1990). We can neutralize the unwelcome uniqueness presupposition in (15a) by supposing that conditionals of this kind involve quantification over *situations* (Berman 1987; Heim 1990; von Fintel 1994). The work in the tradition just cited follows Kratzer (1989) in supposing that situations are parts of possible worlds, comprising individuals and properties of individuals and relations between them. A situation can, however, omit some of the properties of an individual who is in it. Individuals, in this view, are *thin particulars* in the sense of Armstrong 1978—roughly speaking, individuals in the normal sense of the term considered in abstraction from their properties. This conception affords a device that will prove useful, namely the *minimal situation* of a certain kind. The minimal situation in which Angelika Kratzer is tired (at a certain time t, in a certain possible world w), for example, contains nothing but Kratzer's thin particular and, linked with it, the property of tiredness; it does not contain the property of hunger predicated of this thin particular, even if, at time t and in world w, Kratzer was in fact both tired and hungry (Kratzer 1989). The minimal situation in which Kratzer is both tired and hungry, at t in w, is called an *extension* of the previous, smaller situation, since it contains all the individuals and properties that the smaller one did, plus some more. The device of minimal situations is useful because there is an infinite number of situations in which Angelika Kratzer is tired at t in w—the smallest one, plus all the possible extensions of it within that possible world—and yet we sometimes want to have particular distinguished situations corresponding to separate instantiations of some kind of event, so that we can count them and quantify over them. An application will be seen shortly. Situation semantics will play a significant part in this book.

As for the present case, (15a), Heim (1990) follows Berman's (1987) treatment of conditionals and quantificational adverbs. She thus supposes that examples like this involve a phonologically null universal quantifier over minimal situations. A sentence of the form [if α, β] will be true if and only if for every minimal situation s in which α is true, there is an extension of s, s', in which β is true. Furthermore, definites within β, which corresponds to the larger situations s', are allowed to make anaphoric reference back to the smaller situations s. (See chapter 2 for details.) This means that (15a) has the truth conditions in (17).

(17) For every minimal situation s such that there is a man from Athens in s, there is an extended situation s' such that the unique man from Athens in s likes ouzo in s'.

The pronoun *he* contributes the definite description "the unique man from Athens in s" to the truth conditions, meaning that we have a D-type analysis. We can see, however, that within this version the uniqueness presupposition associated with the definite description is not in the least bit counterintuitive. All that is supposed is that each situation s contains only one man from Athens, and this is correct, since the situations s are the *minimal* situations that contain a man from Athens.

At the moment, then, it looks as if the description-theoretic approach to donkey anaphora and related problems has a promising instantiation in the D-type analysis combined with situation semantics. In the next section, however, I describe a number of problems that this approach still faces.

1.3.2   Problems with the Description-Theoretic Approach

The Problem of Indistinguishable Participants   It might seem that the device of minimal situations is such a powerful one that no troublesome uniqueness presuppositions could remain to afflict the D-type hypothesis. This is not the case, however. Hans Kamp has drawn attention to sentences such as (18) (Heim 1990).

(18) If a bishop meets a bishop, he blesses him.

If we try to analyze this example too using situation semantics and D-type pronouns, the objection goes, there are no suitable functions that could be used to interpret the pronouns *he* and *him*. For what could they be? Suppose we once again use the situation variable s for the minimal situations specified by the antecedent, and s' for the extended situations specified by the consequent. If we try to interpret either pronoun as a definite description whose descriptive content is "bishop in s," we do not achieve the right results, because we end up with "the unique bishop in s" when in fact there are two bishops in each situation s. The same happens if we try "bishop who meets a bishop in s"; since meeting is a symmetrical relation, it is alleged that there is not just one bishop who meets a bishop in any situation in which a bishop meets a bishop, and hence no sense can be made of "the unique bishop who meets a bishop in s." Heim (1990) dubs this *the problem of indistinguishable participants*. It is one of the three major problems that face the D-type analysis as rehabilitated by Heim (1990). I will discuss it further in chapter 4.

The Problem of the Formal Link   Another significant problem that the rehabilitated D-type analysis faces is the problem of the *formal link* between donkey pronoun and antecedent (Kadmon 1987, 259; Heim 1990, 165–175). As explained above, a D-type analysis along the lines of Cooper 1979 has the property that the descriptive content of the definite descriptions by which D-type pronouns are interpreted is retrieved from the utterance context; it is simply some contextually salient relation or function. This, however, seems to run afoul of the following examples (Heim 1982, 21–24, 80–81; 1990, 165–175).[9]

(19) a. Every man who has a wife is sitting next to her.
     b. *Every married man is sitting next to her.

It seems uncontroversial to assume that the *married-to* relation is made salient by mention of the word *married* in (19b), and the salience of this relation is all that is needed, according to the D-type analyses currently under consideration, to produce a D-type reading for the pronoun *her* in that example. It should be able to mean "the unique entity married to x," with x bound by the λ-abstractor below the subject. The sentence has no such reading, however, creating a problem for the D-type analysis. It seems that D-type pronouns require an explicit NP-antecedent as the source of their descriptive content. I discuss this problem further in chapter 2 (section 2.4).

The Problem of Pronominal Ambiguity The third and last[10] major problem for the D-type analysis as it currently stands is the very fact that it has pronouns be systematically ambiguous between two kinds of meanings that are not easily related to each other, namely, individual variables and definite descriptions. As already mentioned, no language shows any lexical or morphological difference between pronouns used as individual variables and pronouns used as definite descriptions.[11] Only a theory in which all pronouns had the same semantics, as they do in theories of dynamic binding, would be ultimately satisfying.

The reader is referred to Heim 1990 for more details of the D-type analysis as rehabilitated with situation semantics. My own version is laid out in chapter 2. For now, suffice it to say that I take the three major problems facing this analysis to be those just outlined: those of indistinguishable participants, the formal link, and pronominal ambiguity.

1.4 Dynamic Theories

1.4.1 Outline of the Dynamic Approach
Dynamic theories of anaphora in natural language were first worked out in detail (independently) by Kamp (1981) and Heim (1982), although their work had important precursors in Karttunen 1976 and Stalnaker 1979. The view of meaning on which dynamic theories are based is essentially that of Stalnaker (1979): the meaning of a sentence does not reside in its

truth conditions, but rather in the way it changes the context or *common ground*, which is roughly the information that parties to a dialogue have in common.

To illustrate the dynamic approach to anaphora, I will show how our two donkey sentences (5a) and (14a), repeated below, are treated in Groenendijk and Stokhof's (1991) Dynamic Predicate Logic (DPL). I choose this framework because of the relative perspicuity of its semantics, which shows clearly the way the dynamic view of meaning affects anaphoric possibilities, and also because of the simplicity of the formal language (first-order predicate logic (PL)) for which the semantics is defined. It should be emphasized, however, that DPL is not in itself an adequate compositional account of natural language semantics. For one thing, it can provide a compositional account of meaning only at the clausal level—it can combine PL translations of clauses into larger formulas, and give a semantics for the whole, but it has little to say about how the meanings of the lexical items in a clause combine compositionally within it. (It does insist that indefinites be translated by ∃ and universal quantifiers by ∀, though.) For a more thoroughly compositional dynamic account of natural language semantics based on some of the same principles as DPL, we have to turn to Groenendijk and Stokhof's (1990) Dynamic Montague Grammar. See also van Eijck and Kamp's (1997) compositional version of Kamp's original (1981) Discourse Representation Theory (DRT); the 1981 version of DRT has often been criticized for not incorporating compositionality as a methodological principle.

DPL, then, has the same syntax as ordinary predicate logic.[12] The models on which the semantics is based are also ordinary extensional first-order models, consisting of a domain D of individuals and an interpretation function F, which assigns individuals to individual constants and sets of n-tuples of individuals to the n-place predicates. Variable assignments are also done in the well-known way, being functions from the set of variables to the domain. So far, then, all is familiar.

The innovation comes in the semantics proper. To start with, the semantic values of formulas are represented as sets of ordered pairs of variable assignments. The idea is that a sentence is uttered in the context of a particular (possibly empty) assignment of variables to individuals. After it has been processed, it might leave the assignment different. This ability to change the context (in particular, the variable assignment) is the factor singled out as constitutive of the meaning of a sentence in dynamic theories. But we do not want to consider the effect of a sentence on just one particular variable assignment. The meaning of a sentence will be the way it affects variable assignments in general. Roughly speaking, we might think of the meaning of a sentence on this view as being a function that will take a variable assignment as its argument and give as output another (possibly identical) variable assignment. But the meaning will not actually be a *function*, because a given sentence might leave more than one variable assignment (in association with conditions placed on the properties of the values of the variables) as a possible representation of how the world is claimed to be by the sentence. So we could think of the meaning of a sentence as a function from variable assignments to *sets* of variable assignments. Equivalently, the meaning of a sentence would be a *relation* between variable assignments and variable assignments—a given variable assignment g, considered as the context of utterance of a sentence, could in principle be mapped to more than one possible output assignment. We arrive, then, at the conception of semantic values of formulas as sets of ordered pairs of variable assignments.

Let me illustrate with the case of the formula $\exists x P x$. Uttered in a context that supplies an assignment g, the idea is that this formula will leave as open possibilities those assignments that differ from g at most on the value that they assign to x, and that, furthermore, assign to x an individual that has property P. The semantic value of $\exists x P x$, then, will be that relation between assignments such that the second assignment differs from the first at most with respect to x, and maps x to some individual that is P. Using the notation "$h[x]g$" to indicate that h differs from g at most on its assignment to x, we can express this more concisely as in (20).

(20) $[\![\exists x P x]\!] = \{\langle g, h\rangle \mid h[x]g \ \& \ h(x) \in F(P)\}$

Moving on to the general case, $\exists x \phi$, we must recognize that ϕ too might have dynamic effects. So in effect we first take into account the fact that there is existential quantification by changing the input assignment g to assignments that can differ from g with respect to x, and then allow for this set of assignments to be altered by ϕ, yielding the final output assignments. The rule, then, is (21).

(21) $[\![\exists x \phi]\!] = \{\langle g, h\rangle \mid \exists k : k[x]g \ \& \ \langle k, h\rangle \in [\![\phi]\!]\}$

We need only two more rules, those for atomic formulas and conjunction, before we can give a simple example of DPL in action, capturing an anaphoric dependency that arguably cannot be captured without descriptive pronouns according to other treatments of pronouns. Here are the rules:

(22) $[\![R t_1 \ldots t_n]\!] = \{\langle g, h\rangle \mid h = g \ \& \ \langle [\![t_1]\!]_h \ldots [\![t_n]\!]_h\rangle \in F(R)\}$

(23) $[\![\phi \wedge \psi]\!] = \{\langle g,h \rangle \mid \exists k : \langle g,k \rangle \in [\![\phi]\!] \ \& \ \langle k,h \rangle \in [\![\psi]\!]\}$

Atomic formulas do not produce new variable assignments in and of themselves. They take an assignment and give the same one as output, provided that it meets the condition specified. Formulas that do this are called *tests*. $[\![t]\!]_h$ is $F(t)$, if t is an individual constant, and $h(t)$, if t is a variable.

The conjunction rule, meanwhile, is especially important in DPL, since as well as being used for natural language *and*, it is also used to translate sequences of sentences without *and*. The standard example in the dynamic literature is (24).

(24) A man walks in the park. He whistles.

This seems to have a meaning like that of (25), where the obvious interpretations should be provided for the one-place predicates.

(25) $\exists x(Mx \wedge Px \wedge Wx)$

It is hard to see how a compositional translation procedure could arrive at (25) as a translation of (24), however. Respecting the sentence break, we can only come up with the two separate formulas in (26).

(26) a. $\exists x(Mx \wedge Px)$
     b. Wx

If we allow conjunction, in accordance with intuition, to translate the sentence sequencing procedure, we arrive at (27).

(27) $\exists x(Mx \wedge Px) \wedge Wx$

Now if we interpreted this with a static semantics, the variable in Wx would not be in the scope of the existential quantification. But with DPL semantics, this is not the case. We are now in a position to interpret (27), using the rules we have seen. The calculation is given in (28).[13]

(28) $[\![\exists x(Mx \wedge Px) \wedge Wx]\!]$
   $= \{\langle g,h \rangle \mid \exists k : \langle g,k \rangle \in [\![\exists x(Mx \wedge Px)]\!] \ \& \ \langle k,h \rangle \in [\![Wx]\!]\}$ (by 23)
   $= \{\langle g,h \rangle \mid \exists k : \langle g,k \rangle \in \{\langle g,h \rangle \mid \exists k' : k'[x]g \ \& \ \langle k',h \rangle \in [\![Mx \wedge Px]\!]\}$
   $\& \ \langle k,h \rangle \in [\![Wx]\!]\}$ (by 21)
   $= \{\langle g,h \rangle \mid \exists k : \exists k' : k'[x]g \ \& \ \langle k',k \rangle \in [\![Mx \wedge Px]\!] \ \& \ \langle k,h \rangle \in [\![Wx]\!]\}$
   (by reduction)
   $= \{\langle g,h \rangle \mid \exists k : \exists k' : k'[x]g \ \& \ \langle k',k \rangle \in \{\langle g,h \rangle \mid \exists k'' : \langle g,k'' \rangle \in [\![Mx]\!]$
   $\& \ \langle k'',h \rangle \in [\![Px]\!]\} \ \& \ \langle k,h \rangle \in [\![Wx]\!]\}$ (by 23)
   $= \{\langle g,h \rangle \mid \exists k : \exists k' : k'[x]g \ \& \ \exists k'' : \langle k',k'' \rangle \in [\![Mx]\!] \ \& \ \langle k'',k \rangle$
   $\in [\![Px]\!] \ \& \ \langle k,h \rangle \in [\![Wx]\!]\}$ (by reduction)

$$= \{\langle g,h \rangle \mid \exists k : \exists k' : k'[x]g \ \& \ \exists k'' : \langle k',k'' \rangle \in \{\langle g,h \rangle \mid h = g$$
$$\& \ h(x) \in F(M)\} \ \& \ \langle k'',k \rangle \in \{\langle g,h \rangle \mid h = g \ \& \ h(x) \in F(P)\}$$
$$\& \ \langle k,h \rangle \in \{\langle g,h \rangle \mid h = g \ \& \ h(x) \in F(W)\}\} \qquad \text{(by 22)}$$
$$= \{\langle g,h \rangle \mid \exists k : \exists k' : k'[x]g \ \& \ \exists k'' : k'' = k' \ \& \ k''(x) \in F(M)$$
$$\& \ k = k'' \ \& \ k(x) \in F(P) \ \& \ h = k \ \& \ h(x) \in F(W)\}$$
$$\text{(by reduction)}$$
$$= \{\langle g,h \rangle \mid h[x]g \ \& \ h(x) \in F(M) \ \& \ h(x) \in F(P) \ \& \ h(x) \in F(W)\}$$
$$\text{(by =)}$$

So, if we are to represent the effect that processing (24) has on the information of a hearer, and if we use variable assignments with associated conditions to represent the way the world is being claimed to be, we end up saying the following: that, starting from an assignment g, we can arrive only at assignments h that differ from g at most in the assignment to x, and that are such that $h(x)$ is a man who walks in the park and whistles. In other words, we have introduced a new entity, x, and claimed that x is a man who walks in the park and whistles. This has the effect of altering the information state of the hearer in the same way that processing (25) would. So Wx does in effect end up being bound by the existential quantifier in (27), even though it is not syntactically in its scope.

Implicit in this explanation is the conception of truth in dynamic semantics. I just said that DPL uses variable assignments and associated conditions to represent the way the world is being claimed to be. We can see that in the above case the sentence will be true if there is at least one output assignment h that differs from g at most in the assignment to x, and that is such that the individual to which x is mapped satisfies the conditions given. In fact, this requirement, that there be at least one output assignment h for an input assignment g, is the general criterion of truth in DPL and similar dynamic systems.

(29) ϕ is true with respect to g in a model M iff $\exists h : \langle g,h \rangle \in \llbracket \phi \rrbracket_M$.

As we can appreciate by reviewing the rules introduced so far, and the calculation in (28), DPL works by placing successive conditions on possible output assignments; if any output assignment satisfies all of them, the sentence is true.

The crucial step in the calculation in (28), if one can be isolated, is really the one that derives the second line. This is the step that ensures that, in Groenendijk and Stokhof's terminology, the bindings from the left conjunct of (27) are passed on to the right conjunct. We produce the semantic value for $\exists x(Mx \wedge Px)$, which is a certain set of pairs of assignments $\langle g,k \rangle$; since the assignments k are the outputs of processing this formula, they must contain an entry for x, with associated conditions that x be a man who walks in the park. These assignments k are then the input to processing Wx, which just adds one more condition on x. Groenendijk and Stokhof (1991) call connectives that have this power to pass on bindings from their left argument to their right one *internally dynamic*. Another possible property of connectives or operators is that of being *externally dynamic*, which means being able to pass on bindings outside their arguments to constituents yet to come. Both conjunction and the existential quantifier are both internally and externally dynamic.

Let us now move on to consider implication, which is the final ingredient that we will need to be able to deal with conditional donkey sentences in DPL.

(30) $[\![\phi \to \psi]\!] = \{\langle g, h \rangle \mid h = g \ \& \ \forall k : \langle h, k \rangle \in [\![\phi]\!] \Rightarrow \exists j : \langle k, j \rangle \in [\![\psi]\!]\}$

We can see that implication is internally dynamic, as conjunction is, since it passes on the assignments k from its left argument to its right one. However, it is not externally dynamic: the output assignments h must be identical to the input assignments g. In this respect the rule is like that for the interpretation of atomic formulas (22). The rule for implication is externally static because we cannot have the pronouns *he* and *it* picked up by any binder inside the first sentence in (31).

(31) If a man owns a donkey, he beats it. *He hates it.

Implication, then, will translate natural language *if... then*. It will also be used with universal quantification in the manner familiar from ordinary predicate logic (as in $\forall x(Fx \to Gx)$).

We translate (32) as (33).

(32) If a man owns a donkey, he beats it.

(33) $\exists x(Mx \wedge \exists y(Dy \wedge Oxy)) \to Bxy$

Note that the variable y in Bxy in (33) is not in the syntactic scope of $\exists y$; the translation thus mimics the structure of the natural language sentence and imports the donkey pronoun problem. As a straightforward calculation shows (see appendix A.1), the DPL semantics once more brings it about that the syntactically free variable is in fact bound. We end up with (34).

(34) $\{\langle g, h \rangle \mid h = g \ \& \ \forall k : (k[xy]h \ \& \ k(x) \in F(M) \ \& \ k(y) \in F(D)$
      $\& \ \langle k(x), k(y) \rangle \in F(O)) \Rightarrow \langle k(x), k(y) \rangle \in F(B)\}$

The internally dynamic nature of implication ensures that the assignments k that we end up with after processing the antecedent of the conditional are passed on to be the inputs for processing the consequent. By the time the antecedent is processed, the assignments k contain the variables x and y, and there are associated conditions on the entities that these may be mapped to; the consequent just adds one more condition. Note that the variables x and y in the final subformula Bxy receive identical treatments in (34), even though one of them (x) is syntactically bound in (33) and the other (y) is, as it were, a donkey variable. Thus dynamic semantics can claim to give one semantics to bound pronouns and donkey pronouns, a notable accomplishment.

To deal with the other type of donkey sentence, we need a DPL rule for the universal quantifier. This is as follows.

(35) $[\![\forall x\phi]\!] = \{\langle g,h\rangle \mid h = g \;\&\; \forall k : k[x]h \Rightarrow \exists m : \langle k,m\rangle \in [\![\phi]\!]\}$

Consider the translation (37) for (36).

(36) Every man who owns a donkey beats it.

(37) $\forall x((Mx \wedge \exists y(Dy \wedge Oxy)) \rightarrow Bxy)$

Here again, the variable y in the last atomic formula is not syntactically bound; the existential quantifier does not have scope beyond the translation of the relative clause, as in the English sentence. The donkey problem is replicated, therefore. It will come as no surpise by now, however, that DPL semantics ensures that this variable does end up bound. The semantic value of the formula is that in (38).

(38) $\{\langle g,h\rangle \mid h = g \;\&\; \forall k : (k[xy]h \;\&\; k(x) \in F(M) \;\&\; k(y) \in F(D)$
      $\&\; \langle k(x),k(y)\rangle \in F(O)) \Rightarrow \langle k(x),k(y)\rangle \in F(B)\}$

This is exactly the same as the semantic value in (34), a neat result; the calculation is given in appendix A.2.

Before we leave this introduction to dynamic theories, I wish to bring out the great similarity between DPL and contemporary discourse representation theory. Without going into details of the method of translation and interpretation, let me just state that (39) would have the translation (40) in the formal language of van Eijck and Kamp 1997, and that this structure would have the semantic value in (41).

(39) If a^2 man owns a^3 donkey, he$_2$ beats it$_3$.

(40) $\neg(u_2 \bullet \text{man}(u_2) \bullet u_3 \bullet \text{donkey}(u_3) \bullet \text{own}(u_2,u_3) \bullet \neg\text{beat}(u_2,u_3))$

(41) $\{\langle s,s'\rangle \mid s = s' \wedge \neg \exists s''[s[u_2,u_3]s'' \wedge s''(u_2) \in I(\text{man}) \wedge s''(u_3)$
      $\in I(\text{donkey}) \wedge \langle s''(u_2),s''(u_3)\rangle \in I(\text{own}) \wedge \neg\langle s''(u_2),s''(u_3)\rangle$
      $\in I(\text{beat})]\}$

For the sake of consistency with their article, I have used van Eijck and Kamp's notation in (41). The differences from what we have seen are slight, however: for variables ranging over assignment functions, s and superscripted variants are used; where Groenendijk and Stokhof write "$h[x]g$," van Eijck and Kamp would write "$g[x]h$," and the interpretation function for constants is called I. It can readily be seen that (41) is exactly equivalent to Groenendijk and Stokhof's (34).

1.4.2 Problems with the Dynamic Approach

Let us turn now from the exposition of the basic mechanisms of DPL to the question of what advantages and disadvantages it and related dynamic theories have with respect to the description-theoretic approach, which we examined in section 1.3. One possible advantage immediately springs to mind. Recall that theories that solve the problem of covariation without c-command by positing the existence of D-type pronouns nevertheless continue to translate bound and referential pronouns as simple individual variables. Pronouns are ambiguous in these theories, then, in spite of their uniform surface forms. Dynamic theories, on the other hand, translate bound, referential, and donkey pronouns all as individual variables. It might seem, then, as if they had a significant advantage over D-type theories in this respect.

The question is not so straightforward, however. If dynamic theories could translate all uses of pronouns as individual variables, this would indeed be a notable accomplishment. But as it turns out there are three significant classes of pronouns that can be handled perfectly well by the D-type theory, but that cannot be handled at all, as far as I can see, by dynamic theories.

The Problem of Disjunctive Antecedents The first class is that discussed by Stone (1992), and exemplified in (42).

(42) If Mary hasn't seen John lately, or Ann misses Bill, she calls him.

The D-type theory has the requisite flexibility to deal with this example. Roughly, choosing the definite description "the woman" for *she* and "the man" for *he*, the truth conditions come out to be the following: for every minimal situation s such that *either* Mary hasn't seen John lately in s *or* Ann misses Bill in s, there is an extended situation in which the woman in s calls the man in s.[14] But, as Stone shows, there is no evident way dynamic theories can deal with sentences like this. Pronouns are translated by individual variables in such theories, of course, but in the normal run of things no suitable variables will be introduced by any components of the two sentences in the antecedent of (42), since all the NPs there are definite. It was suggested by Partee and Rooth (1983) that a phrase like *Mary or Ann* be allowed to introduce a new variable, with the condition that its value be either Mary or Ann, but the *or* in (42) does not conjoin names but sentences. Even if we expand our dynamic theories to allow *or* to introduce a propositional variable when it conjoins sentences, no sense can be made of the notion that the value of such a variable could somehow be taken on by the pronouns in the present case. Stone sees no way dynamic theories could handle this type of example, and I do not either, unless they stipulatively introduced D-type pronouns too. On this possibility, see below.

The Problem of Deep Anaphora   Jacobson (2000a, 89, note 12) shows that some pronouns that have a covarying interpretation not only do not have c-commanding antecedents, but do not have any linguistic antecedents at all. In other words, they are *deep anaphors*, according to the well-known distinction of Hankamer and Sag (1976). Jacobson's example is as follows.

(43)   *A new faculty member picks up her first paycheck from her mailbox.*
         Waving it in the air, she says to a colleague:
         Do most faculty members deposit it in the Credit Union?

Note that *it* must have a covarying interpretation here, something like "for most faculty members $x \ldots x$'s paycheck...." All the machinery with which dynamic systems account for covariation without c-command involves certain linguistic expressions introducing new variables into the variable assignments that are used to interpret forthcoming discourse. So there is no evident way they can deal with covariation with no linguistic antecedent whatsoever.

D-type theories, on the other hand, have no difficulty accounting for (43). The relation *paycheck-of* is made salient by the faculty member's waving her paycheck in the air, and we are thus able to interpret the pronoun as "the paycheck of x" (for most faculty members x). It is, of course, open to dynamic theories to account for examples like this by availing themselves of D-type pronouns, as well as dynamic binding. I will examine this possibility below in connection with the next problem.

The Problem of Neontological Pronouns   The third set of examples I have in mind are a subset of the so-called *paycheck pronouns* and *pronouns of laziness*, of which (44) and (45) are classic examples.[15]

(44) John gave his paycheck to his mistress. Everybody else put it in the bank.

(45) This year the president is a Republican. Next year he will be a Democrat.

The relevant readings of these sentences are those according to which everybody else put their own paycheck in the bank, and next year we will have a new president, who, in contrast to the present one, will be a Democrat. No one puts John's paycheck in the bank in (44), and no one switches parties in (45).

A note on terminology before we examine why sentences like these pose a problem for dynamic theories. I am not aware of any precise definition of the term *paycheck pronoun* having been given. It is normally defined by ostension, in connection with sentences like (44). Pronouns of laziness are defined by Geach (1962) as those replaceable in paraphrase with exact repetitions of their antecedents. So both *it* in (44) and *he* in (45) are pronouns of laziness: we could replace them by *his paycheck* and *the president*, and the sentences would mean the same. The class of pronouns I am interested in is not pronouns of laziness, however, since there are some pronouns of laziness that are not particularly problematic; (46) is an example.

(46) I saw the president. He and the secretary of state were talking about their ranches.

In this example, *he* could be replaced without evident change in meaning and with only minimal awkwardness by *the president*, but it could very well be a referential pronoun, and thus (relatively) unproblematic from the standpoint of any theory.

The property of (44) and (45) that I'm interested in is, roughly speaking, that the pronouns *it* and *he* in these sentences introduce wholly new entities. As we have seen in the previous discussion, pronouns in dynamic theories are translated as variables. The system is such that for a pronoun to be coreferential with a previous expression, or to covary on the basis of a previous expression, the same variable that is used to translate the pronoun must have been introduced by the previous expression into the set of assignments that result from processing it. (See, for example, the third line of (28).) But none of this machinery can be of any use here. The intuitive antecedent for *it* in (44) is *his paycheck* in the previous sentence. It is not clear that any dynamic theory would have this expression introduce a variable at all, since it is definite and the power of introducing variables of this kind is normally confined to indefinites. But even if *his paycheck* could somehow introduce a variable in the relevant way, the wrong results would ensue, since *it*, if it was translated by the same variable, would then refer to John's paycheck. An exactly analogous problem arises with *the president* and *he* in (45). The problem for dynamic theories is that these pronouns seem to refer to entities that cannot have had any variable introduced for them by the previous discourse. Since they introduce new entities, I will call such pronouns *neontological pronouns*.

Now the fact that (44) and (45) pose a problem for dynamic theories has not gone unnoticed in the literature, although I don't know if the problem has been explicated as I just did. To my knowledge, two solutions have been proposed for it, which I will now examine.

Chierchia (1992, 1995) proposes that both dynamic binding and the D-type strategy are available in natural language.[16] In many examples, pronouns would be ambiguous between dynamically bound pronouns and D-type pronouns. But neontological pronouns would have to be D-type pronouns. Now as Chierchia himself acknowledges (1995, 117), this approach seems to suffer from an obvious drawback, which is that it is theoretically unparsimonious. Occam's razor dictates that theories that use only one of these two powerful devices are to be preferred to theories that use both. It remains to be seen, of course, whether any nonmixed theory can account for all the facts, but I personally think that the undesirability of using both is so great that our efforts should be concentrated for the forseeable future on finding some way to avoid this. And indeed the present work is an attempt to do just that, since I attempt to show that the D-type approach does not suffer from the problems that seem to affect it, discussed in section 1.3. Of course the D-type approach has no problem with (44) and (45); Cooper 1979 already contains successful D-type analyses of these sentences.

But we should not dismiss Chierchia's mixed strategy as quickly as this. Chierchia himself (1995, 118–119) has given three additional considerations in its favor, and a further interesting argument has been advanced in support of it by Kurafuji (1998, 1999). Let us begin by examining Chierchia's own arguments. First, he says that we can account for the presence of both weak and strong readings of donkey sentences if we let the weak reading be derived by his dynamic binding system (I omit the details) and have the strong reading be derived by a D-type pronoun. The distinction between weak and strong readings is as follows. With some donkey sentences, it seems that the action of the matrix verb is visited on all the relevant donkeys; an example is (47) (Heim 1990, 151).

(47) If a farmer owns a donkey, he deducts it from his taxes.

This is the strong reading (or the ∀-reading, in the terminology of Chierchia 1992, 1995). In other donkey sentences, however, there is no such exhaustivity. The stock example is (48) (Pelletier and Schubert 1989; Chierchia 1992), where it is clearly not being asserted that anyone put *all* their dimes in the meter.

(48) Everyone who had a dime put it in the meter.

This is the weak reading (Chierchia's ∃-reading). The problem, of course, is how to derive both readings, and Chierchia's view, which says that two completely different mechanisms are needed, cannot be taken lightly.

The problem with this argument, however, is the following. Chierchia seems to be taking it for granted that D-type pronouns cannot give rise to weak readings. It is true that the most straightforward implementations of a D-type approach do seem to predict that only strong readings will be available. For (48), for example, following Heim's (1990) approach, we seem to predict that the sentence will be true if and only if for every pair of an individual x and a minimal situation such that x has a dime in that situation, x puts the dime in that situation in the meter. This is a strong reading. This cannot be the whole story, though. The D-type analysis says basically that some pronouns have the semantics of definite descriptions. It makes the prediction, then, that sentences with D-type pronouns will have the readings that the corresponding sentences with overt definite descriptions will have. And it is beyond doubt that the sentence with an explicit definite description corresponding to (48) in fact has a weak reading, as we see in (49).

(49) Everyone who had a dime put the dime in the meter.

While this example is perhaps slightly awkward, it is clearly grammatical, and it clearly does *not* imply that anyone put all their dimes in the meter. There is no problem in principle, here, then, for the D-type theory, since the prediction it makes is fulfilled. There is a problem in that the most straightforward situation semantics used in conjunction with the D-type theory predicts only strong readings. But this is likely to be a technical problem with that situation semantics, perhaps having to do with too rigorous an insistence on strictly *minimal* situations being quantified over. For further discussion, see Heim 1990. I am not convinced, then, by Chierchia's first argument that the D-type theory needs to be supplemented by dynamic binding.

Chierchia's second argument (1995, 118) to this effect is that anaphora in straightforward donkey sentences like (32), (36), and (47) is completely automatic and not affected by what he calls pragmatic factors; the examples where he abandons dynamic binding and turns to D-type pronouns, however, are supposed to be affected by these pragmatic factors. The kind of pragmatic factor that Chierchia appears to have in mind is that certain discourses involving cross-sentential anaphora, for which he would use D-type pronouns, can be made awkward by manipulating the information that the hearer has. He gives the examples in (50) and (51) (1995, 9).

(50) a. ??I hope that John has an apartment in Paris. I believe he hasn't sold it.

    b. I hope that John still has an apartment in Paris. I believe he hasn't sold it.

(51) a. ??John doesn't have a car. Paul has it.

    b. John doesn't have a car anymore. Paul has it.

The (a) examples improve when, in the (b) examples, we are given reason to suppose that certain hypothesized entities do indeed exist. Since regular donkey sentences are not affected by this kind of manipulability by contextual factors, Chierchia says, we have evidence that two different mechanisms are at work.

This argument, however, neglects the fact that contrasts like those in (50) and (51) do in fact surface in ordinary donkey sentences. The slight level of awkwardness (really just a need for a rich context) that is detectable in (50a) and (51a) is also present in (52a) and (53a).

(52) a. ??If a man doesn't have a car, Paul has it.

    b. If a man doesn't have a car anymore, Paul generally has it.

(53) a. ??I believe that every man that I hope has an apartment in Paris hasn't sold it.

    b. I believe that every man that I hope still has an apartment in Paris hasn't sold it.

I find that the facts do not warrant the distinction between straightforward donkey sentences and the rest that Chierchia alleges, then. One might also ask if the two classes of sentence that Chierchia distinguishes here do indeed correspond to the classes of those that can and those that cannot be dealt with by dynamic binding.

The third and final argument that Chierchia makes in support of his mixed approach is as follows. He compares (54), which he would analyze in terms of dynamic binding, to (55), which he claims must involve quantification over events (1995, 119).

(54) When a dog is black, it is always mean.

(55) When John walks in, he always turns on the light.

Chierchia's basic point seems to be that the similarity between (55) and (54), in combination with the idea that (55) involves quantification over events, makes it likely that (54) involves quantification of a similar structure. This is obviously only circumstantial evidence at best. But it also fails to take into account the fact that a D-type analysis that uses situation semantics, along the lines of Heim 1990, would in fact assign similar quantificational structures to these two sentences: both would be true if and only if every member of a certain set of minimal situations (those of a dog's being black, or John walking in) can be extended to a situation with some other property (the dog being mean, John turning on the light). Chierchia's point really has no force.

The argument advanced by Kurafuji (1998, 1999) in favor of a mixed approach is slightly more elaborate. To appreciate it, we must examine the question of what instances of cross-sentential anaphora can and cannot be dealt with by dynamic binding, according to Kurafuji and Chierchia. The diagnostic they use for determining when a pronoun can and cannot be dynamically bound is basically the distinction between externally dynamic and externally static operators that we have already examined above in connection with Dynamic Predicate Logic. Recall that on the basis of examples like (24), repeated here as (56), it is typically assumed in dynamic theories that existential quantification is externally dynamic.

(56) A man walks in the park. He whistles.

The point is that the existential quantifier, which is the operator with greatest scope in the first sentence, also seems to bind *he* in the second sentence. Not all operators have this extended reach, however. In particular, it is assumed by Chierchia and Kurafuji on the basis of examples like (57) and (58) that universal quantifiers and negation do not have this property. That is, they are externally static.[17]

(57) Every man walks in the park. *He whistles.

(58) a. It is not the case that a man walks in the park. *He whistles.
     b. No man walks in the park. *He whistles.

The conclusion is that when we find anaphora that cannot be simple co-reference taking place into a domain closed off by a static operator, like the universal quantifier and negation, the anaphoric element cannot be a dynamically bound pronoun and must be a D-type pronoun.

Kurafuji (1998, 1999), then, makes the important and interesting claim that the distribution of different third-person pronouns in Japanese is governed by whether they occur in a position that can be dynamically bound, according to this conception. Specifically, he claims that the null pronouns are ambiguous between variables and D-type pronouns, and the overt *so*-series of pronouns have to be variables, and hence cannot appear in positions where Chierchia would have a D-type pronoun. To begin with, both types of pronouns can be referential and bound in straightforward examples (Kurafuji 1999, 54–57). In (59) we see that both types of pronouns can be used inside a donkey sentence (1998, 129), as we would expect if Kurafuji is right. (Donkey sentences with quantifiers and relative clauses can also contain either.)

(59) John-wa hon-o   ka-eba,   sore-o/∅ yom-u.
     John-TOP book-ACC buy-COND it-ACC   read-PRES
     'As for John, if he buys a book, he reads it.'

But the situation is different when we have a sequence of two sentences, the first of which is universally quantified, as in (60) and (61) (1998, 130; 1999, 64, 94).

(60) Dono seehin-mo   chuuibukaku kensas-are-ta.
     which product-even carefully   inspect-PASS-PAST
     Soshite ∅/??sore-wa hako-ni tsumer-are-ta.
     and   it-TOP   box-in pack-PASS-PAST
     'Every product was inspected carefully. And they were packed in
     the box.'

(61) John igai-no   dare-mo-ga   jibun-no kurejittokaado-o tsuma-ni
     John except-GEN who-even-NOM self-GEN credit card-ACC   wife-to
     watashi-ta. John-wa ∅/??sore-o aijin-ni   watashi-ta.
     give-PAST   John-TOP   it-ACC mistress-to give-PAST
     'Everyone but John gave a credit card of his to his wife. John gave
     one of his to his mistress.'

Here, and in similar examples, Kurafuji reports that a null pronoun is ac-ceptable while a *so*-series one is not. The same contrast between null and overt occurs when the potential antecedent for a pronoun is in the scope of negation, as in (62) (1998, 131; 1999, 125).

(62) Kono tatemono-ni toire-ga   na-i   ka ∅/??sore-ga henna
    this   building-in   bathroom-NOM not-PRES or   it-NOM funny
    tokoro-ni a-ru   ka-no dochiraka-dea-ru.
    place-in exist-PRES or-COP which(Q)-COP-PRES
    'Either this building doesn't have a bathroom or it's in a funny
    place.'

On the basis of these and similar examples, then, Kurafuji draws the conclusion that the null pronouns can be either variables (referential or dynamically bound) or D-type pronouns, while the *so*-series pronouns must
be variables and cannot be D-type pronouns. If this demonstration were
unproblematic, it would obviously be a rather striking vindication of
Chierchia's mixed approach to anaphora. A D-type approach that used
only static binding would lump donkey sentences like (59) in the same
category as examples like (60), (61), and (62), in that all would use D-
type pronouns, and seems to be confounded by the fact that there is a
pronoun (*sore*) that can be used in one example but not the others. But
Chierchia's approach, according to which (60), (61), and (62) but not
(59) must use D-type pronouns, seems to cut the empirical pie the right way.

Unfortunately, however, there seem to be problems with Kurafuji's se-
lection and handling of the data. Let us begin by taking a closer look at
(60), and the alleged inability of *sore* to be anaphoric back to the products. The first point to note here is that for many speakers the sentence is
in fact completely grammatical, as Kurafuji (1998, 130) acknowledges.
Furthermore, speakers I have consulted who do find *sore* degraded report
that it does not merit the two question marks that Kurafuji gives it; it is
said rather to be basically fine but just slightly awkward, perhaps "?" or
even "(?)." I personally do not get the impression that the data are robust
enough to base any conclusions on.

But let us give Kurafuji the benefit of the doubt and grant the hypothesis that there is a significant contrast here. Note that the interpretation of
the good version of (60) (with the null pronoun) is "... *they* were packed
in the box." Kurafuji (1998, 132; 1999, 65) says that the sentence can describe a situation in which all the products were first inspected and then
all packed, but cannot describe a situation in which each product was
packed as soon as it was inspected. It is not clear, then, that we even
have a D-type interpretation here at all. I cannot see anything wrong
with the hypothesis that we are dealing with a null *referential* pronoun.
But then (60) does not provide any indication that null pronouns and
sore differ in their ability to have a D-type interpretation.

We might still wonder why *sore* is ungrammatical in this sentence. A simple hypothesis that might do the job is that *sore* is a singular pronoun, or at least has a preference for being interpreted as singular. Confirmation for this hypothesis is to be found in the fact that when a plural marker is added to *sore*, as in (63), (60) becomes completely acceptable for all speakers, as Kurafuji acknowledges (1998, 142; 1999, 72).

(63) Dono seehin-mo   chuuibukaku kensas-are-ta.   Soshite
     which product-even carefully   inspect-PASS-PAST and
     sore-ra-wa hako-ni tsumer-are-ta.
     it-PL-TOP   box-in pack-PASS-PAST
     'Every product was inspected carefully. And they were packed in
     the box.'

Since Kurafuji needs to maintain that we need a D-type interpretation in this configuration in order for (60) to be relevant to his project, it seems that (63) poses a problem for his contention that *sore* cannot be a D-type pronoun.

To deal with this problem, Kurafuji does two things. First, he proposes (1998, 142; 1999, 72–77) that in fact the D-type interpretation is provided here not by the pronominal stem but by the plural marker *ra*: *ra* means "the plural entity that is P," where P is a salient property supplied by the context, as in Cooper's version of D-type pronouns, and the stem, *sore*, is still translated as a variable x. But, by a process whose exact justification is unclear, this x is subject to λ-abstraction, yielding the identity function $\lambda x. x$; the identity function takes the semantic value of *ra* as its argument, so we are left with "the plural entity that is P." This account cannot be compelling, I submit, without a justification of the λ-abstraction just mentioned. It also seems rather unintuitive that the plural marker and not the pronominal morpheme itself is the locus of the anaphora.

Kurafuji's second response to (63) is to claim (1999, 87) that there is independent evidence that *sore* can have a plural interpretation without a plural marker. He gives one example, namely (64).

(64) John-wa seezee san satsu-no hon-o   kat-ta.   Soshite
     John-TOP at most three CLASS-GEN book-ACC buy-PAST and
     sore-o yon-da.
     it-ACC read-PAST
     'John bought at most three books. And he read them.'

I do not dispute that this example is basically fine, but the speakers whose judgments I have sought say that there is nevertheless something slightly odd about *sore* here. To be more precise, Shigeru Miyagawa (personal communication) reports a strong intuition that *sore* in (64) can only have a singular interpretation and has to refer to the *collection* of the three books. There is an implication that the three books were all sold at once, perhaps actually in one package. The sentence becomes degraded if it is assumed that there were three separate acts of book buying, and there is some effort to be made in concentrating on the "sold-in-one-package" reading. The slight oddness that results seems, in fact, to be at the same level and of the same kind as that experienced in (60) by the speakers who find that sentence slightly degraded. I see no reason to attribute the slight oddness of (60) to anything other than the fact that here the use of *sore* requires the hearer to zero in on the reading whereby the products are considered as a collection, despite the fact that the inspection (presumably) considers them one by one.

About (61) I can be more brief. Speakers report that *sore* does indeed merit Kurafuji's two question marks (if not more) when it is considered under the interpretation shown, namely "John gave one of his credit cards to his mistress." But if it is presupposed that each man has exactly one credit card, and the sentence is considered under the interpretation "John gave his credit card ...," speakers find that there is an improvement, and that *sore* here becomes only mildly degraded, as above. I would attribute the mild residual effect here to the fact that *sore* is a distal demonstrative, often to be translated as "that" (Kurafuji 1999, 56). Compare English (65).

(65) Everyone apart from John gave his credit card to his wife. John gave it/?that to his mistress.

In the absence of any notable justification for the distal demonstrative features, it is not surprising that some examples like this are slightly awkward.

I can also be fairly brief about Kurafuji's (62). Here speakers report that if *sore-ga* (nominative) is changed to *sore-wa* (topic-marked), the sentence becomes fine.

(66) Kono tatemono-ni toire-ga   na-i   ka sore-wa henna
     this   building-in bathroom-NOM not-PRES or it-TOP funny
     tokoro-ni a-ru   ka-no dochiraka-dea-ru.
     place-in exist-PRES or-COP which(Q)-COP-PRES
     'Either this building doesn't have a bathroom or it's in a funny place.'

It might be interesting to explore the consequences of this fact for our theories of topic marking, but the relevance for the matter at hand is that here too *sore* can in fact be used in an environment where Kurafuji claims it is ungrammatical. It is also worth noting that if we keep the nominative morphology but put focal stress on *sore* by means of *dake* 'only', the sentence becomes grammatical once more.

(67) Kono tatemono-ni toire-ga   na-i   ka sore-dake-ga
      this   building-in bathroom-NOM not-PRES or it-only-NOM
      mitsukara na-i   ka-no dochiraka-dea-ru.
      found   not-PRES or-COP which(Q)-COP-PRES
      'Either this building doesn't have a bathroom or that's the only
      thing that hasn't been found.'

Overall, then, we must conclude that Kurafuji's interesting claim is really not backed up by the data.

Before we leave Kurafuji, however, there is some theoretical interest to be had in revisiting his and Chierchia's notion of why D-type pronouns are needed in addition to dynamic binding. Recall that they are operating under the assumption that D-type pronouns are necessary for anaphora back to domains closed off by externally static operators. This differs, obviously, from the characterization that I gave earlier using the notion of neontological pronouns. I chose to frame the problem the way I did because it is obvious that there is no difficulty in principle in writing down a definition of universal quantification or negation that is externally dynamic, and, indeed, such definitions have already been formulated and proposed for use in natural language semantics by Groenendijk and Stokhof (1990). These authors note the fact that sometimes a sentence following a universally quantified sentence does appear to have its pronouns bound by the preceding universal quantifier. They give the discourse in (68); another, better-known, example is (69) (Partee, cited in Roberts 1987).

(68) Every player chooses a pawn. He puts it on square one.

(69) Each degree candidate walked to the stage. He took his diploma
      from the dean and returned to his seat.

Groenendijk and Stokhof formulate an externally dynamic version of universal quantification to deal with these sentences, along with externally dynamic versions of negation, implication, and disjunction to deal with other examples. As they point out, this leaves the question of when the externally dynamic versions can be used. Externally dynamic universal quantification cannot be used in (57), as we have seen. But it is plausible that there remain to be discovered some conditions that favor one or the other version (see Poesio and Zucchi 1992 for a first attempt), and that a dynamic system could be set up that would use both. But such a system would still not be able to account for the pronouns in (44) and (45), and for similar examples. I maintain that neontological pronouns, then, are the real problem for dynamic theories, and not pronouns anaphoric to domains closed off by allegedly static operators.

Chierchia's mixed system would still be a solution to the problem as I conceive it, of course. But I do not think that he and Kurafuji have shown sufficiently strong evidence for the presence of both dynamic binding and D-type anaphora in natural language for us to disregard the striking lack of theoretical parsimony in such a system.

Let us now leave Chierchia's system and turn to the other solution that I know of to the problem faced by dynamic theories in connection with (44) and (45). It is suggested in passing by Gardent (1991) and in more detail by Hardt (1999) that pronouns that cannot be interpreted as dynamically bound individual variables should be able to obtain their semantic content by the same process that is used in cases of ellipsis.[18] Let us consider (70), which is Hardt's example.

(70) Smith spent his paycheck. Jones saved it.

Hardt supposes that *his paycheck* does indeed contribute a variable to the variable assignments passed on for the evaluation of the following sentence, to talk in the terms we used earlier. Thus he tackles head on one of the problems faced by dynamic systems in connection with these sentences—as noted earlier, dynamic systems do not normally say that definite terms introduce a variable, but would rather say that it is in the nature of definites to be interpreted by variables already introduced, as proposed in Heim 1982. In Hardt's system, NPs like *his paycheck* are translated as generalized quantifiers. So the translation of *his paycheck* is (71).

(71) $\lambda P_2[x_3 \mid x_3 = \lambda P([u_3 \mid \text{of}(u_3, u_0), \text{paycheck}(u_3)]; P(u_3))]; x_3(P_2)$

To explain, this introduces two variables into the variable assignments used for the evaluation of further sentences: u_3, for Smith's paycheck, and the generalized quantifier variable x_3, which is set equal to $\lambda P([u_3 \mid \text{of}(u_3, u_0), \text{paycheck}(u_3)]; P(u_3))$. It is further ensured (by means of "$x_3(P_2)$") that this generalized quantifier will play a role in the interpretation of the current sentence. The variable u_0, meanwhile, is special. Hardt adopts the *centering theory* of Grosz, Joshi, and Weinstein 1995, which at any given time allocates one entity the role of *center* (roughly, topic) of the discourse. Such an entity, in addition to its own variable (say, u_4, u_7) can also be picked out with a special variable u_0, whose value will be set equal to that of different variables at different times, as the center changes. Without going into centering theory, let us just grant Hardt his assumption that in the first sentence of (70) the center is Smith, while in the second it is Jones. The mechanism by which Hardt achieves the "sloppy" interpretation of the pronoun can now be appreciated: because it contains u_0, x_3 means, roughly, "the paycheck of the current center." Since the center changes from Smith to Jones between the introduction of x_3 and the interpretation of it_3 (which takes on the value of x_3), the pronoun ends up designating the paycheck of Jones, as required.

Thus the intuitive content, and part of the formalization, of Hardt's idea. Notice, however, that the actual implementation cannot be as simple as this. The reason is that the variable x_3 specifies that the paycheck whose properties it maps to 1 is the one that is the value of u_3. And that is Smith's paycheck. So if x_3 is in fact used as it stands in the interpretation of the following sentence, we still will not be able to talk about Jones's paycheck. In fact if the center shift does take place, so that the value of u_0 is now Jones, we will end up in the contradictory state of supposing that the center's (Jones's) paycheck is the value of u_3, which is Smith's paycheck. So in fact Hardt only appears to have sidestepped the essential problem that dynamic theories face with neontological pronouns. When we take a closer look, we see that the problem remains.

Hardt makes a curious move at this point. He says that in using the variable x_3 for the interpretation of it_3, we can substitute "an alphabetic variant" of it. We are allowed, then, to insert a variant in which the variable assigned to the paycheck is not u_3 but something else, say u_6. This, of course, would solve the problem if it were permissible: a novel variable is introduced for the entity in question, and it is identified as being the paycheck of the center (who is now Jones). But it is in my opinion most stipulative, if not downright impossible, to make a substitution of an alphabetic variant in this manner. The problem is that dynamic systems, by their very nature, do not allow for the equivalence of alphabetic variants, in the way that more traditional static logics do. It matters whether we say, for example, $\exists x Px$ or $\exists y Py$, since the former but not the latter will be able to bind a syntactically free variable x that occurs in a later formula. As far as I can see, then, it is not only stipulative but actually illegal to solve the problem of neontological pronouns by relying on the notion of alphabetic variance.

One could ask whether Hardt is not just creating unnecessary trouble for himself by introducing this variable u_3 for Smith's paycheck. Would it be possible to do without it, perhaps by having the generalized quantifier variable x_3 mean just "the unique paycheck of the current center," as I first said above? Unfortunately, I don't think this is the case, since it is possible that one would want to refer back to Smith's paycheck with a pronoun without there being a concomitant center shift to Smith, which would allow such a version of x_3 to do the job. The following example seems to work well.

(72) Last year the president was a Democrat. This year he's a Republican. I preferred *him*.

This can easily be taken to mean that I preferred the Democratic president, but there does not seem to have been a center shift back to him before the pronoun that refers to him is actually uttered. So it does seem necessary to have a variable for the actual entity referred to by the first occurrence of *his paycheck* or *the president*. But then the original problem of neontological pronouns remains.

One final note on the approach to the problem taken by Gardent and Hardt. Abstracting away from the technical detail of their implementations, it does in fact seem reasonable to see these authors too as introducing something like D-type pronouns into dynamic systems. They do not state it in those terms, but the fact remains that besides normal dynamically bound individual variables, their systems also include these other pronouns with a lot of descriptive content, whose semantics is really just that of definite descriptions raised to the type of generalized quantifiers. It seems, then, that they are committing furtively the same sin against theoretical parsimony that Chierchia committed more openly. In particular, we must question the need for dynamic binding at all if we have D-type pronouns, since it looks like a reasonable research strategy, which has had a great deal of success, to account for the facts with a mixture of D-type pronouns and ordinary binding.

I do not believe, then, that any of the solutions that have been offered have rescued dynamic theories from the embarrassment they face over neontological pronouns.

1.5   A Variable-Free Theory of Donkey Anaphora

1.5.1   Outline of the Variable-Free Theory

A third, and conceptually quite different, approach to the problem of covariation without c-command is that proposed by Jacobson (2000a). Jacobson (2000a) is working in a framework in which there is no syntactic level like LF at which constituents can appear displaced from their surface positions in order to aid interpretation. Another interesting feature of Jacobson's approach is the hypothesis that no syntactic items are interpreted as free variables. (Jacobson thus calls her theory *variable-free semantics*, but this should not be construed as prohibiting the use of bound variables in the metalanguage to identify various model-theoretic objects.) One advantage of doing away with free variables in the syntax, according to Jacobson, is that the whole apparatus of indices and variable assignments needed to interpret them can be done away with.[19]

Before showing how a donkey pronoun is accounted for by Jacobson's system, I need to introduce some of her technical machinery,[20] and it so happens that a good way to do this is to run through the treatments she gives to ordinary referential and bound pronouns. Let us start, then, with (73), where *he* is referential.

(73) He lost.

As in many other systems, the intransitive verb (or T′) *lost* is simply assumed to have a denotation $[\lambda y.\ y\ \text{lost}]$. But we cannot, in this variable-free system, have *he* simply be a free variable of type e straightforwardly combining with this function. The way Jacobson proceeds is as follows. Pronouns are listed in the lexicon as identity functions over individuals (possibly with some presuppositions built in to deal with ϕ-features, but we will abstract away from this), so *he* in our example has a denotation $[\lambda x.x]$. We combine this with $[\lambda y.\ y\ \text{lost}]$ by subjecting the latter to the type-shifting rule **g**, of which (74) is a slightly simplified version (omitting syntactic concerns).

(74) *The **g** rule*
       For any semantic types a, b and c: if f is a function of type $\langle a, b \rangle$, then $\mathbf{g}_c(f)$ is the following function of type $\langle\langle c, a\rangle, \langle c, b\rangle\rangle$:
       $\lambda V_{\langle c, a\rangle}.\ \lambda C_c.\ f_{\langle a, b\rangle}(V_{\langle c, a\rangle}(C_c))$.

It can be seen that, in effect, **g** is a kind of function composition operator: for any two functions f and h, $\mathbf{g}(h)(f) = h \circ f$. In the present case, we subject the denotation of *lost* to $\mathbf{g}_e$ and then combine the denotations of *lost* and *he* by ordinary functional application and λ-conversion, as shown in (75).

(75) a. $[\lambda y.\, y \text{ lost}]$
       $\rightarrow_{g_e} [\lambda f_{\langle e,e \rangle}.\, \lambda z.\, [\lambda y.\, y \text{ lost}](f(z))]$
       $= [\lambda f_{\langle e,e \rangle}.\, \lambda z.\, f(z) \text{ lost}]$
     b. *he lost*
       $[\lambda f_{\langle e,e \rangle}.\, \lambda z.\, f(z) \text{ lost}](\lambda x.\, x) = [\lambda z.\, z \text{ lost}]$

We arrive at the apparently paradoxical result, then, that the denotation of *he lost* is the same as the denotation of *lost*. This is claimed to be no bad thing by Jacobson. All the audience need do, she points out, is apply the resulting function to some contextually salient individual, and propositional information will be obtained. She points out that more familiar ways of dealing with sentences like (73) do not have a proposition be the immediate outcome of running the semantics on the sentence, either; we obtain, rather, a function from variable assignments or contexts to propositions.

To deal with normal bound pronouns, we need one more piece of machinery. Suppose that we have not (73) but (76), with *he* bound by the subject.

(76) Every man$_i$ thinks he$_i$ lost.

We proceed in exactly the same way as above with regard to *he lost*, with the result that the embedded sentence has the denotation shown in (75). We now need to deal with *thinks*. For simplicity's sake, we will not give even an elementary version of the semantics of propositional attitude verbs. Let us just take the type t to be whatever the type of sentences must be to make things work out correctly. So we can give a simplified denotation for *thinks* as in (77).

(77) $[\![\text{thinks}]\!] = \lambda p_t.\, \lambda x.\, x \text{ thinks } p$

We now need a type-shift rule that will enable us to do binding. The rule is called **z** and is given in (78), again without its proper syntactic correlate.

(78) *The z rule*
     For any semantic types a and b: if f is a function of type
     $\langle a, \langle e, b \rangle \rangle$, then $\mathbf{z}(f)$ is the following function of type
     $\langle \langle e, a \rangle, \langle e, b \rangle \rangle$: $\lambda G_{\langle e,a \rangle}.\, \lambda x.\, f(G(x))(x)$.

Thus if we apply **z** to the denotation of *thinks*, we obtain the result shown in (79).

(79) $\lambda p_t.\, \lambda x.\, x$ thinks p
    $\rightarrow_z \lambda P_{\langle e,t \rangle}.\, \lambda y.\, [\lambda p_t.\, \lambda x.\, x$ thinks $p](P(y))(y)$
    $= \lambda P_{\langle e,t \rangle}.\, \lambda y.\, y$ thinks $P(y)$

We now compose *thinks* and *he lost* in the normal way, as shown in (80).

(80) $[\lambda P_{\langle e,t \rangle}.\, \lambda y.\, y$ thinks $P(y)](\lambda z.\, z$ lost$)$
    $= \lambda y.\, y$ thinks y lost

We see, then, that we end up with the right meaning for *thinks he lost*. The sentence claims that every man has the property we end up with in (80), and the correct meaning is obtained.

We are now in a position to deal with donkey pronouns and related phenomena. For the sake of simplicity in calculation, I will use the second sentence of (81).

(81) Bill immediately put his paycheck in the bank. But every student lost it.

The reading to concentrate on is the one according to which every student lost his own paycheck; it helps to imagine that Bill is not a student, and that there is slight contrastive stress on the word *student*. The pronoun, then, displays the characteristic covariation without c-command that we are trying to explain. To begin with the pronoun, we take its lexically recorded denotation, the identity function over individuals, and subject it to the $\mathbf{g_e}$ rule, as shown in (82).

(82) *it*
       $\lambda x.\, x$
   $\rightarrow_{\mathbf{g_e}} \lambda f_{\langle e,e \rangle}.\, \lambda y.\, [\lambda x.\, x](f(y))$
   $= \lambda f_{\langle e,e \rangle}.\, \lambda y.\, f(y)$
   $= \lambda f_{\langle e,e \rangle}.\, f$

The purpose of this move, as will become clear later, is to create a slot for a function of type $\langle e,e \rangle$ to be taken as argument. This slot will end up being passed up, as it were, so that the denotation of the whole sentence is a function taking arguments of type $\langle e,e \rangle$, and this denotation will end up being applied to the contextually salient function that maps people to their paychecks. So, returning to *it*, we need to turn *lost* into a function that can take this function $[\lambda f_{\langle e,e \rangle}.\, f]$ as argument and pass up the type $\langle e,e \rangle$ slot. This we do by subjecting the meaning of *lost* to $\mathbf{z}$ and $\mathbf{g}_{\langle e,e \rangle}$, as we see in (83).

(83) *lost*

$\lambda x. \lambda y.\ y$ lost x

$\rightarrow_{\mathbf{z}}$ $\quad \lambda f_{\langle e,e\rangle}. \lambda z. [\lambda x. \lambda y.\ y$ lost $x](f(z))(z)$

$=$ $\quad \lambda f_{\langle e,e\rangle}. \lambda z.\ z$ lost $f(z)$

$\rightarrow_{\mathbf{g}_{\langle e,e\rangle}}$ $\lambda F_{\langle ee,ee\rangle}. \lambda g_{\langle e,e\rangle}. [\lambda f_{\langle e,e\rangle}. \lambda z.\ z$ lost $f(z)](F(g))$

$=$ $\quad \lambda F_{\langle ee,ee\rangle}. \lambda g_{\langle e,e\rangle}. \lambda z.\ z$ lost $F(g)(z)$

We now combine *lost* with *it* in the normal way, with the result shown in (84).

(84) *lost it*

$\quad [\lambda F_{\langle ee,ee\rangle}. \lambda g_{\langle e,e\rangle}. \lambda z.\ z$ lost $F(g)(z)](\lambda f_{\langle e,e\rangle}. f)$

$= \lambda g_{\langle e,e\rangle}. \lambda z.\ z$ lost $[\lambda f_{\langle e,e\rangle}. f](g)(z)$

$= \lambda g_{\langle e,e\rangle}. \lambda z.\ z$ lost $g(z)$

We are now nearly done. It is evident from the unexceptionable lexical entries in (85) that *every student* will have, in the first instance, the denotation in the first line of (86). This is then subjected to $\mathbf{g}_{\langle e,e\rangle}$, so it will be able to take the VP denotation we have ended up with as an argument.

(85) a. $[\![$every$]\!] = \lambda P_{\langle e,t\rangle}. \lambda Q_{\langle e,t\rangle}. \forall x(P(x) \to Q(x))$

b. $[\![$student$]\!] = \lambda x.\ x$ is a student

(86) *every student*

$\quad \lambda Q_{\langle e,t\rangle}. \forall x(x$ is a student $\to Q(x))$

$\rightarrow_{\mathbf{g}_{\langle e,e\rangle}} \lambda \mathscr{F}_{\langle ee,et\rangle}. \lambda f_{\langle e,e\rangle}. [\lambda Q_{\langle e,t\rangle}. \forall x(x$ is a student $\to Q(x))](\mathscr{F}(f))$

$= \quad \lambda \mathscr{F}_{\langle ee,et\rangle}. \lambda f_{\langle e,e\rangle}. \forall x(x$ is a student $\to \mathscr{F}(f)(x))$

Now all we have to do is combine the denotations of *every student* (86) and *lost it* (84). The result is shown in (87).

(87) *every student lost it*

$\quad [\lambda \mathscr{F}_{\langle ee,et\rangle}. \lambda f_{\langle e,e\rangle}. \forall x(x$ is a student $\to \mathscr{F}(f)(x))](\lambda g_{\langle e,e\rangle}. \lambda z.\ z$ lost $g(z))$

$= \lambda f_{\langle e,e\rangle}. \forall x(x$ is a student $\to [\lambda g_{\langle e,e\rangle}. \lambda z.\ z$ lost $g(z)](f)(x))$

$= \lambda f_{\langle e,e\rangle}. \forall x(x$ is a student $\to x$ lost $f(x))$

The final line here is the denotation of the sentence. As described above, the hearer has to apply this function to some contextually salient function of the right type in order to obtain propositional information. In this case, the right function is the one that maps people to their paychecks. The sentence thus ends up conveying that every student lost their own paycheck, which is the desired result.

Note, before we go on to examine possible problems with this kind of approach, that this theory does account for the fact that the forms we call pronouns have referential, bound, and D-type uses: one basic denotation, that of the identity function over individuals, suffices to yield all three uses, if we accept the existence of the type-shifting mechanisms postulated.

1.5.2 Problems with the Variable-Free Theory

The current theory seems to share the following two problems with D-type theories. In section 2.5, furthermore, it will be argued that there is a third problem that affects both the variable-free theory and the standard D-type theories, and in section 5.5.2 another problem will arise for variable-free semantics.

The Problem of the Formal Link   It is evident from the description just given that the current variable-free theory suffers from the problem of the formal link, just like the D-type theory. (See section 1.3.2.) That is, there is no evident way that it can distinguish between the grammaticality of (88a) and (88b).

(88) a.   Every man who has a wife is sitting next to her.
     b.   *Every married man is sitting next to her.

Both sentences seem to be well suited to make salient the function mapping people to the people they are married to. Indeed, the vital words *wife* and *married* are very similar from the point of view of a theory that relies only on the contextual salience of functions without reference to syntactic categories, like the present one: both words seem basically to be of type $\langle e, et \rangle$, denoting relations between people and their wives or spouses; both seem to have been transformed into functions of type $\langle e, t \rangle$ in the sentences above. Both, in other words, seem to be equally far away from the function of type $\langle e, e \rangle$ that has to be made salient. It is unclear, then, how the variable-free theory could explain why only one of the sentences is grammatical.

The Problem of Indistinguishable Participants   It is also evident on reflection that the current theory will almost certainly end up suffering from another of the problems that afflict the D-type analysis, namely, the problem of indistinguishable participants (see section 1.3.2), exemplified by the grammaticality of (89).

(89) If a bishop meets a bishop, he blesses him.

In fact, Jacobson does not propose an analysis even of ordinary conditional donkey sentences, and it is far from evident how to deal with them on her theoretical assumptions. So this is an initial problem. But in the spirit of the analysis of *every student lost it* given above, we seem to have to suppose that the denotation of (89) would be a function from functions of some type to a function from functions of that same type to truth values. That is, informally speaking, it would look something like (90), for some type τ.

(90) $\lambda f_\tau. \lambda g_\tau$. if a bishop meets a bishop, $f[\ldots]$ blesses $g[\ldots]$

This function, on the analogy of the above analysis, would be applied by listeners to two contextually salient functions to obtain propositional information, with the two pronouns analyzed by means of these salient functions. (The exact details would presumably depend on exactly how conditionals were handled.) But even with this bare outline of an account, which seems necessary to maintain the same general approach that we have seen, it is evident that the current theory will share the problem of indistinguishable participants: it does not seem to be the case that there are two different functions f and g by which the two bishops could be distinguished.

1.6   Conclusion

To sum up, then, the D-type approach to covariation without c-command says that some pronouns are definite descriptions and, in its latest incarnation, uses situation semantics to neutralize the unwelcome uniqueness presuppositions that this move produces. It is currently faced with three problems: dealing with sentences involving indistinguishable participants, establishing a formal link between D-type pronouns and their intuitive antecedents, and doing away with the thesis of pronominal ambiguity.

Dynamic binding theories attempt to explain covariation without c-command by altering the semantics so that operators can bind variables not syntactically in their scope. They also face three problems, those of disjunctive antecedents, deep anaphora, and neontological pronouns.

The variable-free theory analyzes pronouns as identity functions subject to various type-shifting operations. When it comes to analyzing apparent covariation without c-command, it shares two of the problems of the D-type analyses, those of the formal link and indistinguishable participants.

The rest of this book can be seen as an attempt to clear away the problems that affect the D-type theory. In particular, a new version of the D-type theory will be proposed and defended in chapter 2. The resulting syntax and semantics for D-type pronouns will be unified with that of referential and bound pronouns, and also with that of overt definite descriptions, in chapter 3; and then I will return to the theme of D-type anaphora in chapter 4 and propose a solution for the problem of indistinguishable participants. Chapter 5 will introduce a new problem for dynamic and variable-free theories that leaves the D-type analysis untouched, and chapter 6 will focus on the analysis of proper names, assimilating them to definite descriptions partly on the basis of previously undetected D-type readings that they can be made to display. But first, a novel theory of D-type pronouns.

Chapter 2

D-Type Pronouns

2.1 Introduction

2.1.1 The Proposal in Brief

I will be basing my analysis of D-type pronouns on the observation that pronominal forms can have the semantics of definite determiners of various kinds, including definite articles, as pointed out in a classic paper by Postal (1966) on the basis of examples such as (1).

(1) You troops will embark but the other troops will remain.

There are more details in section 2.1.2 on the evidence that suggests that pronouns should at least occasionally be assimilated to determiners in their semantics and syntax.

Let us examine once more the simple version of the D-type theory suggested by Heim and Kratzer (1998, 290–293), according to which the pronoun in (2) would spell out an LF fragment of the kind in (3).

(2) Every man who owns a donkey beats it.

(3) [the [$R_{\langle 7, \langle e, et \rangle \rangle}$ pro$_{\langle 1, e \rangle}$]]

Recall that the relation variable R would pick up the salient *donkey-owned-by* relation, and the pronoun would denote the donkey owned by x, for every man x who owns a donkey.

My present concern is the following. Given the work that seeks to assimilate pronouns to determiners, it seems that we might be missing a generalization if we adopt a conventional D-type analysis like this, in the following sense. Take (3). It consists of a definite article and some material providing a function of type $\langle e, t \rangle$ for the definite article to take as its argument. But we already have reason to believe that pronouns can be interpreted as definite articles, following Postal. We would reduce donkey anaphora and related phenomena to something we already have to acknowledge, then, if we could say that in these cases the semantic contribution of the donkey pronoun is just a definite article, and the equivalent of the material following *the* in (3) is obtained some other way.

I suggest, then, that $[\![\text{it}]\!] = [\![\text{the}]\!]$, abstracting away from the ϕ-features of *it*. The same goes for the other third-person pronouns. We know, furthermore, that NPs can undergo PF deletion in the environment of an identical NP, as in (4) (Jackendoff 1968, 1971; Perlmutter 1970).

(4) My shirt is the same as his.

Combining these two simple ideas, we see that there could have been deletion of *donkey* after *it* in (2), and that *it* here could mean the same as *the*. This would mean that (2) would have an LF almost or precisely identical to that of (5).

(5) Every man who owns a donkey beats the donkey.

Since (5) does indeed mean the same as (2), it seems that this is an option worth exploring. In fact my claim in this chapter is that D-type pronouns can quite generally be viewed as being definite articles whose complements are subject to NP-deletion. For ease of reference, I call this the NP-deletion theory.[1]

This chapter is structured as follows. The introduction continues with some further remarks on NP-deletion and assimilating pronouns to determiners, and section 2.2 lays out my version of the semantic framework (situation semantics) that I will be adopting. I then concentrate for a while on accounting for donkey anaphora: in section 2.3 I show that the current proposal can obtain the correct truth conditions for donkey sentences, in particular the characteristic covariance without c-command, and in sections 2.4 and 2.5 I examine various ways conventional D-type analyses encounter problems with donkey anaphora, and try to show that the NP-deletion theory improves on them. In section 2.6, I examine the other types of sentence in which linguists have posited D-type pronouns, and show how the NP-deletion theory deals with these data. And in section 2.7, I discuss and dismiss some objections that have already been made to the NP-deletion theory.

2.1.2   The Assimilation of Pronouns to Determiners

To argue that personal pronouns in English are a kind of definite article, Postal (1966) used examples like those in (6), (1) (repeated here as (7)), and (8), where pronouns appear in determiner position.[2]

(6) a. we Americans
   b. us linguists
   c. you Communists
   d. (*dialectally*) them guys, (*Scots*) they Sassenachs

(7) You troops will embark but the other troops will remain.

(8) We Americans distrust you Europeans.

It does not seem plausible to analyze these DPs as involving appositive constructions, as Postal (1966) has already pointed out, with many arguments. One argument is that there is no sign of or requirement for the characteristic "comma intonation" associated with apposition in sentences like (9).

(9) You, troops, will embark.

To distance the *you* in (7) and (8) from the *you* in (9), it might be thought desirable to have the denotation of *you troops* in (7) be the sum[3] of the contextually salient troops. This does not seem advisable, however. The reason is that already when the speaker says *you troops* in (7) "the other troops" are salient; we can tell because the sentence is most naturally delivered with contrastive stress on *you* and *the other*, and there would be no way to get that without the other troops being borne in mind while *you troops* is being said, in order for there to be something to stand in contrast to the denotation of *you troops*. The suggested denotation would give the wrong results in this case, then, incorrectly making *you troops* stand for all the troops who figure in (7). It is more plausible, therefore, that *you* in (7) has a denotation like that in (10); in this formula, g is a variable assigment, a is the addressee, and $\leq_i$ is the *individual part-of* relation of Link 1983.

(10) $[\![you_j]\!]^{g,a} = \lambda f : f \in D_{\langle e,t \rangle} \ \& \ a \leq_i g(j) \ \& \ f(g(j)) = 1 . g(j)$

Basically, then, this plural *you* takes an NP with denotation f and gives as the denotation of the whole DP some contextually salient plural individual j that is conditioned as follows: the addressee a must be part of j, and j must be f. This rather roundabout lexical entry enables us to have the denotation of *you troops* in (7) be the troops being addressed (or of whom representatives are being addressed), and not "the other troops."

There is now a rich tradition of work showing that other empirical and conceptual advantages can be obtained from assimilating pronouns and determiners.[4] Although there are no overt prenominal uses for third-person singular pronouns in English, I submit that it is not a large step to believe that these pronouns too can sometimes have the semantics of a determiner. (In chapter 3 I will be arguing, in fact, that pronouns always have this semantics.) In particular, then, I propose that pronouns have the same denotation as *the*, with the exception that pronouns have ϕ-features. I will be discussing the meaning of *the* in chapter 3, but for the sake of concreteness I give in (11) the views of *the* and *she* (to pick one example) that I will be assuming in this chapter. (*Fx* means "*x* is a female person.")

(11) a. $[\![\text{the}]\!] = \lambda f : f \in D_{\langle e, t \rangle}$ & $\exists! x \, f(x) = 1 . \iota x \, f(x) = 1$
    b. $[\![\text{she}]\!] = \lambda f : f \in D_{\langle e, t \rangle}$ & $\exists! x \, f(x) = 1$ & $\forall x (f(x) = 1 \rightarrow Fx)$.
      $\iota x \, f(x) = 1$

I will not be moving very far from these lexical entries in chapter 3; the main debate will revolve around whether these words should in fact take two arguments and yield the unique entity that satisfies both predicates.

2.1.3 NP-Deletion

NP-deletion, in the guise of N'-deletion, has been around for a long time, at least since Jackendoff 1968, 1971, and Perlmutter 1970. These authors gave examples like the following.

(12) a. Bill's story about Sue may be amazing, but Max's is virtually incredible.
    b. I like Bill's wine, but Max's is even better.

With the advent of the DP-hypothesis, which I follow here, the name became changed to NP-deletion, for obvious reasons (Saito and Murasugi 1989; Lasnik and Saito 1992).

    Under what circumstances is NP-deletion possible? There seem to be two conditions under which it is allowed. The first, most obviously, is when there is a linguistic antecedent, as in the examples we have seen so far.[5] The second is when the deictic aid can be invoked of something in the immediate environment. For example, a visitor being enthusiastically leaped on by his host's dog might nod at it and say, "Mine does the same thing," even if no mention has been made of the word *dog*.[6] It is not possible, however, to reconstruct a suitable NP from the linguistic context alone if it has not actually occurred explicitly. In the following discourse, for example, the second sentence is impossible, even though the relation expressed by the word *husband* has been made contextually salient by the first sentence.

(13) Mary is married. *And Sue's is the man drinking the Martini.

This fact will be of some importance later on, when we examine the problem of the formal link between donkey pronoun and antecedent (section 2.4).

It is not my purpose in this chapter to explain why NP-deletion should be constrained in exactly this way, and I will offer no more than a few speculative remarks. I suspect that there is no unified explanation for the two conditions just described, and that two different processes are involved. The type of NP-deletion that has a linguistic antecedent is obviously parallel to VP-ellipsis, which is widely accepted to be possible only when there is a linguistic antecedent (Hankamer and Sag 1976). NP-deletion in the absence of a linguistic antecedent would rely on some extralinguistic reconstruction by the hearer of what must be meant by the speaker; this explains the fact that it seems limited to cases where there is some immediate cue in the physical environment, which is indicated by some physical gesture for the greatest felicity to result. Any harder task, presumably, would produce the feeling of mental stretching that one has on hearing (13).

Moving away from the global conditions under which NP-deletion is possible, there is also the question of what can make up the immediately adjacent linguistic material. Specifically, one sometimes hears the claim that the deleted NP must be preceded by a genitive phrase, as in (12) (Saito and Murasugi 1989). As far as I can tell, however, this is much too strong. Consider the data in (14).

(14) a. Sue only bought two books, but Mary bought **at least three**.
     b. Most movies bore Mary, but she does like **some**.
     c. Many unicorns were in the garden, but Mary only noticed **a few**.
     d. Most MIT students build robots, and **all** watch *Star Trek*.
     e. The boys came to the party; **each** gave a present to the birthday girl.
     f. The twins showed up too; **both** began to criticize the food.
     g. Mary tried to corral the unicorns, but **many** escaped.
     h. Some students are morning people, but **most** are not.
     i. I don't like either woman; **neither** knows much about *Star Trek*.
     j. Many Athenians went to Sicily, but **few** returned.
     k. Two heads are better than **one**.
     l. *Two heads are better than **no**.
     m. i. *Sue only bought one book, but Mary bought **every**.

        ii. *More than one Athenian went to Sicily, and **every**
             returned.

n.   i. *I wanted to read the best book in the store, so I bought
             the.

        ii. *The giant wanted to eat the children, but **the** escaped.

o.   i. *I wanted to read a book, so I bought **a**.

        ii. *I expected a bird to fly through the mead hall, and **a** did.

After this quick survey, then, it looks like NP-deletion is possible after every determiner except *no, every, a,* and *the* (see Lobeck 1995, 42–45). But it has been argued for some time that, under certain conditions at least, *one* and *a* are phonological variants of the same lexical item (Perlmutter 1970; Stockwell, Schachter, and Partee 1973). I espouse the theory of Stockwell, Schachter, and Partee (1973, 70–71), according to which the word is realized as *one* under the same conditions as those under which *your* is realized *yours*—that is, when there is no NP following overtly; otherwise it is *a/an*. This means that NP-deletion in the environments in (14o) is indeed possible, but the sentences are realized as in (15).

(15) a. I wanted to read a book, so I bought **one**.

      b. I expected a bird to fly through the mead hall, and **one** did.

Under theories like this, there are of course environments where surface *one* does not derive from the indefinite article.

    I suppose that the same thing happens with *no*. The surface forms *no* and *none* seem to be in complementary distribution, with the conditioning environment being that which we have already seen: the presence or absence of a phonologically realized NP sister. This means that NP-deletion in the environment in (14l) would actually produce the sentence in (16).

(16) Two heads are better than **none**.

The determiners *every* and *the*, on this view, would be the only ones that genuinely do not allow NP-deletion after them. It is interesting to note that *every* has at least one other strange property in addition, namely, the inability to appear in partitive constructions (17).

(17) a. All of the boys gave a present to Mary.

      b. Each of the boys gave a present to Mary.

      c. *Every of the boys gave a present to Mary.

It is notable that figuring in partitive constructions involves appearing with no phonologically overt NP sister, just like NP-deletion. But I will not attempt to investigate here why this word should behave in this manner.[7]

It is of course tempting to argue at this point that NP-deletion takes place after *the*, too, with *the* then being spelled out as a "pronoun." That is, we could suppose that in English *the* is not a separate lexical item from the third-person pronouns, as I said above. Instead there are the various third-person pronouns that have the semantics of definite articles with ϕ-features, as shown in (11), but a low-level morphological process spells them out as *the* when they take a phonologically realized NP as complement. In other words, there would be an alternation between the phonological forms *it* and *the* (for example) exactly parallel to the one we have just seen between *yours* and *your*, and, if my suspicion is correct, *none* and *no*.[8] As far as I can see, this could in fact be the case for English, but I am dubious about postulating it here because it obviously does not hold good for a closely related language like German.[9] In German, the definite article *der, die, das* can appear with no overt following NP, as we see in (18).

(18) a. Hans sieht **den** Mann.
          Hans sees the man
          'Hans sees the man.'
      b. Hans sieht **den**.
          Hans sees the
          'Hans sees him.'

Besides *der, die, das* there is a set of normal pronouns *er, sie, es*. We are not, however, obligated to use one of these latter forms in cases like (18b), meaning that pronouns and common or garden definite articles must be distinct lexical items in German. I see little point in identifying the two in English, then, since we have to acknowledge these two sorts of things anyway, although as far as I can see there would be nothing to prevent us from identifying them in English and saying that other languages work differently. But for the purposes of this chapter I will be assuming that what we normally call pronouns and definite articles are distinct lexical items, even though the semantics of pronouns is very like that of *the*. There will be more discussion relevant to this point in chapter 3.

For our present purposes, I hope that the large number of determiners that allow NP-deletion after them will make it seem quite unexceptionable to posit NP-deletion after the alleged determiners *he, she, it*, and *they*.

2.2   Semantics

2.2.1   Background

Recall that I am claiming that (19a) looks like (19b) at LF, abstracting away from irrelevant detail, and therefore obtains its covarying reading in the same way that (19c) does.

(19) a. Every man who owns a donkey beats it.
      b. every man who owns a donkey beats [it donkey]
      c. Every man who owns a donkey beats the donkey.

But now we must ask how (19c) can possibly get a covarying reading, in the absence of any lexical items like pronouns that we normally take to be interpreted as bindable variables. The answer will be that binding does take place in (19c) and (19b), but that it is not individual variables that are bound but situation variables. Hence I will now set out the version of situation semantics that I will be assuming in much of the present work. This semantics is based most directly on the work of Kratzer (1989), Berman (1987), Heim (1990), von Fintel (1994), and Heim and Kratzer (1998), but some details, including the precise formulation of the lexical entries of quantifiers, are novel.

The following semantics is based on the notion of a *situation*, where, as in Barwise and Perry 1983, a situation consists of one or more individuals having one or more properties or standing in one or more relations at a particular spatiotemporal location (Barwise and Perry 1983, 7). I am most directly influenced by the version of this theory set out in Kratzer 1989, where a situation is a *state of affairs* in the sense of Armstrong 1978. Armstrong (1978, 1997) sets up an ontology that is realist about universals: there are certain properties and relations that really occur in the world in different places at once, being instantiated by different individuals, or *n*-tuples of individuals, at the same time. In addition to universals, then, the world contains individuals or *particulars* that instantiate them. Armstrong (1978, 114) distinguishes between two types of particulars: a thick particular, which is a particular with all its properties, and a *thin particular*, which is a particular taken in abstraction from all its properties. A thin particular is identified with the total space-time area occupied by the individual in question (Armstrong 1978, 118).[10] Since the scheme treats (at least some) properties as being ontologically basic, it is evident that we have the option of considering thin particulars in connection with only a proper subset of the properties they instantiate. To use

Kratzer's (1989) example, there is a part of the world that consists only of Angelika Kratzer's thin particular (at a certain time) plus the property (instantiated by the thin particular) of being hungry. A state of affairs or situation, then, is one or more particulars having one or more properties or standing in one or more relations (Armstrong 1978, 113); it need not contain all the properties and relations that the particulars it contains do in fact instantiate at the time in question.

This means that we can define a reflexive part-of relation $\leq$ on the union of the set of situations and the set of thin particulars. A situation s is part of a situation s' if and only if s' contains all the particulars s does, instantiating all the properties and relations that they instantiate in s. For example, the situation that contains just Angelika Kratzer's thin particular instantiating the property of being hungry is part of the situation that contains just Angelika Kratzer's thin particular instantiating the properties of being hungry and being tired. The latter situation is sometimes also said to be an *extension* of the former. This part-of relation will be of some importance in our semantics. So too will be the related notion of a *minimal situation*. A minimal situation such that p is the situation that contains the smallest number of particulars, properties, and relations that will make p true (intuitively speaking). For example, the minimal situation in which John owns Flossy contains just the thin particulars of John and Flossy plus the relation of owning with them instantiating it; no further properties, relations, or particulars are present. A minimal situation in which John owns a donkey (in which, in other words, there is an individual x such that x is a donkey and John owns x) again contains just two thin particulars instantiating the owning relationship, with one of them being John's; the difference is that the situation also contains a property, that of being a donkey, which the second particular instantiates. There may be more than one minimal situation in which John owns a donkey, of course: if John owns more than one donkey, there will be one such minimal situation for each donkey.

2.2.2 Ontological Ingredients (Kratzer 1989)

S a set, the *set of possible situations* (including the set of thick particulars)

A a set, the set of possible thin particulars

$\leq$ a partial ordering on $S \cup A$ (intuitively, the part-of relation) such that at least the following conditions are satisfied:

> (i) For no $s \in S$ is there an $a \in A$ such that $s \le a$;
> (ii) For all $s \in S \cup A$ there is a unique $s' \in S$ such that $s \le s'$ and for all $s'' \in S$: if $s' \le s''$, then $s'' = s'$.

$\wp(S)$ the power set of S, the *set of propositions*

W a subset of S, the set of maximal elements with respect to $\le$, the *set of possible worlds*. For all $s \in S$, let w_s be the maximal element s is related to by $\le$.

To work out the possible-worlds aspect of the semantics properly, it would be necessary to address the relationship between individuals or situations in different possible worlds that are in some sense the same; we might want to introduce the *counterpart* relation, following Lewis 1968, 1973. But in practice I will hardly be dealing with sentences that demand this, and I will generally only talk about situations that are part of the actual world.

2.2.3 Rules (after Heim and Kratzer 1998)

1. *Functional Application (FA)*
If α is a branching node and $\{\beta, \gamma\}$ the set of its daughters, then, for any assignment g, α is in the domain of $[\![\ ]\!]^g$ if both β and γ are, and $[\![\beta]\!]^g$ is a function whose domain contains $[\![\gamma]\!]^g$. In that case, $[\![\alpha]\!]^g = [\![\beta]\!]^g([\![\gamma]\!]^g)$.

2. *Predicate Modification (PM)*
If α is a branching node and $\{\beta, \gamma\}$ the set of its daughters, then, for any assignment g, α is in the domain of $[\![\ ]\!]^g$ if both β and γ are, and $[\![\beta]\!]^g$ and $[\![\gamma]\!]^g$ are of type $\langle\langle s, e \rangle, \langle s, t \rangle\rangle$. In that case, $[\![\alpha]\!]^g = \lambda u_{\langle s,e \rangle}.\lambda s. [\![\beta]\!]^g(u)(s) = 1 \ \& \ [\![\gamma]\!]^g(u)(s) = 1$.

3. *Predicate Abstraction (PA)*
For all indices i and assignments g, $[\![\lambda_i\, \alpha]\!]^g = \lambda u_{\langle s,e \rangle}.[\![\alpha]\!]^{g^{u/i}}$.

4. *Traces (TR)*
If α is a trace, g is a variable assignment, and $i \in \mathrm{dom}(g)$, then $[\![\alpha_i]\!]^g = g(i)$.

Variable assignments will now be functions from the natural numbers to functions of type $\langle s, e \rangle$.

In addition to the above rules that operate on the object language, we also need the following rule to operate on the metalanguage when doing derivations.

- λ-*Conversion (λC)*
For any type τ, $[\lambda x_\tau.\, M](N_\tau) = [N/x]M$, where $[N/x]M$ is the result of substituting N for x in M.

2.2.4 Sample Lexical Entries

$[\![\text{Mary}]\!]^g = \lambda s.\ \text{Mary}$

$[\![\text{laughs}]\!]^g = \lambda u_{\langle s,e\rangle}.\ \lambda s.\ u(s)$ laughs in s

$[\![\text{cat}]\!]^g = \lambda u_{\langle s,e\rangle}.\ \lambda s.\ u(s)$ is a cat in s

$[\![\text{greets}]\!]^g = \lambda u_{\langle s,e\rangle}.\ \lambda v_{\langle s,e\rangle}.\ \lambda s.\ v(s)$ greets $u(s)$ in s

$[\![\text{every}]\!]^g = \lambda f_{\langle\langle s,e\rangle,\langle s,t\rangle\rangle}.\ \lambda g_{\langle\langle s,e\rangle,\langle s,t\rangle\rangle}.\ \lambda s.$ for every individual x: for every minimal situation s' such that $s' \leq s$ and $f(\lambda s.x)(s') = 1$, there is a situation s'' such that $s'' \leq s$ and s'' is a minimal situation such that $s' \leq s''$ and $g(\lambda s.x)(s'') = 1$

$[\![\text{a}]\!]^g = \lambda f_{\langle\langle s,e\rangle,\langle s,t\rangle\rangle}.\ \lambda g_{\langle\langle s,e\rangle,\langle s,t\rangle\rangle}.\ \lambda s.$ there is an individual x and a situation s' such that s' is a minimal situation such that $s' \leq s$ and $f(\lambda s.x)(s') = 1$, such that there is a situation s'' such that $s'' \leq s$ and s'' is a minimal situation such that $s' \leq s''$ and $g(\lambda s.x)(s'') = 1$

$[\![\text{it}]\!]^g = \lambda f_{\langle\langle s,e\rangle,\langle s,t\rangle\rangle}.\ \lambda s : \exists! x\ f(\lambda s'.x)(s)(s) = 1.\ \iota x\ f(\lambda s'.x)(s)(s) = 1$

$[\![\text{the}]\!]^g = \lambda f_{\langle\langle s,e\rangle,\langle s,t\rangle\rangle}.\ \lambda s : \exists! x\ f(\lambda s'.x)(s)(s) = 1.\ \iota x\ f(\lambda s'.x)(s)(s) = 1$

$[\![\text{always}]\!]^g = \lambda p_{\langle s,t\rangle}.\ \lambda q_{\langle s,t\rangle}.\ \lambda s.$ for every minimal situation s' such that $s' \leq s$ and $p(s') = 1$, there is a situation s'' such that $s'' \leq s$ and s'' is a minimal situation such that $s' \leq s''$ and $q(s'') = 1$

$[\![\text{who}]\!]^g = \lambda f_{\langle\langle s,e\rangle,\langle s,t\rangle\rangle}.\ \lambda u_{\langle s,e\rangle} : \forall s\ u(s)$ is a person. $\lambda s.\ f(u)(s) = 1$

$[\![\text{if}]\!]^g = \lambda p_{\langle s,t\rangle}.\ p$

There will be discussion of some situation-semantic technicalities connected with the treatment of quantification proposed here in section 2.3.3, after we have seen the above quantifiers in action in the analysis of donkey sentences.

2.3 The Truth Conditions of Donkey Sentences

2.3.1 Examples with *if*-clauses

Following Berman (1987), I assume that quantificational adverbs (including the silent variant of *always* found in multicase conditionals) impose the structure in (20) on their LFs.

(20) [[always [if α]] β]

This means that the donkey sentence in (21) has the LF structure in (22).[11]

(21) If a man owns a donkey, he always beats it.

(22) [[always [if [[a man] [λ_6 [[a donkey] [λ_2 [t_6 owns t_2]]]]]]] [[he man] beats [it donkey]]]]

A rather lengthy calculation (shown in appendix B.1) reveals that this LF has the truth conditions in (23), according to the semantics set out in section 2.2. It is suggested that the diagram in (24) be used as an *aide-mémoire* when reading these truth conditions.

(23) λs_1. for every minimal situation s_4 such that

$s_4 \leq s_1$ and there is an individual y and a situation s_7 such that s_7 is a minimal situation such that $s_7 \leq s_4$ and y is man in s_7, such that there is a situation s_9 such that $s_9 \leq s_4$ and s_9 is a minimal situation such that

$s_7 \leq s_9$ and there is an individual x and a situation s_2 such that s_2 is a minimal situation such that $s_2 \leq s_9$ and x is a donkey in s_2, such that there is a situation s_3 such that $s_3 \leq s_9$ and s_3 is a minimal situation such that $s_2 \leq s_3$ and y owns x in s_3,

there is a situation s_5 such that

$s_5 \leq s_1$ and s_5 is a minimal situation such that $s_4 \leq s_5$ and $\iota x\ x$ is a man in s_5 beats in s_5 $\iota x\ x$ is a donkey in s_5

(24)

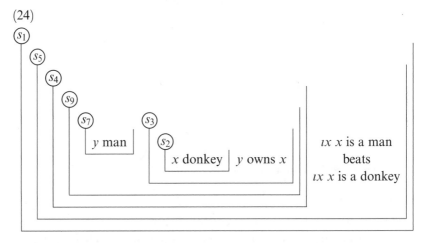

These truth conditions are intuitively adequate. Note in particular that the unique man and the unique donkey in s_5 mentioned at the end must be the man and donkey that figured in s_7 and s_2, since s_5 is an extension of these latter situations. Furthermore, since all situations are defined as the minimal ones of the appropriate kind, no other donkeys or men can sneak in, meaning that the final uniqueness presuppositions with regard to men and donkeys in s_5 are justified.

2.3.2 Donkey Sentences with QP and Relative Clause

The donkey sentence in (25) will have the LF in (26).

(25) Every man who owns a donkey beats it.

(26) [[every [man [who [λ_6 [[a donkey] [λ_2 [t_6 owns t_2]]]]]]] [beats [it donkey]]]

A calculation (shown in appendix B.2) shows that this LF receives the truth conditions in (27). Once again, a diagram is provided (in (28)) to help the reader keep track of the structure of the situations.

(27) λs_4. for every individual y:

for every minimal situation s_5 such that

$s_5 \leq s_4$ and y is a man in s_5 and there is an individual x and a situation s_2 such that s_2 is a minimal situation such that $s_2 \leq s_5$ and x is a donkey in s_2, such that there is a situation s_3 such that $s_3 \leq s_5$ and s_3 is a minimal situation such that $s_2 \leq s_3$ and y owns x in s_3,

there is a situation s_6 such that

$s_6 \leq s_4$ and s_6 is a minimal situation such that $s_5 \leq s_6$ and y beats in s_6 ιz z is a donkey in s_6

(28)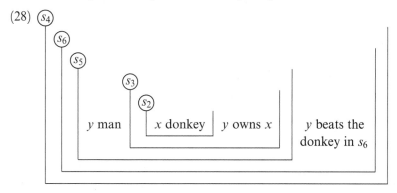

Again, the truth conditions seem intuitively adequate. In particular, the unique donkey in s_6 must be the donkey introduced in s_2, and hence owned by the man y, for each man y, because s_6 is an extension of s_2. As with the preceding truth conditions, the consistent specification of *minimal* situations of each relevant kind means that no other donkeys can be in the situations s_6, and so the uniqueness presupposition is justified.

2.3.3 Discussion of Quantification

For the benefit of those interested in situation-semantic technicalities, I will now point out some of the innovations I have included in the situation-semantics treatment of quantification and discuss one seemingly troublesome feature of the system. For the sake of reference, I repeat in (29), (30), and (31) the definitions of the quantifiers *every*, *a*, and *always*.

(29) $[\![\text{every}]\!]^g = \lambda f_{\langle\langle s,e\rangle,\langle s,t\rangle\rangle} \cdot \lambda g_{\langle\langle s,e\rangle,\langle s,t\rangle\rangle} \cdot \lambda s.$ for every individual x: for every minimal situation s' such that $s' \leq s$ and $f(\lambda s.x)(s') = 1$, there is a situation s'' such that $s'' \leq s$ and s'' is a minimal situation such that $s' \leq s''$ and $g(\lambda s.x)(s'') = 1$

(30) $[\![a]\!]^g = \lambda f_{\langle\langle s,e\rangle,\langle s,t\rangle\rangle} \cdot \lambda g_{\langle\langle s,e\rangle,\langle s,t\rangle\rangle} \cdot \lambda s.$ there is an individual x and a situation s' such that s' is a minimal situation such that $s' \leq s$ and $f(\lambda s.x)(s') = 1$, such that there is a situation s'' such that $s'' \leq s$ and s'' is a minimal situation such that $s' \leq s''$ and $g(\lambda s.x)(s'') = 1$

(31) $[\![\text{always}]\!]^g = \lambda p_{\langle s,t\rangle} \cdot \lambda q_{\langle s,t\rangle} \cdot \lambda s.$ for every minimal situation s' such that $s' \leq s$ and $p(s') = 1$, there is a situation s'' such that $s'' \leq s$ and s'' is a minimal situation such that $s' \leq s''$ and $q(s'') = 1$

Persistence   The first way the above lexical entries for quantifiers contrast with (at least some) previous situation-semantics work on quantification is that the denotations they give do not produce persistent propositions. In the terminology of Barwise and Perry (1983), a proposition is *persistent* just in case, for every situation s in which it is true, it is also true in all situations of which s is a part. Using the present notation, the definition is as follows (Kratzer 1989, 618).

(32) *Persistence*
     A proposition $p \in \wp(S)$ is persistent if and only if for all s and $s' \in S$ the following holds: whenever $s \leq s'$ and $s \in p$, then $s' \in p$.

An example of Kratzer's might help to bring out what is involved here. Suppose that Kratzer has an orchard, and that in showing it off to a visitor she utters (33).

(33) Every tree is laden with wonderful apples.

It is clear from the context that Kratzer is not claiming that every tree in the world is laden with wonderful apples, but only that every tree in her orchard is so laden. The question is how exactly we are to express this fact. According to the lexical entry for *every* given above, (33), if we make no other assumptions, will have the denotation in (34).

(34) $\lambda s.$ for every individual x: for every minimal situation s' such that
$s' \leq s$ and x is a tree in s', there is a situation s'' such that $s'' \leq s$
and s'' is a minimal situation such that $s' \leq s''$ and x is laden with
wonderful apples in s''.

It is clear that this proposition is not persistent. Take the minimal situation containing Kratzer's orchard. If all Kratzer's trees are as good as
she claims, then (34) is true in this situation—that is, this situation is a
member of the set defined by (34). But when we start considering larger
situations, we will soon find one containing a tree that is not laden with
wonderful apples. And (34) will not be true in such a situation. So (34) is
not persistent. The question is whether this matters.

As Kratzer explains (Kratzer 1989, 617), there are basically two positions one could take on this issue. One is the position taken by Barwise
and Perry (1983), who would maintain that the denotation of (33) is indeed something like (34), but that in saying (33) Kratzer only claimed
that (34) was true in a limited part of the world. In other words, it does
not matter that (34) is not true in the world as a whole, because Kratzer
was not trying to talk about the world as a whole. The other position is
that adopted by Kratzer. She says (Kratzer 1989, 617–618) that quantifiers like *every* are interpreted with respect to an implicit restrictor as
well as explicit restrictors like *tree*, and that therefore the restriction to
her orchard (in the present case) makes it into the proposition expressed
in a way that it does not on the first view. It is as if she had said (35),
which on the above situation semantics would have a denotation like
that in (36).

(35) Every tree in my orchard is laden with wonderful apples.

(36) $\lambda s.$ for every individual x: for every minimal situation s' such that
$s' \leq s$ and x is a tree in Kratzer's orchard in s', there is a situation
s'' such that $s'' \leq s$ and s'' is a minimal situation such that $s' \leq s''$
and x is laden with wonderful apples in s''.

So the proposition expressed does end up being persistent, on this second view. The reason is that it contains within it its own restriction to
Kratzer's orchard. Even if we evaluate the situation-semantics denotation
of (35) with respect to situations much bigger than Kratzer's orchard, the
claim made will still be the same—that is, it will still just be a claim about
Kratzer's orchard.

Now it is not immediately clear that there would in fact be any difference between these two theories if the trouble were taken to spell them
out in more detail. After all, Barwise and Perry would presumably also

want to say that in uttering (33) Kratzer has conveyed what she would have conveyed by uttering (35). I suspect that the difference, if a difference is to be found, must lie in whether there is actual linguistic machinery devoted to the narrowing down of the domain of quantification: von Fintel (1994), for example, suggested that, in addition to their overt restrictors, quantifiers take as arguments phonologically null variables that pick up contextually salient properties to provide further restriction of the quantification. If there is such linguistic machinery, then we will arrive at a denotation like (36) in the case of the present example and will never pass through a stage at which the denotation looks like (34). If, on the other hand, there is no such linguistic machinery, then the picture we end up with is that the proposition expressed is (34) and the audience is put in the position of selecting a situation that is plausibly the one meant to be a member of the set of situations thus defined. It does look like it will be possible to elucidate the differences between the two views, then. But it looks as though finding empirical evidence in support of one or the other would be a very difficult task. Kratzer herself (1989, 618) does not attempt to give any empirical arguments for quantified sentences always being persistent. Instead she makes the conceptual points that constraints like persistence narrow the range of possible meanings available to us and produce definitions (of negation, for example) that are consistent with independent concerns. These points are hardly compelling.

All this is merely to say that I am aware that, unlike Kratzer (1989, 620–622), I have not built any special provisions into my denotations of quantifiers to ensure that quantified sentences end up being persistent, but it would be possible to add such provisions were it shown to be necessary, perhaps along the lines of von Fintel 1994.

Definites and the Nuclear Scope   It is perhaps worth noting the contrast between the way I handle quantification using situations in this work and the way Heim does in her 1990 article.[12] Heim assumed that situation variables were present in the syntax. In a quantificational structure, all the predicates in the restrictor would be relativized to one situation variable, say s_1, and those in the nuclear scope would be relativized to another, say s_2, with the exception that definites in the nuclear scope referring back to entities introduced in the restrictor could have the situation variable of the restrictor (Heim 1990, 146). So (37), for example, would look something like (38) at LF. (I ignore the requirement to subject the indefinites in the antecedent to quantifier raising.)

(37) If a man owns a donkey, he always beats it.

(38) [[always [if a man(s_1) owns(s_1) a donkey(s_1)]] [he(s_1) beats(s_2) it(s_1)]]

Such LFs would be interpreted by a rule like (39).

(39) $[[[\text{always } [\text{if } \alpha]] \beta]]^g$ = True iff for every minimal situation s_1 such
     that $[\![\alpha]\!]^{g\,s_1\backslash s_1}$ = True, there is a situation s_2 such that $s_1 \leq s_2$ and
     $[\![\beta]\!]^{g\,s_1\backslash s_1,\,s_2\backslash s_2}$ = True.

In this rule, sequences like $s_1\backslash s_1$ mean that the object-language situation
variables (in normal typeface) are to be replaced by the corresponding
metalanguage situation variables (in boldface) during the calculation of
truth conditions. Applying (39) to (38), we obtain the truth conditions
in (40).

(40) For every minimal situation s_1 such that there is an x such that x is
     a man in s_1 and there is a y such that y is a donkey in s_1 and x
     owns y in s_1, there is a situation s_2 such that $s_1 \leq s_2$ and the unique
     x such that x is a man in s_1 beats in s_2 the unique y such that y is a
     donkey in s_1.

In (38) and (40) I have assumed that the pronouns are to be interpreted as
contextually salient functions from situations to individuals: *he* is interpreted as a function from situations to the unique man in those situations,
and *it* is interpreted as a function from situations to the unique donkey
in those situations.[13] These truth conditions too seem to be intuitively
adequate.

The problem is, of course, that in this approach we have to rely on
syncategorematic rules for quantification. Quantifiers do not have lexical
entries that enter into the compositional semantics like those of any other
word, and this special treatment is surely methodologically undesirable.
The reason such rules are necessary is the assumed desirability of truth
conditions like those in (40), in which the donkeys and men of the restrictor are picked out in the nuclear scope using the situation variable of the
restrictor (s_1 in this case). This means that we must be able to differentiate
between the predicates in the nuclear scope that have s_1 and those that
have s_2, and this in turn means that these variables must be present in
the syntax. It seems impossible to write any *semantic* rule, a rule operating on denotations, that would take the denotation of the nuclear scope
of a donkey sentence, computed in such a way as to use the same situation variable at all times, and go through and change the situation variables on the definites to those of the restrictor, while leaving those on the
other predicates alone. The reason is that the denotation is just a function

from situations to truth values (in cases like (37)); there are no "definites" in it, properly speaking, even though we might use definites in our meta-language when we write it down. We have to have situation variables in the syntax, then, in order to have truth conditions of the type in (40).[14] But now let us consider the consequences of this for any attempt to have a normal denotation for a word like *always*, a denotation that will take as arguments a certain number of semantic objects (two propositions in this case) and operate on them. We see that no such denotation will be possible in this case: the nuclear scope, to repeat, is going to look like the LF fragment in (41).

(41) $[he(s_1) \; beats(s_2) \; it(s_1)]$

Since there are two different situation variables here, we cannot arrive at a proposition: we could abstract over s_1 and leave s_2 free, or abstract over s_2 and leave s_1 free. Either way, we do not arrive at a proposition, but only at something that denotes a proposition relative to an assignment function. So there is no proposition derived from the nuclear scope that could be taken as an argument by a putative denotation of *always* that would take two propositions as arguments and still have the required distribution of situation variables. The only way to get the desired result seems to be the kind of syncategorematic rule used by Heim.

In an attempt to rectify this situation, I have replaced the syncategorematic rules by lexical entries of the type already given and exemplified. In this new system, the donkeys and men of the nuclear scope must be the ones introduced in the restrictor, because of two principles: the situations introduced to describe the nuclear scope are extensions of the ones introduced by the restrictor, meaning that the donkeys and men of the latter must be present in the former; and each new situation introduced has been specified to be the minimal situation that meets the conditions laid down, meaning that no other men or donkeys can be present in the nuclear-scope situations. I hope to have shown in the discussion following the truth conditions for donkey sentences in sections 2.3.1 and 2.3.2 that the mechanisms introduced are sufficient to deal with the normal cases.

There are still some harder examples to deal with, however. According to Heim (personal communication), LFs with both s_1 and s_2 present in the nuclear scope were introduced to deal with sentences like (42).

(42) If a donkey is lonely, it talks to another donkey.

The nuclear-scope situations created by this sentence must contain two donkeys. One of them was not present in the restrictor situations, however. So it looks as if it will be advantageous to be able to analyze the sentence as meaning something like (43), which we can do in the approach of Heim 1990.

(43) For every minimal situation s_1 such that there is an x such that x is a donkey in s_1 and x is lonely in s_1, there is a situation s_2 such that $s_1 \leq s_2$ and there is a y such that y is a donkey in s_2 and the unique x such that x is a donkey in s_1 talks to y in s_2.

Crucially, it looks as if we do not want to have to analyze *it* as meaning "the unique donkey in s_2," because there is no such unique donkey. The device of using both s_1 and s_2 in the description of the nuclear-scope situations makes it possible to distinguish the two donkeys here.

There certainly seems to be an advantage to the Heim 1990 system, then, when it comes to (42) and similar examples. However, I believe that this particular advantage is not worth pursuing. The reason is that even the devices just explained cannot help us when it comes to dealing with the indistinguishable participant sentences, which were described in section 1.3.2, and of which (44) is the most famous example.

(44) If a bishop meets a bishop, he blesses him.

The problem here is that the indistinguishable participants are both introduced in the restrictor, and hence cannot be distinguished by situation variables s_1 and s_2. Notice the similarity between (44) and (42). Both involve participants that look hard to distinguish. But it is obvious that (44) is the harder case: in (44), both participants are bishops, and both meet another bishop, and that is all we know about them when we get on to talking about blessing. In (42) only one of the donkeys is said to be lonely, and, of course, only one of them appears in the restrictor. So since (44) is similar to (42) in the problem it poses, but much harder, it is likely that whatever mechanism ultimately explains (44) will be able to explain (42) too. We should not, then, introduce a mechanism to explain the one that cannot explain the other, especially when that mechanism involves a retreat from the most constrained and satisfactory type of semantic compositionality. See chapter 4 for discussion of the indistinguishable participant cases.

Existentially Quantified Situations and the Nuclear Scope   I now wish to address another apparent problem concerning the treatment of definites in the type of situation semantics I have given above. That is that a sentence like (45) comes dangerously close to meaning (46).[15]

(45) Every man likes the woman.

(46) Every man likes a woman.

To show how this comes about, I give the LF of (45) and the calculation of its denotation.

(47) [[every man] [λ_2 [t_2 loves [the woman]]]]

(48) 1. $[\![[\text{every man}] [\lambda_2 [t_2 \text{ loves [the woman]}]]]\!]^\emptyset$

2. $= [\![\text{every}]\!]^\emptyset ([\![\text{man}]\!]^\emptyset) ([\![[\lambda_2 [t_2 \text{ loves [the woman]}]]]\!]^\emptyset)$ (FA)

3. $= [\![\text{every}]\!]^\emptyset ([\![\text{man}]\!]^\emptyset) (\lambda u.[\![[t_2 \text{ loves [the woman]}]]\!]^{[2 \to u]})$ (PA)

4. $= [\![\text{every}]\!]^\emptyset ([\![\text{man}]\!]^\emptyset) (\lambda u.[\![\text{loves}]\!]^{[2 \to u]} ([\![\text{the}]\!]^{[2 \to u]} ([\![\text{woman}]\!]^{[2 \to u]}))$
$([\![t_2]\!]^{[2 \to u]}))$ (FA)

5. $= [\![\text{every}]\!]^\emptyset ([\![\text{man}]\!]^\emptyset) (\lambda u.[\![\text{loves}]\!]^{[2 \to u]} ([\![\text{the}]\!]^{[2 \to u]} ([\![\text{woman}]\!]^{[2 \to u]}))$
$(u))$ (TR)

6. $= [\![\text{every}]\!]^\emptyset ([\![\text{man}]\!]^\emptyset) (\lambda u. [\lambda u''.\lambda u'''.\lambda s. u'''(s) \text{ loves } u''(s) \text{ in } s]$
$([\lambda f_{\langle\langle s,e\rangle, \langle s,t\rangle\rangle}.\lambda s' : \exists! x f(\lambda s''.x)(s') = 1. \iota x f(\lambda s''.x)(s') = 1]$
$(\lambda u'. \lambda s'''. u'(s''') \text{ is a woman in } s'')) (u))$ (Lex)

7. $= [\![\text{every}]\!]^\emptyset ([\![\text{man}]\!]^\emptyset) (\lambda u. [\lambda u''.\lambda u'''.\lambda s. u'''(s) \text{ loves } u''(s) \text{ in } s]$
$(\lambda s' : \exists! x\ x \text{ is a woman in } s'. \iota x\ x \text{ is a woman in } s') (u))$ (λC)

8. $= [\![\text{every}]\!]^\emptyset ([\![\text{man}]\!]^\emptyset) (\lambda u.\lambda s. u(s) \text{ loves in } s$
$[\lambda s' : \exists! x\ x \text{ is a woman in } s'. \iota x\ x \text{ is a woman in } s'](s))$ (λC)

9. $= [\![\text{every}]\!]^\emptyset ([\![\text{man}]\!]^\emptyset) (\lambda u.\lambda s. u(s) \text{ loves in } s\ \iota x\ x \text{ is a woman in } s)$
(λC)

10. $= [\lambda f_{\langle\langle s,e\rangle, \langle s,t\rangle\rangle}.\lambda g_{\langle\langle s,e\rangle, \langle s,t\rangle\rangle}. \lambda s. \text{ for every individual } x: \text{ for every}$
minimal situation s' such that $s' \leq s$ and $f(\lambda s.x)(s') = 1$,
there is a situation s'' such that $s'' \leq s$ and s'' is a minimal
situation such that $s' \leq s''$ and $g(\lambda s.x)(s'') = 1]$
$(\lambda u'. \lambda s'''. u'(s''') \text{ is a man in } s''') (\lambda u.\lambda s. u(s) \text{ loves in } s\ \iota x\ x$
is a woman in s)   (Lex)

11. $= \lambda s. \text{ for every individual } x: \text{ for every minimal situation } s' \text{ such}$
that $s' \leq s$ and x is a man in s', there is a situation s'' such
that $s'' \leq s$ and s'' is a minimal situation such that $s' \leq s''$
and $[\lambda u.\lambda s. u(s) \text{ loves in } s\ \iota x\ x \text{ is a woman in } s](\lambda s.x)(s'') = 1$
(λC)

12. $= \lambda s. \text{ for every individual } x: \text{ for every minimal situation } s' \text{ such}$
that $s' \leq s$ and x is a man in s', there is a situation s'' such
that $s'' \leq s$ and s'' is a minimal situation such that $s' \leq s''$
and x loves in $s''\ \iota x\ x$ is a woman in s'' (λC)

The concern can be expressed as follows. Take the truth conditions in line 12. They stipulate a set of minimal man-containing situations s', and then make a claim about a set of situations s'', extensions of s'. This much is uncontroversial. The question is what we should make of the claim that for every individual x, every minimal situation s' in which x is a man can be extended to a situation s'' in which x loves the unique woman in s''. The discomforting possibility is that sense can be made of this as follows. We take each of the minimal man-containing situations s' and look for some way of extending it to a situation containing a woman and the information that the man of s' loves the woman, and nothing else. Then there will indeed be extensions s'' of each s' such that it makes sense to say "x loves in s'' ιx x is a woman in s''." However, the objection continues, no restrictions are placed on how we are to expand the situations s' into situations s'' of this kind; we can just do it any way that works. The sentence claims that for each s' there is an s'' of the sort described. And this is just equivalent to saying that for every man there is a woman he loves. This would be a less than welcome result.

Fortunately, I think there are grounds for rejecting this objection. The basis of the counterargument is that in the truth conditions in line 12 it is presupposed and not asserted that each situation s'' contains exactly one woman. Thus it is necessary that this presupposition be accommodated. Now it might seem that there will be no difficulty in making the accommodation: the truth conditions only claim, after all, that for each minimal man-containing situation s' there is *an* extended situation s'' that contains exactly one woman; and this is obviously true, whatever set of men we take to be used in the restrictor. (Things would be different if the claim was that *all* extended situations had this property.) However, it is not the case that all presuppositions that are obviously true are automatically accommodated, as Kripke has pointed out in an unpublished manuscript by means of the following example, quoted by Beaver (1997, 992).

(49) Tonight Sam is having supper in New York, too.

A common analysis of *too* would analyze (49) as having the presupposition (50).

(50) Somebody other than Sam is having supper in New York tonight.

Now (50) will obviously be true, in the absence of extraordinary circumstances, for any given individual Sam and evening in New York. And yet if there is no previous explicit mention of someone other than Sam having supper in New York, (49) is infelicitous. The fact that the presupposition is obviously true is not in itself a sufficient condition for it to be accommodated. But it was an implicit assumption of the argument against the current situation semantics that such presuppositions would be automatically accommodated. Therefore the argument is not sound.

Can we make any positive proposals about what is going on in (49) and (45)? It has in fact already been suggested by van der Sandt (1992), Zeevat (1992), and Beaver (1997, 991–996) that sentences like these two share the property of having presuppositions that are *anaphoric*. The idea is that it is not enough for us to be able to work out on purely general grounds that people other than Sam are having supper in New York, or that there will be situations s'' containing exactly one woman; in order for the presuppositions to be satisfied in the right way, the necessary information must somehow be contextually salient. This is obviously not the case in utterances of (49) and (45) out of the blue.

I think that this idea is along the right lines, although it must be recognized that the differences between information that is and information that is not contextually salient are sometimes rather fine, especially in the case of definites. The presupposition carried by *too* seems to be such that some explicit previous utterance or perceptual stimulus is required as the basis for the anaphora. But the existence and uniqueness presuppositions of definites can sometimes be satisfied without direct immediately preceding input of this kind. For example, it is well known that sentences like the following are acceptable.

(51) Every time a ship enters rough weather, the captain orders the sails to be trimmed.

(52) When John calls at a house, he rings the bell twice.

These sentences are perfectly felicitous when uttered out of the blue, when there is no previous assertion that ships generally have exactly one captain and houses generally have exactly one bell (per door). Presumably, however, the definites are justified here because these propositions are generally known and have been previously encountered—in other words, they are part of the common ground. The general proposition that there are situations that contain exactly one woman, however, while it is true, is of a much more abstract kind, and is presumably not one that is explicitly formulated or contemplated very often. It will therefore generally not be part of the common ground in utterance situations. Thus, since the uniqueness presupposition incorporated by definites is an anaphoric presupposition, this proposition will not be able to be accommodated for an utterance of (45) out of the blue.

The details of the theory of anaphoric presuppositions are less important for our present purposes than the basic empirical observation, and I will not attempt to defend any particular proposal here. See the authors cited above for discussion. But two loose ends should be tied up. First, we should contrast (45) with the donkey sentences we have previously examined. For example, let us review the truth conditions for (25) (repeated here as (53)), given in (27) (repeated here as (54)).

(53) Every man who owns a donkey beats it.

(54) λs_4. for every individual y:

for every minimal situation s_5 such that

$s_5 \leq s_4$ and y is a man in s_5 and there is an individual x and a situation s_2 such that s_2 is a minimal situation such that $s_2 \leq s_5$ and x is a donkey in s_2, such that there is a situation s_3 such that $s_3 \leq s_5$ and s_3 is a minimal situation such that $s_2 \leq s_3$ and y owns x in s_3,

there is a situation s_6 such that

$s_6 \leq s_4$ and s_6 is a minimal situation such that $s_5 \leq s_6$ and y beats in s_6 ιz z is a donkey in s_6

In this case, we do not predict that there will be any difficulty with the anaphoric existence and uniqueness presuppositions of definites, since the donkeys necessary for the existence presupposition of "ιz z is a donkey in s_6" have been explicitly introduced, and the stipulation that minimal situations are to be considered takes care of the uniqueness presuppositions. So this sentence and similar ones differ in the right way from (45).

We can finally note that the solution given here makes the prediction that a sentence like (45) might in fact have a reading where the denotation of *the woman* covaries with the men. Such a reading is not absolutely ruled out. All that is necessary is that there be some prior reason to suppose that there will be women in the situations s''. In other words, the current approach makes the prediction that whether or not a sentence like (45) has covarying reading is a pragmatic matter, not a semantic matter. To test this prediction, let us construct a context that would be expected to favor such a reading, and see whether it emerges. The scenario in (55) seems to work.

(55) Each man was paired with a different woman for the training exercise. Fortunately, every man liked the woman, and things went smoothly.

Here, the sentence *every man liked the woman* does indeed have a reading of the type described. It is not equivalent to *every man liked a woman*, as the objection first claimed was predicted. Nor should we expect it to be, given the considerations we have now weighed. The requirement for a prior reason to presuppose the existence of women in the relevant situations makes it impossible that the reading should turn out to be equivalent to that obtained with *a woman*, because the latter normally implicates novelty or an inability to specify further.

I tentatively conclude, then, that the version of situation-semantics quantification adopted here makes the right predictions about cases like (45) and (55), as well as for the donkey sentences for which it was principally designed.

2.4   The Problem of the Formal Link

2.4.1   The Problem
As I mention in section 1.3.2, the D-type analysis has difficulty distinguishing between pairs of sentences like those in (56) and (57) (Heim 1982, 21–24, 80–81; 1990, 165–175).

(56) a.   Every man who has a wife is sitting next to her.
     b.   ?*Every married man is sitting next to her.

(57) a.   Someone who has a guitar should bring it.
     b.   ?*Some guitarist should bring it.

In the terms of the contextual versions of D-type pronouns sketched in section 1.3.1, utterance of (56b) should make salient the relation $[\lambda x. \lambda y. y$ is married to $x]$, which would suffice to yield a D-type denotation for *her*: the sentence would be able to be paraphrased, "For all x such that x is a married man, x sits next to the unique y such that y is married to x." The sentence has no such reading, however, creating a problem for these versions of the D-type strategy. Heim (1990, 165), following Kadmon (1987, 259), dubs this the problem of the *formal link* between donkey pronoun and antecedent: intuitively, *a wife* in (56a) seems to be acting as the antecedent to *her*, and (56b) is bad because here there is no such antecedent to which the donkey pronoun can be linked. In general, there seems to have to be an NP antecedent from which a D-type pronoun can derive its descriptive content.

2.4.2   Previous Solutions
There seem to be two routes that one could in principle take: one could keep the apparently problematic idea that D-type pronouns obtain their descriptive content by containing a variable over functions, or one could

reject it in favor of a syntactic procedure that extracts a predicate or predicates from the surrounding linguistic material in a mechanical fashion, as mentioned briefly under the heading of *linguistic* D-type theories in section 1.3.1. The first strategy is used by Chierchia (1992) and the second by Heim (1990) and Neale (1990). Both face problems of their own, as we will see.

Keeping the Variable Over Functions   The trouble with keeping the variable over functions is that, in order for the facts to be accounted for, a constraint must be imposed to the effect that this variable can only take on a value that is based, somehow, on the denotation of a Noun Phrase in the context. This is what Chierchia does, when he introduces the following principle (Chierchia 1992, 159):

(58) In a configuration of the form $NP_i \ldots it_i$, if it_i is interpreted as a function, the range of such functions is the (value of the) head of NP_i.

(He further needs to ensure that D-type pronouns *must* be coindexed with an NP; otherwise there would be nothing to prevent one from not being so indexed and picking up the "married-to" relation on the basis of the occurrence of *married* in (56b).) This kind of constraint does the job, of course, but at the cost of pure stipulation. Given a theory in which D-type pronouns denote functions from individuals to individuals (or from situations to individuals), it does not fall out naturally that the range of these functions should be determined by some NP in the linguistic environment, as opposed to a scenario in which some functions are available to be used because they are suggested by the semantic values of other types of words in the linguistic environment, or because they are contextually salient in some other way. Compare the case of referential pronouns: contextual salience alone is enough to provide a value for these free variables.

Using a Syntactic Procedure   The advantage of using a syntactic procedure is that we account naturally for the restriction to NPs. Making a free variable over functions only look at NPs is a strange thing to do; making a syntactic procedure target a particular category label, however, is eminently natural. That is just the kind of thing that syntactic procedures do.

The difficulty is in making the necessary procedure natural and, if possible, independently justified. I think it is fair to say that these desiderata have not been met by the solution proposed in Heim 1990. Heim proposes that NPs are freely indexed, thus allowing NPs to be the antecedent of pronouns by being coindexed with them; then a pronoun whose antecedent is not definite and does not have scope over it is rewritten according to the transformational rule in (59).

(59) X S Y NP$_i$ Z $\Rightarrow$ 1 2 3 4+2 5
 $\quad$ 1 2 3 4 $\quad$ 5
 $\quad$ conditions: 4 is a pronoun
 $\qquad\qquad\quad$ 2 is of the form [$_S$ NP$_i$ S]
 $\qquad\qquad\qquad\qquad\qquad$ 6 $\quad$ 7

Thus a copy of the antecedent (term 6) plus its sister (term 7) is inserted in the position of the pronoun. Heim assumes the material is Chomsky-adjoined to the pronoun. Thus (59) converts (60) into the LF in (61).

(60) [every$_{x_1}$ [man(x_1) that [[a$_{x_2}$ donkey(x_2)]$_2$ [x_1 owns x_2]]]]$_1$ [x_1 beats it$_2$]

(61) [every$_{x_1}$ [man(x_1) that [[a$_{x_2}$ donkey(x_2)]$_2$ [x_1 owns x_2]]]]$_1$ [x_1 beats [it$_2$[[a$_{x_2}$ donkey(x_2)]$_2$ [x_1 owns x_2]]]]

We furthermore need a semantic rule to give the right interpretation to the sequence [it$_2$[[a$_{x_2}$ donkey(x_2)]$_2$ [x_1 owns x_2]]]. The rule that accomplishes this is in (62).

(62) $[\![$it [[Det$_x$ α]β]$]\!]^g$ = the unique $\mathbf{x}$ such that $[\![\alpha]\!]^{gx\backslash \mathbf{x}} = [\![\beta]\!]^{gx\backslash \mathbf{x}}$ = True (undefined if there is no such individual)

With this machinery in place, we can see that we no longer predict a D-type reading for (56b) and similar examples. Example (56b) simply does not meet the structural description for (59).

   As Heim (1990, 171) points out, this approach to D-type pronominalization is reminiscent of theories of VP-ellipsis that have material copied and inserted at the site of the empty VP (Williams 1977). It is thus in fact very similar to the theory advocated in this chapter. The similarities between our two approaches might be thought to extend even to the claim that third-person pronouns can be interpreted the same way as the definite article: the rule in (62) is syncategorematic and does not specify a particular semantic contribution for the pronoun, but what intuitive plausibility the production of the definite description has derives from the fact that pronouns, like definite articles, are definite.

   Heim's solution is very similar to some ideas arrived at contemporaneously but independently by Neale (1990). It is perhaps not necessary to go into all the details of Neale's system here. Briefly, he translates sentences into a formal language RQ, a modification of first-order logic that includes restricted quantifiers, and then calculates the truth conditions of these RQ translations. The crucial rule he uses for donkey sentences is (63) (Neale 1990, 182–183).[16]

(63) If x is a pronoun that is anaphoric on, but not c-commanded by, a nonmaximal quantifier "$[Dx : Fx]$" that occurs in an antecedent clause "$[Dx : Fx](Gx)$," then x is interpreted as "$[$the $x : Fx$ & $Gx]$."

Take (64), and the RQ translation of its subject, (65).

(64) Every man who bought a donkey vaccinated it.

(65) [every x: man x & [a y: donkey y](x bought y)]

The antecedent clause for the pronoun *it*, anaphoric on *a donkey*, is (66). Applying (63) to the pronoun, therefore, we get (67).

(66) [a y: donkey y](x bought y)

(67) [the y: donkey y & x bought y]

This means that the RQ translation of the whole sentence (64) is (68).

(68) [every x: man x & [a y: donkey y](x bought y)]([the y: donkey y & x bought y](x vaccinated y))

This seems to get the truth conditions correct. Moreover, even though Neale does not explicitly mention the problem of the formal link, it is evident that the sentences we want to rule out do not meet the structural description in (63), because in subjects like *every married man* and *some guitarist* there is no antecedent clause of the form "$[Dx : Fx](Gx)$." So we can see Neale's system as another solution to the current problem, albeit perhaps an unintentional one.

It can be seen that these solutions of Heim and Neale, although they have the advantage of being syntactic procedures (one on the object language, the other on the metalanguage), cannot be said to be particularly natural and are not independently justified. They are complicated procedures that come into play only in the case of D-type pronouns, with the specific intention of arriving at the right interpretation for these pronouns. Although they arguably achieve the right results in the end, they do not seem particularly explanatory, therefore.

This is not to say that no solution using a syntactic procedure could work. I advocate a procedure that might broadly be called syntactic in the next section.

2.4.3   The Solution According to the NP-Deletion Theory

The theory that donkey anaphora is NP-deletion has a simple and natural way of explaining (56) and similar contrasts. We have seen in section 2.1.3 that, in the absence of any cue in the immediate physical environment, NP-deletion requires a linguistic antecedent, just like VP-ellipsis. There is a suitable linguistic antecedent in (56a), namely, *wife*. There is no suitable linguistic antecedent in (56b). No more need be said. Note that this solution uses an independently needed mechanism, and falls out naturally from the rest of the theory of donkey anaphora, in a way that the previous syntactic solutions do not.

2.5   Donkey Sentences and Strict/Sloppy Identity

2.5.1   A New Problem for the D-Type Analysis

The NP-deletion theory of donkey anaphora can claim another empirical advantage over standard D-type analyses when it comes to dealing with certain VP-elliptical continuations of donkey sentences. This data has not been examined before, to my knowledge.

Standard D-type analyses claim that D-type pronouns give covarying readings because they contain a bound individual variable. One variant (Heim and Kratzer 1998) has the variable be present at LF, producing a VP that looks like (69). Another (Cooper 1979) has the pronouns be syntactically simplex and introduces a bindable variable in their denotations. But whatever choices are made about LF, the denotation of a VP containing a D-type pronoun ends up like the one in (70).

(69) $[t_{\langle 1,e \rangle}$ beats $[$the $[R_{\langle 7,\langle e,et \rangle \rangle} \text{ pro}_{\langle 1,e \rangle}]]]$

(70) $\lambda x . x$ beats the unique z such that z is a donkey owned by x

Given this denotation, we then predict that a continuation sentence with a type e subject and VP-ellipsis (or a downstressed VP) will have a sloppy reading. We do not need to commit ourselves to any particular theory of VP-ellipsis in order to see this. All that is necessary is that the rules that directly or indirectly determine the availability of strict and sloppy readings should make reference to the denotation of the antecedent VP (or some constituent containing the antecedent VP). This seems virtually unavoidable, and is certainly the case in treatments such as those of Rooth 1992a, Tomioka 1997, Fox 2000, and Merchant 2001. Given this one basic assumption, we then only have to look at (71).

(71) a. In this town, every farmer who owns a donkey beats the donkey
        he owns, and the priest *beats the donkey he owns* too.
     b. In this town, every farmer who owns a donkey beats the donkey
        he owns, and the priest does too.

The antecedent VP *beats the donkey he owns* spells out as closely as possible in idiomatic English the denotation in (70). Its own denotation will certainly be equivalent to (70). We just have to observe now that the two sentences in (71) have sloppy readings: they can be read as presupposing that the priest has a donkey and stating that he beats it. But now notice the prediction: the sentences in (71) have sloppy readings; the VPs of these sentences have denotations equivalent to the postulated VP-denotations of donkey sentences; distribution of strict and sloppy readings relies on the denotations of the antecedent VPs; so we predict, if we believe standard D-type accounts, that donkey sentences followed by elliptical continuation sentences with type e subjects will have sloppy readings.

We will now examine the data relevant to this prediction, and show it to be false.[17] Consider the pair of sentences in (72).

(72) a. In this town, every farmer who owns a donkey beats the donkey
        he owns, and the priest *beats the donkey he owns* too.   (sloppy, strict)
     b. In this town, every farmer who owns a donkey beats it, and the
        priest *beats it* too.   (*sloppy, strict)

Example (72a) repeats (71a). In (72b) we have a donkey sentence followed by a sentence with subject of type e and a repeated, phonologically reduced version of the VP of the first sentence. Given (70), we predict that a sloppy reading will be possible. But (and this is an extremely sharp judgment) it is not possible. Note that we cannot explain the lack of a sloppy reading in (72b) by appealing to any difficulty in accommodating the presupposition that the priest owns a donkey, because we have no trouble accommodating the identical presupposition in (72a), and standard D-type analyses claim that (72a) is identical to (72b) in all relevant respects.[18]

The corresponding pair of sentences with VP-ellipsis instead of phonological reduction is in (73).

(73) a. In this town, every farmer who owns a donkey beats the donkey
        he owns, and the priest does too.   (sloppy, strict)
     b. In this town, every farmer who owns a donkey beats it, and the
        priest does too.   (?*sloppy, strict)

Exactly the same contrast surfaces.[19] The same judgments are obtained, and similar comments apply, when we investigate conditional sentences, as in (74) and (75).

(74) a. In this town, if a farmer owns a donkey he beats the donkey he
           owns, and the priest *beats the donkey he owns* too.   (sloppy, strict)
     b. In this town, if a farmer owns a donkey he beats it, and the
           priest *beats it* too.   (*sloppy, strict)

(75) a. In this town, if a farmer owns a donkey he beats the donkey he
           owns, and the priest does too.   (sloppy, strict)
     b. In this town, if a farmer owns a donkey he beats it, and the
           priest does too.   (?*sloppy, strict)

Sloppy readings do not seem to be possible in these sentences.[20] This falsifies the prediction we made earlier. The standard D-type analysis cannot be correct.

2.5.2   The Consequences for Variable-Free Semantics

It is worth noting that the data just examined seem also to raise a problem for Jacobson's (2000a) variable-free semantics account of donkey anaphora. Recall from (84) in section 1.5.1 that the denotation of the VP *lost it* in (76) comes out to be (77).

(76) Bill immediately put his paycheck in the bank. But every student
       lost it.

(77) $\lambda g_{\langle e,e \rangle}.\, \lambda z.\, z$ lost $g(z)$

So here too we see that an individual variable (z) in the argument position of the paycheck pronoun ends up being bound by the λ-abstractor that closes off the VP-denotation. Jacobson's system gives results equivalent to a traditional D-type account, then, in this respect.

Let us briefly go through example (74b) in Jacobson's system. By the mechanisms given in section 1.5.1 that lead to (77), the VP of the second sentence (78) will have the denotation (79).

(78) ... the priest beats it, too.

(79) $\lambda g_{\langle e,e \rangle}.\, \lambda z.\, z$ beats $g(z)$

Jacobson assumes with many other researchers that items of type e can undergo a type-raising process that will convert them into generalized quantifiers (Jacobson 1999, 120). So the subject *the priest* will be able to have the denotation in (80).

(80) $\lambda P_{\langle e,t \rangle}. P(\imath x \; x \text{ is a priest})$

In section 1.5.1, we saw how application of $\mathbf{g}_{\langle e,e \rangle}$ enabled the basic denotation of *every student* to shift to a function that can take as argument a function like (79) and pass up the type $\langle e, e \rangle$ slot. Similarly, we can shift (80) to (81).

(81) $\lambda \mathcal{F}_{\langle ee,et \rangle}. \lambda f_{\langle e,e \rangle}. \mathcal{F}(f)(\imath x \; x \text{ is a priest})$

We now combine the denotations of *the priest* and *beats it* in the normal way.

(82) $\quad [\lambda \mathcal{F}_{\langle ee,et \rangle}. \lambda f_{\langle e,e \rangle}. \mathcal{F}(f)(\imath x \; x \text{ is a priest})] \; (\lambda g_{\langle e,e \rangle}. \lambda z. z \text{ beats } g(z))$
$\quad = \lambda f_{\langle e,e \rangle}. [\lambda g_{\langle e,e \rangle}. \lambda z. z \text{ beats } g(z)](f)(\imath x \; x \text{ is a priest})$
$\quad = \lambda f_{\langle e,e \rangle}. \imath x \; x \text{ is a priest beats } f(\imath x \; x \text{ is a priest})$

As with other examples in Jacobson's system, we should now be able to apply this function to the contextually salient function mapping people to their donkeys. This would result in a reading whereby the priest beats his own donkey, of course. But we have seen that the sentence actually has no such reading.

2.5.3   A Solution Using the NP-Deletion Theory

The Solution for Examples with *if*-Clauses   Let us consider the LF structure of our example (74b), repeated here with the addition of an explicit quantificational adverb as (83).

(83)   In this town, if a farmer owns a donkey he always beats it, and the
         priest *beats it* too.   (*sloppy, strict)

We have already seen the structure of *If a farmer owns a donkey he beats it* in (22). The LF structure of (83) depends on what the two conjuncts of *and* are. The sentence *the priest beats it too* must form one of the conjuncts. Since it is a sentence, there seem to be two possibilities for the overall structure. Either *the priest beats it too* is conjoined with *he beats it*, and thus forms a continuation of the consequent of the conditional, or it is conjoined with *If a farmer owns a donkey he beats it*. I will examine both possibilities, the object being to show that both options yield up only strict readings if the semantics advocated in this chapter is adopted.

   The structure of the first option, where the sentence with the phonologically reduced VP simply forms part of the consequent of the conditional, is shown in (84). Applying our semantics, we obtain the truth conditions in (85), given in simplified form to aid exposition.

(84)

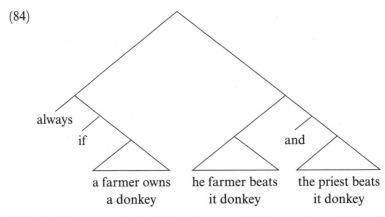

always

if   and

a farmer owns   he farmer beats   the priest beats
   a donkey   it donkey   it donkey

(85) λs_1. for every minimal situation s_2 such that $s_2 \leq s_1$ and there is an
individual x such that x is a farmer in s_2 and there is an individual
y such that y is a donkey in s_2 and x owns y in s_2, there is a
situation s_3 such that $s_3 \leq s_1$ and s_3 is a minimal situation such that
$s_2 \leq s_3$ and the unique farmer in s_3 beats in s_3 the unique donkey in
s_3 and the unique priest in s_3 beats in s_3 the unique donkey in s_3.

These truth conditions are intuitively correct. In particular, the donkeys
beaten by the priest are the same as the ones beaten by the farmers, and
were introduced in the definition of the situations s_2 as belonging to the
farmers. The correct strict reading is obtained, therefore.

The only matter still potentially problematic with regard to this structure is the status of the priest or priests who figure in the truth conditions.
The example is most naturally read as talking about only one priest, the
priest who serves the town. But the truth conditions do not necessitate
this, and in fact leave open the possibility that there could be many
priests, covarying with the farmers. I actually do not think this is problematic, because this reading does exist for the sentence, although it is
marginal: one has to imagine that we are talking about an extremely reli-
gious neighborhood, with one priest stationed in every farmhouse. Compare (86), where there is obvious covariance in the denotation of the
subject of the ellipsis sentence.

(86) If a farmer owns a donkey he beats it, and his wife does too.

It is entirely appropriate, then, that the truth conditions leave this matter
vague: in the religious-neighborhood scenario, we can take the priest in
each extended situation s_3 to be the priest stationed in the farmhouse of
the farmer in each situation s_2. But if we know that such a scenario is unlikely, we can imagine the priest in each situation s_3 to be the same person

each time, the priest of the town, or some other contextually salient priest.

Let us move on, then, to the other possible structure, which is shown in (87). In this structure, *the priest beats it* is not in the scope of the overt

(87)

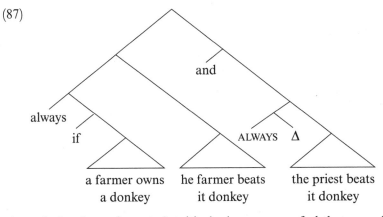

always

if   ALWAYS   Δ

a farmer owns   he farmer beats   the priest beats
a donkey   it donkey   it donkey

always in *he always beats it*. Intuitively, however, we feel that some kind of universal applicability is being claimed for the beating handed out by the priest, as well as for that given by the farmers. To account for this intuition, then, a proponent of this general structure would have to make the move shown in (87), whereby a phonologically null quantificational adverb with universal force (here written ALWAYS) is postulated for the second conjunct. Recall from section 2.3.1 that Berman and others have already proposed that such a thing exists in order to deal with examples like (74b), where there is universal force but no overt quantificational adverb.[21] This quantificational adverb will of course require a restrictor, and I have indicated a syntactic slot for one in (87) with the branch whose terminal is Δ. We can be agnostic about the nature of Δ. We could imagine that it is an ellipsis site, with material equivalent to the previous restrictor *if a farmer owns a donkey* syntactically present, or we could imagine it to be merely a propositional variable that will receive as denotation the salient proposition that is the meaning of *a farmer owns a donkey*. Either way, I think that by this stage it will be evident on reflection (the calculation could easily be performed) that (87) will have a denotation equivalent to that of the previous structure (84). In particular, the meaning of the last sentence *the priest beats it* will be, roughly: for every minimal situation in which a farmer owns a donkey, there is an extended situation in which the unique priest in that situation beats the unique donkey in that situation. And the donkeys of the extended situations must be the donkeys of the smaller situations, as before, in order for the uniqueness presuppositions not to be violated. So the correct strict reading is obtained once more.

Although it is not essential for the current project, there may be some interest in asking which of the above structures is correct, or if they are both available. The first structure, (84), certainly seems more straightforward, without the phonologically null and seemingly redundant structure posited by the second one, (87). But note that the structure in (87) will certainly be necessary when another overt quantificational adverb is introduced in the sentence with the phonologically reduced or elided VP, as in (88).

(88) If a farmer owns a donkey he beats it, and the priest usually *beats it* too.

Given also that we need a null universal quantificational adverb to deal with examples like (74b), it is hard to rule out the structure in (87). I tentatively conclude, then, that both structures are available.

Be that as it may, it seems that both the conceivable structures for (83) yield only a strict reading, in accordance with the facts, if analyzed according to the view of donkey anaphora advocated in this chapter, and the accompanying situation semantics.

The Solution for Examples with QP and Relative Clause   Let us go on to consider the interpretation of relative-clause donkey sentences plus continuations with ellipsis or phonological reduction, as in (72b), repeated here as (89).

(89) In this town, every farmer who owns a donkey beats it, and the priest *beats it* too.   (*sloppy, strict)

The surface structure of this example seems to be something like (90).

(90)

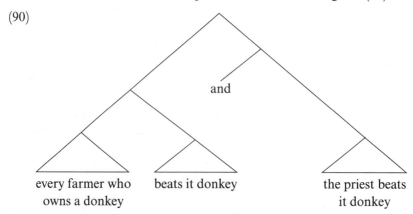

There is a question, then, as to how a covarying reading for the final *it* is to be obtained. Again, there seem to be two possibilities.

First, one could reproduce the second solution, (87), given for examples with conditionals. That is, one could suppose that before *the priest beats it* there is a null quantificational adverb, as shown in (91). Note that if

(91)

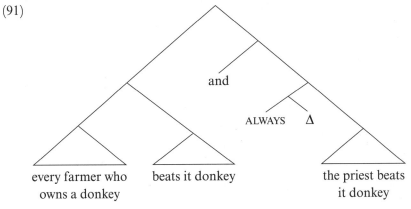

this is how things work, Δ must not need a syntactically present sentential antecedent, since there is no suitable antecedent in (91). A suitable proposition must be able to be the value of Δ through contextual salience alone, but I cannot see any immediate problem with such an approach. Assuming that the value of Δ here can be what it was in (87), we see that *the priest beats it* comes out to mean what it did in this earlier sentence, and that the correct strict reading is obtained.

The question now becomes whether any other plausibly obtainable value of Δ would give rise to an unwelcome sloppy reading. If there is to be a sloppy reading, the donkey beaten by the priest must belong to the priest, and so, in order for [it donkey] to pick this out, the value of Δ must somehow introduce situations in which the priest owns a donkey. But it is plausible to claim that there is no way this could come about, since there has been no previous mention of priests owning donkeys. It seems, then, that the solution in (91) predicts correctly that only a strict reading will be available.

Let us move on, then, to examine the other way the final *it* in (89) could possibly achieve a covarying reading. If it does not come under the scope of a quantificational element in its own sentence, the second conjunct, as just suggested, the only other possibility is that it comes under the scope of such an element in the first conjunct. The quantificational element there, of course, is the determiner *every*.

It looks, then, as if the second solution needs the QP *every farmer who owns a donkey* to raise and adjoin to the whole ConjP, making *the priest beats it* part of the nuclear scope of its quantificational structure. But this seems immediately to run foul of the Coordinate Structure Constraint (CSC) of Ross (1967), which forbids movement of or out of a conjunct. The CSC is exemplified by such crashingly bad sentences as those in (92) and (93), where movement has taken place overtly.

(92) a. *Which surgeon did Kim date *t* and a lawyer?
     b. *Which surgeon did Kim date a lawyer and *t*?

(93) a. *Which surgeon did Kim date friends of *t* and a lawyer?
     b. *Which surgeon did Kim date a lawyer and friends of *t*?

More importantly for the present discussion, there is also evidence that the CSC holds at LF, forbidding QR of a conjunct or out of a conjunct (Lakoff 1970; Rodman 1976; May 1985). This is shown in (94).

(94) a. A student likes every professor.   ($\exists > \forall, \forall > \exists$)
     b. A student [[likes every professor] and [hates the dean]]
                                                              ($\exists > \forall, *\forall > \exists$)

When *every professor* is in a conjunct, in (94b), it cannot raise at LF and have scope over *a student*.

It would seem, then, that we cannot resolve our difficulty by having *every farmer who owns a donkey* in (90) raise at LF and bind into the second conjunct. But actually there does exist evidence that such movement is possible in limited circumstances. Ruys (1993) has observed that when there is a bindable variable in the second conjunct a QP in the first conjunct *can* raise at LF in order to bind it.[22] Compare (95a) (= (94b)) with (95b).

(95) a. A student [[likes every professor] and [hates the dean]]
                                                              ($\exists > \forall, *\forall > \exists$)
     b. A (different) student [[likes every professor$_1$] and [wants her$_1$ to be on his committee]]   ($\exists > \forall, \forall > \exists$)

This, then, is a very good parallel for the situation presented to us by (90): we are hard put to make any sense of the *it* of the second conjunct without putting a covarying interpretation on it, and that can be achieved by construing it as a donkey pronoun and having the subject of the first conjunct raise and bind the situation variable of the following (phonologically null) NP. We end up with the structure in (96) at LF. According to

(96)

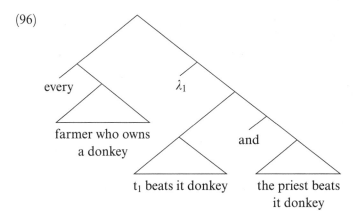

our semantics, (96) has the truth conditions in (97), again simplified so as to be more readily comprehensible.

(97) λs_1. for every individual x: for every minimal situation s_2 such that $s_2 \leq s_1$ and x is a farmer in s_2 and there is an individual y such that y is a donkey in s_2 and x owns y in s_2, there is a situation s_3 such that $s_3 \leq s_1$ and s_3 is a minimal situation such that $s_2 \leq s_3$ and x beats in s_3 the unique donkey in s_3 and the unique priest in s_3 beats in s_3 the unique donkey in s_3.

Once more, only a strict reading is obtained.

This concludes the main part of the discussion of the problem of donkey sentences and continuations with phonologically reduced VPs. It can be seen that in the analysis of these data the theory that donkey anaphora is NP-deletion scores a significant empirical point over conventional D-type analyses.

Some Related Data   In the interest of strict accuracy, we should note that there is a further complication in the judgments given by speakers on strict and sloppy identity in continuations of donkey sentences with VP-ellipsis or phonologically reduced VPs. In the examples used in section 2.5.1, the type e subject of the continuation sentence was not a member of the set denoted by the NP in the QP subject of the donkey sentence. It is an interesting fact that when it *is* a member of this set, sloppy readings suddenly become available, as we see in (98).[23]

(98) a. Almost every student who was awarded a prize accepted it, but
    the valedictorian didn't *accept it*.   (sloppy, ?strict)

   b. Almost every student who was awarded a prize accepted it, but
    the valedictorian didn't.   (sloppy, ?strict)

We can tell that membership by the second subject in the set denoted by the NP of the first is indeed an important factor by means of the following (admittedly awkward) minimal pair. (Father Giles is the priest of the town being described.)

(99) a. In this town, almost every farmer who owns a donkey beats it, but Father Giles doesn't *beat it*.   (*sloppy, ?strict)

    b. In this town, almost every farmer who owns a donkey beats it, but Farmer Giles doesn't *beat it*.   (?sloppy, ?strict)

What should we make of these facts?

I think that the answer to this puzzle is as follows. The strict readings in the above examples are obtained in one of the ways we have just been examining, of course: insertion of a null quantificational adverb in the second sentence or QR of the QP subject of the first sentence. The sloppy readings are obtained simply by refraining from utilizing these mechanisms and yet still having the *it* of the second sentence be followed by an NP: so we have [it prize] or [it donkey] in the second sentence. So the second sentence of (99b), for example, has the structure in (100a) and the denotation in (100b).

(100) a. [[Farmer Giles] [does [not [beat [it donkey]]]]]

    b. λs. Farmer Giles does not beat in s the unique donkey in s

Let us start by noting that, if (100a) is how the second sentence of (99b) looks at LF, both it and the first sentence of (99b) will have VPs with the denotation in (101).

(101) $\lambda u_{\langle s,e \rangle}. \lambda s. u(s)$ beats in s the unique x such that x is a donkey in s

This, presumably, is what allows the VP-ellipsis to take place.

But now what are we to make of "the unique donkey in s"? There will not necessarily be a problem with the presuppositions of uniqueness and existence. To make sensé of the sentence, it suffices to interpret "the unique donkey in s" as being the donkey owned by Farmer Giles; presumably we use the well-known mechanism of narrowing down the universe of discourse in order to make sense of "improper" definite descriptions. Now if we did not previously know that Farmer Giles had a donkey, we will be helped in accommodating this presupposition by the fact noted above about membership in the set denoted by the NP of the subject of the first conjunct: Farmer Giles, since he is a farmer, could be a member of the set of farmers who own donkeys, just introduced, and realization of this possibility is ipso facto a tentative accommodation of the presupposition that Farmer Giles owns a donkey. We are not only helped in this accommodation by the explicit mention of the set of farmers who own donkeys, but also by the fact that, if Farmer Giles did own a donkey, the second sentence would then be an explanation of why the first sentence says *almost every* instead of the stronger *every*. (For whatever reason, there is an expectation that an explanation of this type will be following when we say *almost every ... but*.) All in all, then, there are powerful factors that enable us to accommodate the presupposition that Farmer Giles has a donkey, and thus to allow the sloppy reading of (99b). But when in (99a) we substitute Father Giles for Farmer Giles, no analogous factors are present: no set of donkey-owning priests has just been explicitly introduced, and the supposition that Father Giles has a donkey will not enable us to make sense of the *almost every ... but* locution. Thus we are not able to accommodate the presupposition that Father Giles has a donkey, and no sloppy reading is available for (99a), even if we give it a structure and content isomorphic to (100a) and refrain from raising the QP subject of its first conjunct at LF.[24]

2.6   The Other Uses for D-Type Pronouns

So far this chapter has concentrated exclusively on donkey anaphora, for the very good reason that the majority of the work on D-type pronouns seems to be concerned with this particular manifestation of them. But there are of course other types of sentence in which linguists have posited the existence of these pronouns, and it remains to be shown that the approach being advocated can deal with these too. I will take the following to be an adequate sample: Bach-Peters sentences, quantificational subordination, modal subordination, and paycheck sentences.

2.6.1   Bach-Peters Sentences

Bach and Peters observed that there is no way both pronouns in sentences like (102) can be bound at the same time (Bach 1970). Either *every pilot who shot at it* c-commands *him* or *the MiG that chased him* c-commands *it*, but not both.

(102) Every pilot who shot at it hit the MiG that chased him.

Jacobson subsequently proposed that these sentences be handled by having the first pronoun, *it* in (102), be derived from a full NP, *the MiG that chased him* (Jacobson 1977).

Essentially the same solution can be maintained under the theory that D-type pronouns are in fact definite articles. We simply suppose that an

NP *MiG that chased him* has been deleted by NP-deletion after the definite article *it*, as illustrated in (103). We thus predict that (102) means exactly the same as (104), which is correct.

(103) every pilot who shot at [it ~~MiG that chased him~~] hit [the MiG that chased him]

(104) Every pilot who shot at the MiG that chased him hit the MiG that chased him.

Note that the "antecedent" for NP-deletion does not literally come before the deleted phrase on this occasion. This is unproblematic, since it is easy to construct examples of uncontroversial NP-deletion where the same thing happens, as in (105). If we start with the same underlying sentence and use NP-deletion to erase the second NP instead of the first, we end up with (106), which also means the same as (102), in accordance with our hypothesis.

(105) John's was an awful fate.

(106) Every pilot who shot at the MiG that chased him hit it.

There is no problem, then, in accounting for Bach-Peters sentences on the NP-deletion theory.

2.6.2 Quantificational and Modal Subordination

As the term is normally used in the literature,[25] quantificational subordination is the phenomenon exhibited by (107) (Heim 1990, 139).

(107) Most books contain a table of contents. In some, it is at the end.

It is immediately evident that examples like this pose no problem for the NP-deletion theory. We only have to suppose that NP-deletion has taken place twice in the second sentence of (107), the antecedents being in the previous sentence. This second sentence, then, is predicted to have the same LF as (108).

(108) In some books, the table of contents is at the end.

And, as predicted, (108) means exactly the same as the second sentence in (107). If there is any problem at all here, then, it is not one that concerns the interpretation of pronouns.

We can say the same about the phenomenon of modal subordination (Roberts 1989, 1996), exemplified in (109).

(109) John wants to catch a fish. He hopes I will grill it for him.

The present theory simply predicts that (109) will mean the same as (110), which is correct.

(110) John wants to catch a fish. He hopes I will grill the fish for him.

We can leave aside, given our present purposes, the problem of how *the fish* in the second sentence of (110) comes to talk about the putative fish that John may or may not catch.

2.6.3 Paycheck Sentences

The use of D-type pronouns to analyze paycheck sentences is one of their oldest applications, dating back to Cooper's 1979 paper. The classic example is from Karttunen 1969:

(111) The man who gave his paycheck to his wife was wiser than the man who gave it to his mistress.

To the supposition that there is a problem here, one might object that the paycheck of the man who gave his paycheck to his mistress has become contextually salient, meaning that it could just be picked up by a referential pronoun. The following variant of the sentence, introduced by Cooper (1979, 77), makes the problem explicit, however.

(112) John gave his paycheck to his mistress. Everybody else put it in the bank.

Here we are faced with the familiar problem of covariance without c-command. Cooper solves the problem in the normal way by treating *it* as a definite description meaning "the paycheck of *x*," with the individual variable bound by *everybody else*.

Let us now see how the NP-deletion theory handles this case. At first there seems to be a problem in that *his* in *his paycheck* is in [Spec, DP], according to contemporary syntactic accounts (Abney 1987). This would mean that the NP deleted in the second sentence of (112) could consist of at most the word *paycheck*, which would seem to give no basis for the necessary covariance.

One could explore two options at this stage. One would be to take advantage of situation semantics and see if a situation variable on *paycheck* could give the desired effect, as we saw earlier with donkey anaphora. That is, we could just suppose that the second sentence of (112) has a (simplified) LF like that in (113).

(113) [[everybody else] [put-in-the-bank [it paycheck]]]

We would then get truth conditions like those in (114) (slightly simplified).

(114) λs. for every individual x: for every minimal situation s' such that
$s' \leq s$ and x is person not identical with John in s', there is a
situation s'' such that $s'' \leq s$ and s'' is a minimal situation such
that $s' \leq s''$ and x put in the bank in s'' the unique y such that y is
a paycheck in s''.

It is possible that this strategy might work. If this is the correct account, a
listener would be put in the position of having to accommodate the existence of paychecks in the situations s'' (one for each person x), as is done
with women in the example *Every man liked the woman* (55) discussed in
section 2.3.3. It is plausible that this could happen. After all, (112) explicitly contrasts the behavior of John and other people with respect to their
paychecks, and is most naturally delivered with contrastive stress on both
John and *to his mistress*, which would warn the listener that some other
kind of location for other people's paychecks is forthcoming. It is plausible, then, that the LF could simply be (113), and that (112) works like
(55).

The second option we should explore is that the *his* in *his paycheck* is in
fact within NP at LF. Let us assume that, in cases where NP-deletion is
licensed by a linguistic antecedent (see section 2.1.3), the process of veri-
fying that a suitable antecedent is present takes place at LF, as has been
argued to be the case in the related phenomenon of VP-ellipsis. Then we
could have the individual variable *his* as part of the deleted material
in the second sentence of (112), and the necessary covariance could be
achieved by having this bound by *everybody else*. Roughly, then, the relevant structure at LF would be like that in (115).

(115) John gave [$_{DP}$ the [$_{NP}$ paycheck of him]] to his mistress.
       Everybody else put [$_{DP}$ it [$_{NP}$ paycheck of him]] in the bank.

We see that there is an antecedent for the deleted NP *paycheck of him*,
and that straightforward variable binding in the second sentence achieves
the attested reading.

What reason do we have to believe that possessive DPs can be within
the NP they modify at LF? The answer is found in work by Larson and
Cho (1999), who examine the ambiguity of DPs like *John's former house*
and *John's old car*. The former phrase, for example, can refer either to the
object John owns that was formerly a house (the "N-modifying reading"
of *former*) or to the house John used to own (the "POSS-modifying reading"). Larson and Cho plausibly explain this ambiguity as structural,
depending on the order in which the elements in possessive DPs combine
with each other in the semantics. Very informally, if *former* is the first

thing to compose with *house*, we get a former house, something that was once a house; add *John's* and we have the object of this kind owned by John, and the N-modifying reading above. But if *John's* is the first thing to compose with house, we get a house owned by John; add *former* and we have something that was formerly a house owned by John, and the POSS-modifying reading above. (The reader is referred to Larson and Cho's 1999 paper for a technical implementation.) The point of relevance for the analysis of paycheck sentences is that in order for *John's* to compose with *house* before *former* does, it is most plausibly in a low position, within NP. We have every reason to believe, then, that something like (115) could indeed show the relevant structure in paycheck sentences, which means that the covariance is achieved simply by *his* being bound by *everybody else*.[26]

2.7 Some Objections

In this section I analyze some apparently problematic cases that have been brought to my attention. I do not in fact think that they constitute serious objections to the NP-deletion theory, but they do highlight the fact that there is a lot we still do not know about some of the topics dealt with in this chapter.

2.7.1 Weak Readings

Some commentators have objected to the NP-deletion theory on the grounds that it could not deal with so-called weak readings of donkey sentences. As we have seen in section 1.4.2, with some donkey sentences, we have the intuition that it is being asserted that the owners of the donkeys execute their depraved wishes upon all of their charges, as in (116) (Heim 1990, 151).

(116) If a farmer owns a donkey, he deducts it from his taxes.

This is the strong reading (or the ∀-reading, in the terminology of Chierchia 1992, 1995). In some donkey sentences, however, our intuitions tell us that some of the animals have a lucky escape. The standard example is (117) (Pelletier and Schubert 1989; Chierchia 1992, 1995), where no one has to put *all* their dimes in the meter.

(117) Everyone who had a dime put it in the meter.

This is the weak reading (Chierchia's ∃-reading). It is claimed that if donkey pronouns have the semantics of a definite these nonexhaustive readings are not expected.

This view rests on an inadequate assessment of the semantics of definiteness, however. Let us see how the NP-deletion theory fares in these cases by testing the prediction that it makes, that the corresponding sentences with explicit definite descriptions will also have weak readings. Some relevant examples are in (49).

(118) a. Everyone who had a dime put the dime in the meter.
      b. Everyone who has a credit card will pay their bill with the
         credit card.

While these examples are perhaps slightly awkward, they are clearly grammatical, and they clearly do *not* imply that anyone put all their dimes in the meter or will pay with all their credit cards. There is no problem here, then, for the NP-deletion theory. It claims that (48) has the same LF as (118a), and the meanings of the two sentences are indeed identical.

This is not to say that there is no problem here at all. The semantics for *every* given in section 2.2 does indeed predict prima facie that (118a) should mean that everyone put all their dimes in the meter. It is just that the problem is not a problem with the NP-deletion theory per se. I will not make an attempt to solve it here.

2.7.2   Split Antecedents

Donkeys and Disjunction   Consider (119) and (120), which were first brought to my attention by Bernhard Schwarz. (For similar examples, see Groenendijk and Stokhof 1991, 88; Stone 1992; Chierchia 1995, 71.)

(119) If Mary sees a donkey or a horse, she waves to it.

(120) If Mary sees John or Bill, she waves to him.

According to the NP-deletion theory, there must have been deletion of an NP after *it* in (119). But what could the antecedent possibly be? To get the meaning to come out right, we presumably need something like *donkey or horse*. ("If Mary sees a donkey or a horse, she waves to the donkey or horse.") But this is nowhere to be found. The nearest we have is *a donkey or a horse*, but this is not an NP but a disjunction of two DPs. Things seem, if possible, to be even worse with (120), where there are not even any words that we would ordinarily feel comfortable putting after a definite article in English at all.[27]

A similar difficulty exists with conjunction, of course, in a case like (121).

(121) If Mary sees a donkey and a horse, she waves to them.

But naturally, the corresponding example with *John and Bill* creates no problems, because there the pronoun could be referential.

This difficulty is interesting, in that it provides a new twist to the much-discussed problem of how to constrain the descriptive content of D-type pronouns. Examples like (56) seem to show that the normal D-type theories are too lax in what they allow. But examples like (119) and (120) caution us against going too far the other way: we need to strike a very fine balance.

Ellipsis, Disjunction, and Conjunction I claim, however, that the NP-deletion theory already has within it the necessary flexibility to deal with these disjunction facts. All we need to do is to revise some implicit and unfounded assumptions about the nature of "NP-deletion," and the problem presented by (119) and (120) begins to dissolve.

It has actually been known for some time, though the fact is usually passed over in embarrassed silence, that VP-ellipsis is possible when the antecedent is discontinous and distributed over the two halves of a disjunction or conjunction. The observation goes back at least to Webber (1978), and Fiengo and May (1994, 195–200) discuss the phenomenon.

Let us first consider (122) and (123), which are taken from Fiengo and May 1994.

(122) What an inconvenience! Whenever Max uses the fax or Oscar uses the Xerox, I can't.

(123) I did everything that Mary did. Mary swam the English Channel, and Mary climbed Kilimanjaro, and I did, too.

Notice that the VP understood for (122) is "use the fax or use the Xerox," and the VP understood for (123) is "swam the English Channel and climbed Kilimanjaro." However, there is no constituent matching these in the previous linguistic environment. In both cases, the linguistic environment provides exact matches for each disjunct or conjunct individually, but no constituent with them both conjoined in the way they are understood at the ellipsis site.

We might pause here to consider what might possibly be the explanation of this phenomenon, even though for my present purposes the explanation of it is less important than its existence. On this point, in fact, I am content to admit total bafflement; I wish merely to point out that the only explanation I have read seems to face problems. Fiengo and May in the passage cited above are not entirely explicit, but they seem to be operating under the assumption that in these cases there are three separate operations of reconstruction or copying (1994, 200, note 7): the two antecedent VPs are separately copied and inserted at the ellipsis site, and the conjunction *and* or *or* is copied and put in there too. In this way, the VP-disjunction or conjunction that we understand is supposed to be built up in stages from material overtly present.

This cannot be the correct story, however, because there are examples of this phenomenon that do not include *and* or *or*. Take (124) and (125), for example, which are simple variants of the examples we have just seen.

(124) Max is always using the fax. Oscar is always using the Xerox machine. I can't, of course, when they are.

(125) Mary swam the English Channel. Mary climbed Kilimanjaro. I did, too.

In (124), we understand "use the fax or use the Xerox machine" after *can't* and "using the fax or using the Xerox machine" after *they are*; in (125), we understand "swam the English Channel and climbed Kilimanjaro." We understand exactly the same VP-disjunctions or conjunctions, that is, even though the words *and* and *or* are not present. It seems that we have the ability simply to supply these words between VPs for which there are overt antecedents. This fact presumably will have consequences for our theories of VP-ellipsis, indicating that any theory that relies only on a literal-minded process of copying or deletion under identity is too strict, but it is not the purpose of this chapter to pursue these implications.

The discussion so far has been of VP-ellipsis, which is of course not directly relevant to the NP-deletion theory of donkey anaphora. As far as I know, no one has previously pointed out that an exact analogue to the phenomenon just described can in fact be observed in NP-deletion too. Once one thinks about it, however, examples are not hard to construct:

(126) Mary needs a hammer or a mallet. She's hoping to borrow Bill's.

(127) Mary needs a hammer and a mallet. She's hoping to borrow Bill's.

In (126), we understand "Bill's hammer or mallet"; in (127), we understand "Bill's hammer and mallet." We can also observe that here too we do not actually need an overt *and* or *or* to obtain these readings:

(128) I think Mary needs a hammer. No, wait, maybe John needs a mallet. . . . In any case, they're going to borrow Bill's.

(129) Mary needs a hammer. John needs a mallet. They're going to borrow Bill's.

Again, I have no explanation for these data. I am merely pointing out that so-called NP-deletion is characterized by them.

An Explanation for the Disjunction Difficulty It is obvious now that at least the first and third of our tricky examples no longer present any difficulty.

(130) If Mary sees a donkey or a horse, she waves to it.

(131) If Mary sees John or Bill, she waves to him.

(132) If Mary sees a donkey and a horse, she waves to them.

Example (130) is in fact precisely parallel to (126). Just as we understand "Bill's hammer or mallet" in (126), so we understand "the donkey or horse" in (130), with the postulated definite-article meaning for *it*. And (132) is exactly parallel to (127), in the same way. Since one must admit cases of reconstruction of disjunctions and conjunctions of NPs from split antecedents in cases of uncontroversial (i.e., donkey-free) NP-deletion, there is no harm whatsoever in positing them in other alleged cases of NP-deletion, even if one is entirely baffled, as in the present instance, by how they come about. In fact, since this phenomenon is indubitably a property of NP-deletion, it would be a point *against* my theory if there were *no* examples like (130) and (132).

It is admittedly more difficult to deal with (131), even with the insight to be gleaned from this section. But the following does not seem like an extravagant account of the problem. There is in fact a substantial amount of evidence that proper names can sometimes be predicates. We know that in some languages, for example, proper names are commonly preceded by the definite article, as in German *der Hans*. (Other languages that spring to mind in this connection are Spanish and classical Greek.) Two accounts of this are found in the literature. The first is a type-shifting principle that converts entities of type e to the property of being identical with them.[28] So *Hans* in German would have as its denotation either the person Hans or the property $[\lambda x. x = \text{Hans}]$; the latter, of course, is necessary in *der Hans*. Semanticists have also postulated this operation for languages like English, where proper names usually cannot be preceded by a definite article. Von Fintel, for example, develops a semantics for exceptive *but* according to which its complement must be a set, meaning that the normal type e denotation of *John* in (133) must be raised in this manner (von Fintel 1993, 128).

(133) Every student but John attended the meeting.

Positing this operation for English, then, we can suppose that at the alleged ellipsis site in (131) it is possible to construct the predicates $[\lambda x. \, x = John]$ and $[\lambda x. \, x = Bill]$, on the basis of the previous occurrences of *John* and *Bill*; and *or* can be understood there by whatever mechanism it is understood in examples (126) and (128). This makes (131) parallel to (130): while in the one case we have "waves to the donkey or horse," in the other case we have "waves to the (person) identical with John or (person) identical with Bill."

The second account of the predicatival uses of names is that of Burge (1973), modified by Larson and Segal (1995, 351–355). According to this account, proper names are always predicates meaning "entity called X." So *John*, for example, means "entity called 'John.'" Something like this is surely necessary to account for usages like those in (134).

(134) a. There are two Aristotles.
      b. Which Aristotle do you mean?
      c. I meant that Aristotle.
      d. The Aristotle standing over there?
      e. No, the other Aristotle.

Burge suggests that this meaning is the only meaning we need to posit for proper names. Conventional uses as in *John saw Mary* would result from these predicates being combined with a phonologically null demonstrative like *that*. Larson and Segal (1995, 354–355) basically support this view, but give good evidence to suggest that the phonologically null determiner is a definite article, not a demonstrative. For one thing, this allows unification of the English facts with the crosslinguistic constructions like *der Hans*. But whatever the case may be with regard to the determiner, and whether or not we want to have the names in *John saw Mary* be (modified) predicates, it is clear that the facts in (134) and others like them give powerful support to the hypothesis that proper names can sometimes mean "entity called X." We can suppose, then, that this meaning is the one understood at the ellipsis site in (131), and the problem is solved: we would have "waves to the entity called 'John' or entity called 'Bill.'" See chapter 6 for further discussion of Burge's theory.

Another Split Antecedent   It is worth pointing out that the explanation given for (132) generalizes to one other type of sentence that at first glance seems impossible to deal with on the NP-deletion theory. An example is (135).[29]

(135) If a man has a wife who owns a donkey, he always loves them.

Many speakers can interpret this example to mean, "... he loves his wife and her donkey," although for a few people it is distinctly awkward. Again, the question is how this is possible on the NP-deletion theory. And the answer is that the examples we have looked at give us reason to believe that NP-ellipsis can sometimes take the form of supplying in the ellipsis site a conjunction of two NPs from the linguistic environment, even when the word *and* does not actually occur. (See example (129).)

2.7.3 Tomioka Sentences

Another apparent problem for the NP-deletion theory is posed by examples like the following, which were first discussed by Tomioka (1997, 193; 1999).[30]

(136) Every police officer who arrested a murderer insulted him, and
        every police officer who arrested a burglar did too.

Interestingly, this sentence has a sloppy reading: roughly, every police officer who arrested a murderer insulted the murderer he arrested and every police officer who arrested a burglar insulted the burglar he arrested. The problem for the current theory is this: I am committed to having the first VP in (136) have the LF in (137). But then it might be thought that ellipsis, however it works, should end up producing the same meaning for the elided VP as that which is yielded by (137), and that would incorrectly have the second set of police officers insulting murderers.

(137) [insulted [him murderer]]

Previous versions of the D-type analysis, meanwhile, do not have this trouble. Tomioka (1997, 1999) points out that versions that rely on a contextually salient relation to supply the descriptive content of the D-type pronoun can use the relation that obtains between people and people they arrest; informally, the antecedent VP would then mean something like "insulted the person he arrested," and the sloppy reading is correctly obtained if the elided VP means this too.

We can tell that Tomioka's explanation cannot be correct, however, by repeating the test that we used in section 2.5.1, the interpretation of elliptical continuations with type e subjects. Consider the examples in (138) and (139), assuming that Officer Jones did arrest someone but did not arrest a murderer.

(138) a. Every police officer who arrested a murderer insulted the
           person he arrested, and Officer Jones *insulted the person he arrested*
           too.   (sloppy, strict)

   b. Every police officer who arrested a murderer insulted him, and
      Officer Jones *insulted him* too.   (*sloppy, strict)

(139) a. Every police officer who arrested a murderer insulted the
         person he arrested, and Officer Jones did too.   (sloppy, strict)
      b. Every police officer who arrested a murderer insulted him, and
         Officer Jones did too.   (*sloppy, strict)

If the antecedent VPs in (138b) and (139b) could behave for ellipsis in the
same manner as the antecedent VPs in (138a) and (139a), which is the
hypothesis under consideration, we would expect the elided or downstressed VPs in these pairs of sentences to have the same range of interpretations. They do not, however. So *insulted him* cannot behave for
ellipsis in the same manner as *insulted the person he arrested*, contrary to
what Tomioka's explanation requires.

   But how does the NP-deletion theory deal with examples like (136)?
Again, by pointing out that the prediction it makes is fulfilled: sentences
isomorphic to (136) with uncontested NP-deletion instead of a D-type
pronoun also allow sloppy readings. To see this, however, it will be convenient to alter the example slightly, since the indefinite *a murderer* in
(136) is singular, while those determiners that allow NP-deletion after
them generally take plural NPs. Let us examine (140).

(140) Every police officer who arrested some murderers insulted them,
      and every police officer who arrested some burglars did too.

Like (136), this has a sloppy reading. The sentence is not problematic,
however. Consider the sentences in (141).

(141) Every police officer who arrested some murderers insulted ...
      a. at least three
      b. some
      c. a few
      d. ?most
      e. one
      ... and every police officer who arrested some burglars did too.

These sentences too have sloppy readings. Thus there is no difficulty in
supposing that NP-deletion is responsible for (140) meaning that every
police officer who arrested some murderers insulted those murderers, and
every police officer who arrested some burglars insulted those burglars. So
Tomioka sentences are not problematic for the NP-deletion theory of
D-type anaphora; in fact they are predicted to exist by this theory.

It is worth noting that the examples in (141) are simply analogues in the realm of NP-deletion of a phenomenon that has already been observed and discussed with respect to VP-ellipsis. The following examples are taken from Hardt 1999 and Schwarz 2000. (Example (143) is attributed to Carl Pollard.)

(142) When John had to cook, he didn't want to. When he had to clean, he didn't, either.

(143) I'll help you if you want me to. I'll kiss you even if you don't.

Take (142). This seems to mean that when John had to cook he didn't want to cook, and when he had to clean he didn't want to clean. This is in spite of the fact that, since the matrix VP of the first sentence means "didn't want to cook," straightforward ways of theorizing about VP-ellipsis would have the matrix VP of the second sentence mean the same thing. Let us note the parallel between (142) and (141). Both contain two sentences that themselves contain subordinate clauses: Embedded S_1, Matrix S_1, Embedded S_2, Matrix S_2. In Matrix S_2, there is an ellipsis site, whose antecedent appears to be in Matrix S_1, but this antecedent in Matrix S_1 itself contains an ellipsis site, with the antecedent in Embedded S_1. Instead of understanding the ellipsis site in Matrix S_2 as we would if we simply supplied all the material we understand in the antecedent in Matrix S_1, we understand the ellipsis site in Matrix S_2 as if it contained the material from the antecedent in Matrix S_1 as it would be if its own ellipsis site was filled in not from an antecedent in Embedded S_1 but from one in Embedded S_2. It is as if the larger ellipsis captures the nature of the dependency or link between the ellipsis site in the antecedent and this smaller ellipsis site's antecedent, and this dependency is copied (or whatever) into the ellipsis site in Matrix S_2. One is reminded of Fiengo and May's (1994) notion of a β-occurrence of an anaphoric element, which is such (roughly) that the dependency between it and its antecedent will be copied in ellipsis. But this is not the place to discuss this intuition, or the mechanisms that Hardt and Schwarz propose to deal with this problem. Whatever the correct treatment of (142) turns out to be, there is a good chance that it will be extendable to deal with (141) and, if I am correct, (140).

2.8 Conclusion

My primary concern in this chapter is reductive: since the process of recovering the descriptive content of a D-type pronoun displays exactly the same possibilities and restrictions that NP-deletion does, we should not assume that these are separate mechanisms, but should rather identify them. Concomitantly, we should assume that D-type pronouns are actually definite articles. Such an analysis has a number of empirical advantages over standard D-type accounts. These advantages include ways of dealing with the problem of the formal link between donkey pronoun and antecedent, and the pattern of strict and sloppy readings shown by donkey sentences with phonologically reduced continuations of various kinds.

The theory put forward in this chapter should not be seen only in the context of previous D-type theories, of course. If the solution given to the problem of the formal link is on the right track, then one of the problems that affected D-type theories in general, as opposed to dynamic theories, has been removed. Furthermore, the next chapter will attempt to remove another of these problems mentioned in section 1.3.2, namely, the problem of pronominal ambiguity.

Chapter 3

On the Semantics of Pronouns and Definite Articles

3.1 Introduction

Let us now stand back a bit from D-type pronouns and remind ourselves of the overall project set out in chapter 1. The idea was to lay out a unified syntax and semantics for expressions of type e, based on the syntax and semantics of normal definite descriptions. So far, then, only a small part of the task has been accomplished, since only D-type pronouns have been considered. However, it will turn out to be fairly simple to adapt the standard semantics for bound variable and referential pronouns so as to make it consistent with that given for D-type pronouns. I will lay out the basic mechanism that does this in section 3.2. Then I will address in more detail the question of what we should consider the syntax and semantics of ordinary definite descriptions to be (section 3.3). It will turn out that the overt definite article *the*, in English at least, has to take two arguments, one an index and the other a normal Noun Phrase, making it different from what I have been assuming so far for pronoun definite articles, which I have assumed to be standard Fregean definite articles taking only one argument. The question then arises whether we should change the semantics for pronouns to make it accord with that which we seem to need for overt definite articles. I discuss this question in section 3.5.

3.2 Bound and Referential Pronouns

The standard semantic analysis of bound variable and refential pronouns makes the following basic assumptions: bound and referential pronouns are variables; variable names are provided by numerical subscripts (indices); indices are interpreted by variable assignments or Tarskian sequences; variable assignments are functions from the natural numbers to the domain of individuals. I will provide a summary of a specific implementation of these assumptions in section 3.2.1; then I will show that with a few simple modifications this implementation can be converted into a system compatible with the view of D-type pronouns set out in chapter 2, thus providing a unified semantics for pronouns of the sort described in chapter 1.

3.2.1 Pronouns as Variables: Heim and Kratzer 1998

As a jumping-off point, I will take the theory of bound and referential pronouns in Heim and Kratzer 1998, which is a neat and recent version of the treatment of these items as individual variables. To review briefly, we adorn each pronoun (and each trace) with a subscript natural number called an index. Sentences are interpreted with respect to variable assignments—that is, functions that map indices to individuals, whose mappings are supposed to be created by the context (and by the rule of predicate abstraction, which we will see in a moment). There is a special rule of interpretation to deal with these items, which is given in (1). Example (2) shows a simple referential case.

(1) *Traces and Pronouns Rule*
    If α is a pronoun or a trace, a is a variable assignment, and $i \in \text{dom}(a)$, then $[\![\alpha_i]\!]^a = a(i)$.

(2) $[\![\text{he}_2 \text{ left}]\!]^{[2 \to \text{John}]}$
    $= [\![\text{left}]\!]^{[2 \to \text{John}]}([\![\text{he}_2]\!]^{[2 \to \text{John}]})$
    $= [\![\text{left}]\!]^{[2 \to \text{John}]}(\text{John})$
    $= [\lambda x.\, x \text{ left}](\text{John})$
    $= 1 \text{ iff John left}$

(The third line is achieved by (1).) Bound pronouns are produced by variable assignments in combination with special indices that occupy a node by themselves. For example, it is proposed that one effect of movement is to create such an index, which is adjoined to the target of movement; the same index is put on the trace of the moved item, and can optionally be put on pronouns in the sentence. So (3a) might have an LF (3b), assuming either QR of the subject or movement of it from a VP-internal subject position.

(3) a. Every girl thinks she's smart.
    b. [every girl] [2 [t_2 thinks she$_2$ is smart]]

We now need a rule to interpret these special indices. This is given in (4).

(4) *Predicate Abstraction Rule*

Let α be a branching node with daughters β and γ, where β dominates only a numerical index i. Then, for any variable assignment a, $[\![\alpha]\!]^a = \lambda x \in D. [\![\gamma]\!]^{a^{x/i}}$.

($a^{x/i}$ is that variable assignment which is exactly like a, except that i is mapped to x.) Given this rule, the nuclear scope in (3b) will be interpreted as in (5). ($\emptyset$ is the variable assignment that contains no mappings.)

(5) $\quad [\![[2 \ [t_2 \ \text{thinks she}_2 \ \text{is smart}]]\!]^{\emptyset}$
$\quad = \lambda x \in D. [\![[t_2 \ \text{thinks she}_2 \ \text{is smart}]]\!]^{\emptyset^{x/2}}$
$\quad = \lambda x \in D. [\![[t_2 \ \text{thinks she}_2 \ \text{is smart}]]\!]^{[2 \to x]}$
$\quad = \lambda x \in D. x \text{ thinks that } x \text{ is smart}$

The first step is achieved via the predicate abstraction rule, and the second simply by definition of the notation. The third is an abbreviation, relying on many applications of rules, including the traces and pronouns rule twice. Note that the end result is that both the trace and the pronoun in the nuclear scope end up being bound by the lambda abstractor, and (3a) will be true if and only if every individual who is a girl satisfies the predicate in the last line of (5). This is what we want, of course.

3.2.2 Unifying the Variable and Definite-Article Analyses

Let us take the Heim and Kratzer system, then, as a representative of theories that unify bound and referential pronouns by treating them both as individual variables interpreted by variable assignments. Let us furthermore assume that there is something right about the theories that do this, and also about the treatment of D-type pronouns as definite articles that has been laid out in chapter 2. We can then propose a first pass at a unified theory of the semantics of third-person pronouns along the following lines.

Pronouns are definite articles, and D-type anaphora works as previously described. Bound and referential pronouns occur when these definite articles take an index as an argument. Instead of being entities of obscure ontological status,[1] signified by subscripts, indices will now be phonologically null NPs, which can be taken as arguments by determiners. What will their interpretation be, now that they have changed type? There are two ways of arriving at the answer. One route that could be followed is that which leaves variable assignments the same as they were and introduces the following rule, a revision of the traces and pronouns rule of Heim and Kratzer 1998.

(6) *Traces and Pronouns Rule, Mark II*

For all indices i and variable assignments a such that $i \in \mathrm{dom}(a)$,
$[\![i]\!]^a = [\lambda x.\, x = a(i)]$.

To distinguish our new lexical indices from the special indices created by movement in the Heim and Kratzer system, we will have to write the latter a different way: I will write "λ_i" for the object-language item whose effect in the semantics is to abstract over index i.[2] We will then need a trivially revised version of the predicate abstraction rule, which I give in (7).

(7) *Predicate Abstraction Rule, Mark II*

Let α be a branching node with daughters β and γ, where β dominates only a lambda abstractor λ_i. Then, for any variable assignment a, $[\![\alpha]\!]^a = \lambda x.\, [\![\gamma]\!]^{a^{x/i}}$.

We can now go back and see how this revised system deals with the examples we looked at previously. Instead of (2), we will now have the LF and semantic derivation shown in (8).

(8)　　$[\![[\text{he } 2]\ \text{left}]\!]^{[2\to\text{John}]}$

$= [\![\text{left}]\!]^{[2\to\text{John}]}([\![\text{he}]\!]^{[2\to\text{John}]}([\![2]\!]^{[2\to\text{John}]}))$

$= [\![\text{left}]\!]^{[2\to\text{John}]}([\![\text{he}]\!]^{[2\to\text{John}]}(\lambda x.\, x = \text{John}))$

$= [\lambda x.\, x\ \text{left}]([\lambda f : f \in D_{\langle e,t\rangle}\ \&\ \exists! x\, f(x) = 1.\, \iota x\, f(x) = 1]$
$(\lambda x.\, x = \text{John}))$

$= [\lambda x.\, x\ \text{left}]\ \iota x\ x = \text{John}$

$= 1\ \text{iff John left}$

The second line is obtained by functional application, as usual, and the third by (6). The fourth, as before, comes from consulting the lexicon—note that the lexical entry for *he* is a Fregean definite article. (I abstract away from ϕ-features.) The remaining steps are trivial. The truth conditions, of course, are the same as those obtained in (2).

The bound-variable example also works straightforwardly. The nuclear scope of (3a) now receives the LF and derivation in (9). Note that traces in this system (until we begin to consider the copy theory of movement) are complexes of the form [THE i].[3]

(9)　　$[\![[\lambda_2\ [[\text{THE } 2]\ [\text{thinks}\ [[\text{she } 2]\ \text{is smart}]]]]]\!]^{\emptyset}$

$= \lambda x.\, [\![[[\text{THE } 2]\ [\text{thinks}\ [[\text{she } 2]\ \text{is smart}]]]]\!]^{\emptyset^{x/2}}$

$= \lambda x.\, [\![[[\text{THE } 2]\ [\text{thinks}\ [[\text{she } 2]\ \text{is smart}]]]]\!]^{[2\to x]}$

$= \lambda x.\, \iota y\ y = x\ \text{thinks that}\ \iota y\ y = x\ \text{is smart}$

$= \lambda x.\, x\ \text{thinks that}\ x\ \text{is smart}$

The same truth conditions emerge as before.

As mentioned above, there are two possible ways to achieve the kind of results we are looking for. The one just illustrated uses the traces and pronouns rule, mark II (6), and the predicate abstraction rule, mark II (7), and leaves variable assignments as partial functions from the natural numbers to individuals. The second approach says that variable assignments are in fact partial functions from the natural numbers to a subset of the functions of type $\langle e, t \rangle$, namely those, like $[\lambda x.\, x = \text{John}]$, that are the characteristic functions of singleton sets. This approach puts into the variable assignments the work done in the traces and pronouns rule, mark II, on the first theory, which means that its own interpretation rule for indices, traces and pronouns rule, mark III, can be simpler.

(10) *Traces and Pronouns Rule, Mark III*
      For all indices i and variable assignments a such that $i \in \text{dom}(a)$,
      $[\![i]\!]^a = a(i)$.

There will have to be a corresponding change in lambda abstraction too, of course. The new rule is given in (11).

(11) *Predicate Abstraction Rule, Mark III*
      Let α be a branching node with daughters β and γ, where β
      dominates only a lambda abstractor λ_i. Then, for any variable
      assignment a, $[\![\alpha]\!]^a = \lambda x.\, [\![\gamma]\!]^{a^{[\lambda y.\, y = x]/i}}$.

I will not go through examples in detail to illustrate this second theory. I think it is evident on reflection that its results will be equivalent to those of the first.

Whichever version is chosen, the changes made to the Heim and Kratzer system (and, by extension, to all comparable systems) are quite minor.[4] Pronouns and traces combined with indices are still of type e, and have the same overall meanings that they always did; it is just that they get there by a different road. The real difference is that now we have a unified theory of the semantics of pronouns.

3.2.3 Summary

According to the current view, then, all third-person pronouns are Fregean definite articles with the addition of presuppositions about ϕ-features. For example, *she* would have a denotation as in (12).

(12) $[\![\text{she}]\!] = \lambda f : f \in D_{\langle e, t \rangle}$ & $\exists! x\, f(x) = 1$ & $\forall x (f(x) = 1 \rightarrow \text{FEMALE}(x))$.
      $\iota x\, f(x) = 1$

Furthermore, the NP complement of third-person pronouns must be phonologically null. There are two ways this can happen: the complement can be a common or garden NP affected by NP-deletion, in which case we get D-type anaphora; or it can be an index, an NP that is always phonologically null, in which case we get referential or bound-variable anaphora.

It is possible, however, that this system might have to be changed slightly in light of the investigation of the semantics of the overt definite article *the*, to which I now proceed.

3.3 The Semantics of the Definite Article

3.3.1 Fregean versus Russellian Approaches

The Distinction Let me acknowledge from the outset that I will not be examining every issue that has arisen in the voluminous literature on definite descriptions.[5] But I do wish to set out my view, and the reasoning behind it, on one major division, perhaps the most significant overall division, between different theories of the semantics of the definite article. That division is the one between Fregean and Russellian approaches to its semantics.

There is a passage in Frege's famous 1893 paper "Über Sinn und Bedeutung" in which he analyzes the phrase *the negative square root of 4* as a compound proper name (that is, a syntactically complex expression referring to an individual) formed from the "concept expression" *negative square root of 4* combined with the definite article. He adds that such a combination is permissible when exactly one object falls under the concept. Later philosophers and linguists have elucidated these remarks in such a way as to produce the meaning in (13) for sentences involving definite descriptions (Heim 1991, 495–496), which gives the definite article the lexical entry in (14) in simple extensional systems (Heim and Kratzer 1998, 73–82).[6]

(13) Regardless of the utterance context, [[the ζ] ξ] expresses that proposition that is
  • true at an index i, if there is exactly one ζ at i, and it is ξ at i,
  • false at an index i, if there is exactly one ζ at i, and it is not ξ at i,
  • truth-valueless at an index i, if there is not exactly one ζ at i.

(14) $\lambda f : f \in D_{\langle e,t \rangle}$ & $\exists! x\, f(x) = 1 . \iota x\, f(x) = 1$

Note that the requirement for uniqueness is incorporated as a presupposition in this lexical entry. Informally, it is presupposed that exactly one thing is f; and the definite description refers to this thing if the presupposition is true (and has no semantic value otherwise). This contrasts with Russell's famous analysis of definite descriptions. According to Russell (1905), a sentence of the form *the F is G* has the truth conditions in (15).

(15) $\exists x(Fx \ \& \ \forall y(Fy \rightarrow y = x) \ \& \ Gx)$

As Neale (1990, 44–45) has pointed out, it falls out naturally on this view to consider the contribution of *the* as being that of a quantifier of a certain sort. Sticking closely to Russell's original proposal, we might represent *the* as having the meaning in (16).

(16) $\lambda f_{\langle e,t\rangle} . \lambda g_{\langle e,t\rangle} . \exists x(f(x) = 1 \ \& \ \forall y(f(y) = 1 \rightarrow y = x) \ \& \ g(x) = 1)$

The difference between the Russellian and the Fregean view, then, is that existence and uniqueness are presupposed on the Fregean view and asserted on the Russellian.[7]

Some Preliminary Considerations   I will ultimately be coming down in favor of the Fregean analysis of the definite article. Before I can give what I take to be the strongest argument for this position, however, there is a certain amount of clearing of the undergrowth to be undertaken, in that some considerations that have been taken to tell against the Fregean account must be dismissed.[8] I will concentrate on two areas: data that the Russellian explains by having definite descriptions take different scopes with respect to various operators, and data involving what for a Fregean would be nondenoting definite descriptions that nevertheless do not produce presupposition failure.

Since Russell (1905, 52), it has been claimed that the Russellian analysis can deal with the *de re/de dicto* ambiguity as it arises in sentences containing definite descriptions by having the descriptions take wider or narrower scope than the relevant operator. To take an example involving a propositional attitude predicate, we can analyze the *de re* and *de dicto* readings of (17) as in (18) and (19) (Neale 1990, 121):

(17)   Mary believes that the man who lives upstairs is a spy.

(18)   *De dicto*
       [Mary believes that [[the man who lives upstairs] [is a spy]]]
       'Mary believes that there is an individual x such that x is a man who lives upstairs and x is the only man who lives upstairs and x is a spy.'

(19) *De re*
  [the man who lives upstairs] λ_2[Mary believes [t_2 is a spy]]
  'There is an individual x such that x is a man who lives upstairs
  and x is the only man who lives upstairs and Mary believes that x
  is a spy.'

The same strategy is alleged to be able to account for *de re/de dicto* ambiguities in sentences containing modal operators (Smullyan 1948; Neale 1990, 121), as in (20)–(22).

(20) The number of the planets is necessarily greater than 7.

(21) *De dicto*
  [necessarily [the number of the planets is greater than 7]]
  'For all possible worlds w, there is an individual x such that x is a
  number of the planets in w and x is the only number of the planets
  in w and x is greater than 7 in w.'

(22) *De re*
  [the number of the planets] λ_2[necessarily [t_2 is greater than 7]]
  'There is an x such that x is a number of the planets and x is the
  only number of the planets and, for all possible worlds w, x is
  greater than 7 in w.'

Assume that the utterer of (20) means "planets orbiting Sol at the present time" by *planets*, and that there are nine planets orbiting Sol in the actual world at the present time. Then (21) and (22) correctly predict that this sentence will have a reading on which it is true and a reading on which it is false. The *de dicto* reading is false, since there are possible worlds in which there are seven or fewer planets orbiting Sol at the present time, and the *de re* reading is true, since nine is greater than seven in all possible worlds. Thus it seems as if the Russellian analysis of the definite article is an attractive one, since it allows an empirically robust account of *de re/de dicto* ambiguities in terms of scope.

   This is not the only way to deal with these data, however. It has been recognized at least since Bäuerle 1983 that it is possible, if not advantageous, to handle *de re/de dicto* ambiguities by means of directly manipulating the world or situation variables that indicate the truth-supporting circumstances with respect to which various predicates are evaluated (Bäuerle 1983; Heim 1991; Farkas 1997; Heim, Kratzer, and von Fintel 1998; Percus 2000). This will allow definite descriptions to be interpreted in situ at all times with Fregean meanings. I will first illustrate this idea with a formal system that involves world variables in the syntax, in the fashion of Heim 1990, 1991, Heim, Kratzer, and von Fintel 1998, and Percus 2000.

In this system, each predicate (verb, noun, adjective, and preposition) has an argument place for a possible world variable, and a world-variable binder is located somewhere around the C projection. Examples (23) and (24) show simplified LFs for two simple sentences, and some lexical entries are shown in (25).

(23) [$_{\text{CP}}$ λw [$_{\text{S}}$ Mary [$_{\text{VP}}$ yawns w]]]

(24) [$_{\text{CP}}$ λw [$_{\text{S}}$ John [$_{\text{VP}}$ [likes w] Mary]]]

(25) a. $[\![$quiet$]\!] = \lambda w.\lambda x.x$ is quiet in w
     b. $[\![$likes$]\!] = \lambda w.\lambda x.\lambda y.y$ likes x in w

The world binders in the syntax are interpreted by means of the special rule of *intensional abstraction*, shown in (26). Note that $g^{w/w}$ is the assignment that is just like g except that w is mapped to w; world variables in the syntax are written in the normal font and ones in the meta-language are written in italics. This allows us to proceed with calculations like the one in (27), where the second line is obtained by intensional abstraction.

(26) *Intensional Abstraction*
     If α is of the form $[\lambda w\ \beta]$, then, for any variable assignment g, $[\![\alpha]\!]^g = \lambda w.[\![\beta]\!]^{g^{w/w}}$.

(27) $[\![[_{\text{CP}}\ \lambda w\ [_{\text{S}}\ \text{John}\ [_{\text{VP}}\ [\text{likes w}]\ \text{Mary}]]]]\!]^\emptyset$
      $= \lambda w.[\![[_{\text{S}}\ \text{John}\ [_{\text{VP}}\ [\text{likes w}]\ \text{Mary}]]]\!]^{[w \to w]}$
      $= \lambda w.[\![\text{likes}]\!]^{[w \to w]}([\![\text{w}]\!]^{[w \to w]})([\![\text{Mary}]\!]^{[w \to w]})([\![\text{John}]\!]^{[w \to w]})$
      $= \lambda w.[\lambda w'.\lambda x.\lambda y.y$ likes x in $w'](w)(\text{Mary})(\text{John})$
      $= \lambda w.$ John likes Mary in w

This means that a sentence like (28) will have an LF like that in (29), and by means of the lexical entry in (30) we arrive at the meaning in the last line of (31).

(28) John believes that Mary yawns.

(29) [$_{\text{CP}}$ λw [$_{\text{S}}$ John [$_{\text{VP}}$ [believes w] [$_{\text{CP}}$ λw′ that [$_{\text{S}}$ Mary [$_{\text{VP}}$ yawns w′]]]]]]

(30) $[\![$believes$]\!] = \lambda w.\lambda p_{\langle s,t\rangle}.\lambda x.$ all worlds w' compatible with x's beliefs in w are such that $p(w') = 1$

(31) $[[_{CP}\ \lambda w\ [_S\ John\ [_{VP}\ [believes\ w]\ [_{CP}\ \lambda w'\ that\ [_S\ Mary\ [_{VP}\ yawns$
$w']]]]]]^{\emptyset}$

$= \lambda w.[[_S\ John\ [_{VP}\ [believes\ w]\ [_{CP}\ \lambda w'\ that\ [_S\ Mary\ [_{VP}\ yawns$
$w']]]]]]^{\emptyset^{w/w}}$

$= \lambda w.[[_S\ John\ [_{VP}\ [believes\ w]\ [_{CP}\ \lambda w'\ that\ [_S\ Mary\ [_{VP}\ yawns$
$w']]]]]]^{[w\to w]}$

$= \lambda w.[believes]^{[w\to w]}([w]^{[w\to w]})([[_{CP}\ \lambda w'\ that\ [_S\ Mary\ [_{VP}\ yawns$
$w']]]]^{[w\to w]})\ ([John]^{[w\to w]})$

$= \lambda w.[believes]^{[w\to w]}(w)(\lambda w'.Mary\ yawns\ in\ w')(John)$

$= \lambda w.\begin{bmatrix}\lambda w''.\lambda p_{\langle s,t\rangle}.\lambda x.\ all\ worlds\ w'''\ compatible\ with\\ x\text{'s beliefs in }w''\ are\ such\ that\ p(w''') = 1\end{bmatrix}(w)(\lambda w'.Mary$
yawns in w')(John)

$= \lambda w.$ all worlds w''' compatible with John's beliefs in w are such
that Mary yawns in w'''

Now we are in a position to see how a system like this might be able to deliver the *de re/de dicto* distinction without using syntactic scope. The simplest way to go about things is to assume that there is a special variable w_0 that is referential and picks out the actual world. Then we could represent the difference between *de re* and *de dicto* readings of a definite description embedded under a propositional attitude verb by means of the following LFs and interpretations:

(32) *De dicto*
   a. $[\lambda w_1\ Mary\ believes\ w_1\ [\lambda w_2[[her\ [neighbor\ w_2]]\ [is\ a\ spy\ w_2]]]]$
   b. The proposition true of world w_0 iff all worlds compatible with Mary's beliefs in w_0 are members of the set of worlds w_2 such that the unique x such that x is Mary's neighbor in w_2 is a spy in w_2.

(33) *De re*
   a. $[\lambda w_1\ Mary\ believes\ w_1\ [\lambda w_2[[her\ [neighbor\ w_0]]\ [is\ a\ spy\ w_2]]]]$
   b. The proposition true of world w_0 iff all worlds compatible with Mary's beliefs in w_0 are members of the set of worlds w_2 such that the unique x such that x is Mary's neighbor in w_0 is a spy in w_2.

Note that according to the meaning given for the *de re* reading, Mary need not think that the person she thinks is a spy lives next door to her. This is just what we need. Extension of this solution to the other *de re/de dicto* cases is straightforward.[9]

It will not have gone unnoticed that the analysis just sketched is inconsistent with the syntax and semantics I set out in chapter 2. In particular, I did not there posit world or situation variables in the syntax. But as it happens we can achieve the result just described by means of the system of chapter 2. We just need to posit the operator in (34).

(34) $[\![s_0]\!]^g = \lambda f_{\langle se, st\rangle}.\lambda u_{\langle s,e\rangle}.\lambda s.f(u)(g(0)) = 1$

This is designed to take a noun or NP as argument and give back the denotation of this nominal modified so as to take as its second argument a contextually salient situation. For example, the denotation of *neighbor of Mary* in the system of chapter 2 is shown in (35). The result of attaching the s_0 operator to this with a variable assignment in which 0 is mapped to the actual world w_0 (which is, recall, just a big situation) is shown in (36).

(35) $[\![\text{neighbor of Mary}]\!]^0 = \lambda u_{\langle s,e\rangle}.\lambda s.u(s)$ is a neighbor of Mary in s

(36) $[\![[[\text{neighbor of Mary}]\,s_0]]\!]^{[0\to w_0]} = \lambda u_{\langle s,e\rangle}.\lambda s.u(w_0)$ is a neighbor of Mary in w_0

The lexical entry of the definite article in chapter 2 was (37). Let us assume, as in section 2.6.3, that *her neighbor* is underlyingly something like *the neighbor of her*. Then the denotation of *her neighbor* is (38) if it is accompanied by the s_0 operator, and (39) if it is not.[10]

(37) $[\![\text{the}]\!]^0 = \lambda f_{\langle\langle s,e\rangle, \langle s,t\rangle\rangle}.\,\lambda s : \exists! x\ f(\lambda s'.x)(s) = 1.\iota x\ f(\lambda s'.x)(s) = 1$

(38) $[\![[\text{the }[\text{neighbor of her}]\,s_0]]]\!]^{[0\to w_0]} = \lambda s.\iota x\ x$ is a neighbor of Mary in w_0

(39) $[\![[\text{the }[\text{neighbor of her}]]]\!]^0 = \lambda s.\iota x\ x$ is a neighbor of Mary in s

For simplicity's sake, let us just assume that *is a spy* has the denotation in (40), like any other predicate.

(40) $[\![\text{is a spy}]\!]^0 = \lambda u_{\langle s,e\rangle}.\lambda s.u(s)$ is a spy in s

This means that *her neighbor is a spy*, in our example, will have the denotation in (41) if s_0 is used and the denotation in (42) if not.

(41) $\lambda s.\iota x\ x$ is a neighbor of Mary in w_0 is a spy in s

(42) $\lambda s.\iota x\ x$ is a neighbor of Mary in s is a spy in s

By means of the lexical entry in (43) for *believes*, we arrive at the following LFs and meanings for the *de dicto* and *de re* readings of our example.

(43) $[\![\text{believes}]\!]^0 = \lambda p_{\langle s,t\rangle}.\lambda u_{\langle s,e\rangle}.\lambda s.$ all worlds w compatible with the beliefs of $u(s)$ in s are such that $p(w) = 1$

(44) *De dicto*
    a. [Mary believes [her neighbor is a spy]]
    b. The proposition true of world w_0 iff all worlds w compatible
       with Mary's beliefs in w_0 are such that the unique x such that x
       is Mary's neighbor in w is a spy in w.

(45) *De re*
    a. [Mary believes [her neighbor s_0 is a spy]]
    b. The proposition true of world w_0 iff all worlds w compatible
       with Mary's beliefs in w_0 are such that the unique x such that x
       is Mary's neighbor in w_0 is a spy in w.

It can be seen that we have reproduced our earlier result. The Fregean definite article is still capable of handling the data that are dealt with by means of scope according to the standard Russellian theory.

Moreover, Bäuerle (1983) has argued that systems like the ones just explored are actually empirically superior to ones that account for the relevant ambiguities by means of scope. For example, he points out that a sentence like (46) can accurately describe a scenario like that in (47).

(46) George believes that a Mancunian woman loves all the Manchester United players.

(47) George sees some men on a bus in Manchester who happen to constitute the current Manchester United soccer team. He does not know who they are; that identification is provided by the speaker. He forms the belief that there is at least one Mancunian woman who loves all of these men, without believing *of* any particular woman that *she* does.

The indefinite DP is opaque in this scenario—that is, we cannot scope it out of the belief context, since it is not the case that there is a Mancunian woman x such that George believes that x loves all these men. But the universally quantified DP is transparent: George does not know that these men are the Manchester United soccer team, and this information therefore forms no part of his belief. The traditional story must say, therefore, that *all the Manchester United players* scopes out of the belief context. But this does not lead to the reading in question: since *a Mancunian woman* must stay within the scope of *believes*, we would end up saying that for each Manchester United player y, George believes there is a Mancunian woman who loves y, which has the wrong order for the universal and existential quantifiers. If we try to capture the relevant reading in terms of scope, in other words, it seems as if the indefinite must scope below the attitude verb and above the universal, but the universal must scope above the attitude verb. This, of course, is impossible.

On the kind of system we just examined, however, things are much easier. The relevant reading would be arrived at in the first variant by the following indexing:

(48) [λw George believes w [that λw$'$ a Mancunian woman w$'$ loves w$'$ all the Manchester United players w$_0$]]

An utterance of this LF is true in w_0 if and only if all worlds w' compatible with George's beliefs in w_0 are such that there is a Mancunian woman in w' who loves all the men who are the Manchester United players in w_0. This accurately captures the reading in question.

Other considerations can be brought to bear to supplement Bäuerle's argument. As we just noted, the standard approach involves the relevant DP raising (or otherwise scoping) out of the embedded clause to achieve *de re* readings. This predicts straightforwardly that *de re* readings should not be available when the relevant DP is embedded inside an LF scope island. As discussed in section 2.5.3, it is known that the Coordinate Structure Constraint holds at LF—for example, as illustrated in (49).

(49) Someone thinks that there's champagne in those glasses and that everyone drinking water is getting drunk.   ($\exists > \forall$, *$\forall > \exists$)

Although *everyone drinking water* cannot scope out of the conjunct, (49) has a reading on which the person reported does not necessarily have strange beliefs about the intoxicating effects of water. That is, (49) has a reading in which the universal is understood *de re*. This must be by [-one drinking water] being indexed w_0. Similarly, to return to definite descriptions, (50) has a reading in which no strange beliefs about water are attributed, which also requires the use of w_0 in the syntax.

(50) John believes that there's vodka in that glass and that the man drinking water is getting drunk.

These effects can be replicated using other islands.

Another test for the position of the relevant DP in *de re/de dicto* configurations involves scope freezing. Fox (2000) has shown that a type e subject of an ellipsis sentence freezes in place a QP subject of the antecedent sentence, as in (51).

(51) An American runner seems to Bill to have won a gold medal, and Sergey does too.   ($\exists >$ seems, *seems $> \exists$)

Given this, we might expect that if the standard account of the *de re/de dicto* ambiguity were correct, no *de re* reading would be available for the following sentence.

(52) John thinks that a man drinking water is getting drunk and that Bill is too.

The sentence is ambiguous in the normal way, however.

Finally, suppose that Tom, Dick, and Harry are spies, but John does not know this. John thinks that it is certain that one of these three will assassinate the Grand Mufti, but it is not the case that there is one of them such that he thinks that *he* is certain to. We can report his belief as follows:

(53) John thinks that one of the spies is certain to assassinate the Grand Mufti.

Note that, given John's belief, *one of the spies* must scope below *certain* here. This means that it cannot scope above *thinks*. For this sentence to be able to be used about the given scenario, then, *spies* must be indexed w_0. Scope cannot do everything that is needed.[11]

I take it to be definitively established that the kind of mechanism needed to cope with *de re/de dicto* ambiguities using the Fregean definite article does in fact form part of the grammar of natural language. One could go further and inquire whether the above considerations actually constitute an argument against the Russellian treatment of the definite article. I do not think they do, in fact, since the Russellian could presumably borrow a tactic from the Fregean and say that the predicates that previously were scoped out of harm's way are now to be indexed w_0. But the Russellian theory does not have any advantage over the Fregean theory in this area.

Let us move on to the second of the two considerations that could be taken to tell against the Fregean definite article, namely, the existence of data involving what for a Fregean would be nondenoting definite descriptions that nevertheless do not produce presupposition failure. I have in mind sentences like the following (Neale 1990, 27):[12]

(54) Ponce de León thought the fountain of youth was in Florida.

(55) John thinks that the highest prime number is odd.

Let us follow contemporary educated opinion and assume that there is no fountain of youth and no highest prime number. If we are Fregeans, then, we must admit that *the fountain of youth* and *the highest prime number* do not denote anything. One would expect, according to the Fregean theory, that these sentences containing nondenoting definite descriptions would suffer from presupposition failure (see (13)). But they do not. We can say them perfectly happily, even though we do not believe that there is a fountain of youth or a highest prime number. Therefore it appears that there is a significant problem for the Fregean theory.

Again, however, it turns out that a perfectly viable solution to this problem was proposed many years ago. Karttunen (1974) maintained that in cases of propositional attitude verbs whose sentential complements carry presuppositions, the presuppositions of the complement come to form part of a new presupposition carried by the whole sentence, namely, that the subject of the propositional attitude verb believes the presuppositions of the embedded sentence. For example, it is commonly assumed that (56) carries the presupposition shown:

(56) John has stopped drinking.
     Presupposition: John used to drink.

According to Karttunen, then, when we embed (56) under a propositional attitude verb, as in (57), the presupposition of the embedded sentence will be transmogrified into the presupposition that the subject of the attitude verb believes it:

(57) Mary believes that John has stopped drinking.

This seems to be correct. The proposition that John used to drink is certainly not a presupposition of (57), since we can felicitously continue as in (58). Compare the infelicity of (59).

(58) Mary believes that John has stopped drinking. But in fact John never drank.

(59) #John has stopped drinking. But in fact John never drank.

And it seems infelicitous now to add that Mary believes that John never drank:

(60) #Mary believes that John has stopped drinking. But she never believed he did drink.

It seems, then, that (57) presupposes that Mary believes that John used to drink. So Karttunen is correct: the presupposition of the embedded sentence has been taken and made into a component of the presupposition of the sentence as a whole.

For simplicity's sake, let us suppose that the semantic values of sentences can consist of pairs of propositions, one representing the asserted content and the other representing the presupposed content (Karttunen 1973, 1974; Karttunen and Peters 1979).[13] Then *believes* would have as its semantic value a function that takes such a pair of propositions and maps it to a function that takes an individual x and maps x to the pair of propositions characterized as follows: the asserted content is that x believes the asserted content in the initial pair, and the presupposed content is that x believes the presupposed content of the initial pair.

It is now obvious how the supporter of the Fregean definite article will analyze cases like (54), repeated here as (61).

(61) Ponce de León thought the fountain of youth was in Florida.

The embedded sentence (62) has the presupposition that there exists exactly one fountain of youth:

(62) The fountain of youth is in Florida.
Presupposed content: λw. there is exactly one fountain of youth in w
Asserted content: λw. the unique fountain of youth in w is in
Florida in w

It is important that the nature of this two-part semantic value be clearly understood. We could construe it as determining a partial proposition, one that is defined for some worlds (those in the set defined by the presupposed content) but not others, as in (13) above. Imagine it as a procedure that takes each world w and examines it to see how many fountains of youth (on earth, at a given time) there are in that world; if there are no fountains of youth or more than one, it returns no semantic value; if there is exactly one, it returns 1 if that fountain is Florida in that world, and 0 otherwise. For example, if the fountain of youth is fountain A in world w_1, the proposition returns 1 if we give it w_1 and fountain A is in Florida in w_1, and so on. The contribution of the definite description is an individual concept, a function from worlds to individuals.[14] More revealingly, then, the content of (62) is that proposition that maps worlds w to 1 if and only if applying the fountain-of-youth concept to w yields an object and that object is in Florida in w, maps worlds w to 0 if and only if applying the fountain-of-youth concept to w yields an object and that object is not in Florida in w, and returns no value if and only if applying the fountain-of-youth concept to the given world does not yield any object.[15]

The attitude verb in (61) will take as its two arguments (i) the pair of propositions in (62) and (ii) Ponce de León, and will produce as the semantic value of the whole sentence the pair of propositions characterized as follows:

(63) Presupposed content: all worlds compatible with Ponce de León's beliefs are members of the set of worlds w such that there is exactly one fountain of youth in w.

Asserted content: all worlds compatible with what Ponce de León thinks are members of the set of worlds w such that the unique fountain of youth in w is in Florida in w.

If we like we can once more see this pair of propositions as jointly constituting a partial proposition:

(64) λw: all worlds compatible with Ponce de León's beliefs in w are members of the set of worlds w' such that there is exactly one fountain of youth in w'. all worlds compatible with what Ponce de León thinks in w are members of the set of worlds w' such that the unique fountain of youth in w' (i.e., the result of applying the fountain-of-youth concept to w') is in Florida in w'

This result seems to be in accordance with our intuitions. And, crucially, the definite description *the fountain of youth* is not evaluated with respect to the actual world, but only with respect to possible worlds consistent with the misguided thoughts and beliefs of Ponce de León, meaning that we no longer expect presupposition failure. So the Fregean analysis of the definite article faces no problems with sentences like (61).

Heim's Argument   I now wish to move on to an argument that seeks to show that the Fregean analysis of the definite article is empirically superior to the Russellian analysis. It is due to Irene Heim (1991).

Heim (1991, 493) draws our attention to examples like the following.

(65) Hans wants the banshee in his attic to be quiet tonight.

(66) Hans wonders whether the banshee in his attic will be quiet tonight.

(67) If the banshee in his attic is quiet tonight, he will hold a party.

She points out that the Russellian analysis of definite descriptions predicts that (68a), in an appropriate context, should mean (68b).

(68) a. The banshee in his attic will be quiet tonight.
    b. There is exactly one banshee in Hans's attic, and that banshee will be quiet tonight.

But then this predicts that (65)–(67) should have the readings in (69)–(71), respectively. We simply embed the truth conditions in (68b) under the relevant operators, closely following the syntactic form of the sentences.

(69) Hans wants there to be exactly one banshee in his attic, and for it
     to be quiet tonight.

(70) Hans wonders whether the following is the case: there is exactly one
     banshee in his attic, and that banshee will be quiet tonight.

(71) If there is exactly one banshee in Hans's attic, and that banshee is
     quiet tonight, Hans will hold a party.

The plain fact is, however, that none of (65)–(67) have these predicted
readings. In saying (65), for example, we would not be attributing to
Hans the perverse desire to have a banshee in his attic. It seems that the
Russellian analysis makes clear predictions in these cases that are
straightforwardly false.

The Fregean analysis, on the other hand, seems perfectly well equipped
to deal with these examples. Take (67), and imagine this to be said of
Hans. It is clear, intuitively, that the speaker is not making the party conditional on the *existence* of a banshee in Hans's attic; rather, the speaker
seems to be presupposing the existence of such a banshee, and saying that
if it is quiet, there will be a party. In other words, the meaning of this sentence seems to favor exactly the Fregean approach to definite descriptions,
which, as we observed earlier, differs from the Russellian approach precisely in that it makes the existence and uniqueness of the entity in question
presuppositions, not assertions. Examples (65) and (66) are slightly more
complex, in that they involve propositional attitude verbs. Following Karttunen 1974 once more, we can postulate that the presupposition that there
is exactly one banshee in Hans's attic, carried by the embedded sentence, is
manipulated by the propositional attitude verb and contributes to a proposition carried by the whole sentence to the effect that Hans believes that
there is exactly one banshee in his attic, as described in the previous section. This, again, seems to be in accordance with our intuitions.

I can think of only one possible counterargument that the Russellian
might make to the above considerations, and that is to suggest that the
definite descriptions must have wide scope with respect to the operators
in question.[16] Perhaps some scopal properties of definite descriptions
could be stipulated somehow in the lexical entry of the (Russellian) definite article. However, I think there are serious problems with such a move.
Let us consider (65) again, here repeated as (72).

(72) Hans wants the banshee in his attic to be quiet tonight.

If we were to scope *the banshee in his attic* out above *wants*, as in (73a), to
avoid the problem of attributing to Hans the desire for a haunted attic,

then we would be predicting that the sentence could only have the reading in (73b).

(73) a. [the banshee in his attic] [λ_2 [Hans wants t_2 to be quiet tonight]]
b. There is an x such that:
   i. x is a banshee in Hans's attic, and
   ii. for all y, if y is a banshee in Hans's attic, then $y = x$, and
   iii. Hans wants x to be quiet tonight.

The truth conditions in (73b) seem inadequate. In particular, the wide scope for the definite description means that we rule out *de dicto* readings for *the banshee in the attic*—that is, we predict that the sentence cannot be felicitous when speaker and hearer know that in fact there is no banshee in Hans's attic, and are merely discussing Hans's confused beliefs and baseless desires. But this seems to run counter to our intuitions. The following utterance is quite coherent.

(74) Hans wants the banshee in his attic to be quiet tonight. Silly guy! There is no banshee in his attic.

This utterance would not be coherent if the first sentence in it had the truth conditions in (73b).

A second problem with the suggestion that the definite descriptions in our examples might be forced to take wide scope is that we can construct similar examples with the definite descriptions embedded in islands, without the sentences becoming ungrammatical or suddenly acquiring Russellian readings. An example is (75), where the definite description is inside a conjunct.

(75) Hans wants the banshee in his attic to be quiet and the party to go ahead.

(76) One man wants every banshee to be quiet and the party to go ahead.

As we have already seen, it is known that the Coordinate Structure Constraint generally holds at LF as well as for overt movement. So (76) cannot be read as stating that for every banshee there is one man who wants it to be quiet and the party to go ahead, as it could if *every banshee* could QR out of its conjunct. (See also examples (92), (93), and (94) in section 2.5.3.) Thus in (75), *the banshee in his attic* cannot scope above *want*, so the Russellian falsely predicts that the sentence will state that Hans wants to have a banshee in his attic.

As far as I can see, then, the examples adduced by Heim (1991) constitute a serious problem for the Russellian view of definite descriptions, and
provide support for the Fregean view.

3.3.2   The Argument Structure of the Definite Article

Having come down basically on the Fregean side of the debate about the
semantics of the definite article, I now wish to argue that the Fregean semantics in (14) is not quite correct after all, but must be replaced by one
that has the definite article taking two arguments, one of which will be an
index with the semantics given in section 3.2.2, while the other is a normal NP. The argument comes from the consideration of bound definite
descriptions.

It is well known that definite descriptions can be bound.[17] An example
is (77), which can have the truth conditions in (78).

(77) Mary talked to no senator before the senator was lobbied.

(78) There is no individual x such that x is a senator and Mary talked to
x before x was lobbied.

I will here investigate three possible accounts of this phenomenon.[18]

First, we could follow Heim (1991, 507–508), who suggests that we
arrive at the covarying interpretation for (77) in the following in way.
The semantics of quantifiers is expressed in terms of variable assignments. So, to take a simple example first, (79) has a logical form (80),
which will be interpreted by the rule in (81). Its truth conditions will be
those in (82).

(79) Mary talked to no senator.

(80) [no senator]$_x$ [Mary talked to x]

(81) $[\![[\text{no } \alpha]_x\, \beta]\!]^g = 1$ iff there is no assignment g' differing from g only
in the assignment to x such that $g'(x) \in [\![\alpha]\!]^{g'}$ and $[\![\beta]\!]^{g'} = 1$.

(82) $[\![[\text{no senator}]_x\, [\text{Mary talked to } x]]\!]^g = 1$ iff there is no assignment g'
differing from g only in the assignment to x such that $g'(x)$ is a
senator and Mary talked to $g'(x)$.

The LF of (77), according to Heim's proposal, is (83).

(83) [no senator]$_x$ [Mary talked to x before the senator was lobbied]

Suppose that in the evaluation of sentences by (81) we choose a different
domain $\mathbb{U}_{g'}$ along with each assignment g'. $\mathbb{U}_{g'}$ contains in each case
$g'(x)$ but excludes other members of $[\![\alpha]\!]^{g'}$. In the case of (83), for each

assignment g', $\mathbb{U}_{g'}$ contains only one senator, namely $g'(x)$. We then obtain the truth conditions in (84), which seem to be correct.

(84) $[\![[\text{no senator}]_x [\text{Mary talked to } x \text{ before the senator was lobbied}]]\!]^g$
= 1 iff there is no assignment g' differing from g only in the
assignment to x such that $g'(x)$ is a senator and Mary talked to
$g'(x)$ before the unique senator in $\mathbb{U}_{g'}$ (i.e., $g'(x)$) was lobbied.

As Heim acknowledges, this proposal is not yet thoroughly worked out, but enough has hopefully been said to give some idea.

The intuitive ideas that form the other two types of accounts can be summarized as "Add an individual variable to the NP" and "Add an individual variable to the determiner." In spelling these out, it is natural to take advantage of the new conception of indices advanced in section 3.2.2. In constructing the chain caused by QR of *no senator* in (77), we need to insert a trace [THE i] in the base position of this phrase and adjoin a lambda abstractor λ_i to the target of movement. The "Add an individual variable to the NP" account points out that the right truth conditions could be obtained if we were also to adjoin an index i to the NP in the covarying definite description, assuming these expressions of type $\langle e, t \rangle$ can combine in the semantics by a rule like Heim and Kratzer's predicate modification (Heim and Kratzer 1998, 65). So we would end up with the LF (86), and the truth conditions (87).

(85) *Predicate Modification*
If α is a branching node, $\{\beta, \gamma\}$ is the set of α's daughters, and $[\![\beta]\!]$
and $[\![\gamma]\!]$ are both in $D_{\langle e, t \rangle}$, then $[\![\alpha]\!] = \lambda x \in D_e. [\![\beta]\!](x) = [\![\gamma]\!](x) = 1$.

(86) [no senator] [λ_2 [Mary talked to [THE 2] before the [senator 2] was lobbied]]

(87) There is no individual x such that x is a senator and Mary talked to x before the unique z such that z is a senator and $z = x$ was lobbied.

The "Add an individual variable to the determiner" account, on the other hand, is more radical. It says that *the* takes two arguments, not just one, and that an index occupies one of these argument positions (the inner one, I argue in section 3.3.3). So instead of the semantics in (88), *the* should actually have the denotation in (89).[19] Pronouns, meanwhile, and the silent definite article THE used in traces (until we adopt the copy theory of movement) will continue to have the semantics in (88).

(88) $\lambda f: f \in D_{\langle e, t \rangle} \ \& \ \exists! x \ f(x) = 1 . \iota x \ f(x) = 1$

(89) $\lambda f_{\langle e,t \rangle}. \lambda g : g \in D_{\langle e,t \rangle}$ & $\exists! x(f(x) = 1$ & $g(x) = 1). \iota x(f(x) = 1$ & $g(x) = 1)$

On this account, then, we end up with the LF in (90) and the truth conditions in (91).

(90) [no senator] [λ_2 [Mary talked to [THE 2] before [[the 2] senator] was lobbied]]

(91) There is no individual x such that x is a senator and Mary talked to x before the unique y such that $y = x$ and y is a senator was lobbied.

Again, the correct truth conditions are obtained.

The question, then, is whether we can distinguish empirically between these three conceivable accounts. It turns out that we can.

The crucial data concerns genitival definite descriptions like *Mary's cat*. Since *Mary's cat* seems to mean something like "the cat of Mary's," we might expect that it would display the kind of bound use that we have been discussing. This is not the case, however, as shown by the following data.[20]

(92) a.   John fed no cat of Mary's before the cat of Mary's was bathed.
b.   *John fed no cat of Mary's before Mary's cat was bathed.

(93) a.   Mary gave every child of John's something which the child of John's already had.
c.   *Mary gave every child of John's something which John's child already had.

The (b) cases in these examples are ungrammatical not just on the covarying reading but overall, presumably because quantifiers like *no* and *every* presuppose or implicate that there is more than one entity that satisfies the predicate in their restrictor,[21] while genitives like *Mary's cat* presuppose that there is only one such entity.

How do the three rival hypotheses fare with respect to these data? Heim's suggestion, to start with that, fares badly. The LF of (92b) on this proposal would be (94).

(94) [no cat of Mary's]$_x$ [John fed x before Mary's cat was bathed]

Since *Mary's cat* basically means "the cat of Mary", there is no reason, on Heim's assumptions, why the domain $\mathbb{U}_{g'}$ of each assignment g' should not be able to be narrowed down to contain only one cat of Mary's, namely $g'(x)$ in each case, just as happened with senators in

(84). Then everything should work out perfectly—the uniqueness condition of *Mary's cat* should be satisfied and the right truth conditions should result. The example is ungrammatical, however, meaning that Heim's suggestion must be incorrect.

Nor does the "Add an individual variable to the NP" account fare any better. Whatever one may want to say about the syntax and semantics of *Mary's*, it surely cannot be denied that there is a respectable NP lurking somewhere in *Mary's cat*. If the "Add an individual variable to the NP" account were correct, then, it would be entirely mysterious that (92b) was ungrammatical, since it would not differ in any relevant respect from perfectly grammatical variants with the covarying reading.

We are left, then, with the "Add an individual variable to the determiner" theory. The (b) examples in (92) and (93) do not differ from the (a) examples in any way which would lend support to the other two hypotheses. Moreover, they do differ in the determiners in the definite descriptions, which is precisely the locus of the ability of definite descriptions to be bound according to the "Add an individual variable to the determiner" theory. We must conclude, then, that this theory is on the right lines, and as a concrete implementation I offer the semantics in (89), repeated here as (95), for the definite article.[22]

(95) $\lambda f_{\langle e,t\rangle}. \lambda g : g \in D_{\langle e,t\rangle}$ & $\exists! x(f(x) = 1$ & $g(x) = 1). \imath x(f(x) = 1$ & $g(x) = 1)$

Of course, we still must ensure that it is indices, as opposed to other items of type $\langle e, t\rangle$, that appear in the relevant argument slot. It seems not unreasonable to stipulate that being an index is a property visible to the mechanisms of syntactic sub-categorization. This can also account for the impossibility of structures like [cat 2], which were posited by the "Add an individual variable to the NP" account—predicate modification is only possible between those expressions of type $\langle e, t\rangle$ which the syntax allows to combine (and so not between two NPs, for example, or between PP and T′), and we can say that [cat 2] is ruled out mechanically by syntactic sub-categorization in the same way as some other combinations.

3.3.3 Two Consequences of the New Argument Structure

The Referential-Attributive Debate   Let us examine the consequences of the view advocated here for those occasions when a definite description is *not* bound. Is there any advantage to be had from the index on these occasions? Those familiar with the philosophical literature on definite descriptions might be reminded by the current proposal of Peacocke's (1975) suggestion that so-called 'referential' uses of definite descriptions be assimilated to demonstrative phrases like *that man*, with demonstratives interpreted by Tarski-style sequences and variables in a manner essentially equivalent to the use of indices and variable assignments. But Kripke (1979) and others have cast doubt on the position that we need a distinct "referential" semantics for definite descriptions in Donnellan's (1966) sense.[23] So it looks as if the view that definite articles incorporate an argument place for an index cannot draw any support from the alleged "referential" examples of definite descriptions.[24]

On the other hand, it is possible that the theory that there are distinct referential and attributive uses of definite descriptions, taken in a strong form to imply distinct referential and attributive *semantics*, might actually gain some support from the current theory of indices. Let us begin by noting that a problem arises because of the index on *the* in examples like (96).

(96) Every man who owns a donkey beats the donkey.

If there was an index in the inner argument position of *the* in this example, it seems that the sentence would surely crash, because the index could be neither bound nor referential. It seems best to admit a special item into the syntactic class of indices: let us say that the index 0 will have the anodyne interpretation $[\lambda x : x \in D_e. x \in D_e]$; the others, the positive integers, will be interpreted according to the rules in section 3.2.2. So in examples like (96) we have the index 0.

This conclusion suggests a new take on the old referential-attributive debate. We now have reason to believe that a definite description like *the murderer* can have two different sorts of indices on it: either the normal ones or the new index 0 just introduced. So we could have either (97) or (98).[25]

(97) $[\![[\text{the 1}] \text{ murderer}]\!]^g =$ the unique individual x such that x is a murderer and $x = g(1)$

(98) $[\![[\text{the 0}] \text{ murderer}]\!]^g =$ the unique individual x such that x is a murderer

And this, it seems to me, is a plausible reconstruction of the referential-attributive distinction. According to Donnellan (1966), a speaker who uses a definite description *the* ϕ attributively says something about whoever or whatever is the ϕ. To adapt one of Donnellan's examples slightly, a detective examining footprints at a gory crime scene might say (99).

(99) Well, we know one thing: the murderer is a size 10.

Since, by stipulation, no other personal details are known about the murderer at this stage, we must presumably have (98) in use here: there is no particular individual who could be $g(1)$, as required in (97). On the other hand, it is plausible that a nontrivial index is involved in Donnellan's other scenario, where we look at Jones, on trial for Smith's murder, and, convinced of his guilt, say (100).

(100) The murderer is insane!

Here, *the murderer* could mean "the unique individual x such that x is a murderer and $x = $ Jones."

Let me emphasize once more that I am not convinced by Donnellan's arguments that we *need* something like (97) for the cases he brought up in his classic paper (if, indeed, he meant to argue for something like (97) at all). My current point is simply that we have independent reason, in bound definite descriptions, to suppose that definite descriptions incorporate an index, and we then cannot reasonably stipulate that speakers cannot make use of this index in other linguistic contexts too. If the theory advocated here is on the right lines, we get a distinction between referential and non-referential definite descriptions for free, on independent grounds.

Is there any evidence, then, to show that we actually *need* the index in definite descriptions which are not bound? I believe that there is. Consider (101), which we would easily accept as a felicitous opening to a newspaper article.

(101) Senator Thad Cochran, the Mississippi Republican, announced
        today that ...

In this sentence, the phrase *the Mississippi Republican* seems to be ambiguous. We could take it to imply (falsely, at the time of writing) that Mississippi has only one Republican senator; let us call this the *uniqueness reading*. On the other hand, there is a natural reading of the sentence whereby this is not implied: the phrase is merely taken to remind us of Senator Cochran's home state and party affiliation, without any suggestion that there is no other senator with these characteristics; let us call this the *no uniqueness reading*. A natural hypothesis, given the above argumentation, is that the uniqueness reading comes about by (102) and the no uniqueness reading comes about by (103).

(102) *Uniqueness Reading*
        [[the 0] Mississippi Republican]

(103) *No Uniqueness Reading*
         [[the 1] Mississippi Republican]

In the case of (102), we get the meaning "the unique x such that x is a Mississippi Republican senator," and the presupposition that there are no other Mississippi Republican senators. In the case of (103), assuming the index 1 to be mapped to Thad Cochran in the variable assignment, we get "the unique x such that x is a Mississippi Republican senator and x is identical to Thad Cochran." We do not now take the reporter to be strangely ignorant of the existence of Senator Trent Lott (R-MS).[26]

Now the normal strategy for justifying the uniqueness presupposition (or assertion) in the semantics of the definite article is to say that definite descriptions are often interpreted with respect to narrow universes of discourse, within which the uniqueness presupposition or assertion is in fact justified. In the case of (101), if one wanted to avoid the outcome in (102) and (103), and suppose that the basic semantics of *the Mississippi Republican* was always what we would get from (102), one would have to say that the sentence could be interpreted with respect to two kinds of universes of discourse: one kind would include Trent Lott, and would give us the uniqueness reading (and the feeling of surprise at the reporter's ignorance); the other kind would have to exclude Trent Lott, and would produce the no uniqueness reading. The question comes down to this, then. Is it possible to explain the no uniqueness reading of (101) by supposing that it could be evaluated with respect to a universe of discourse that excludes Trent Lott, even when the very mention of Mississippi Republicans would seem to make it likely that Trent Lott would be made salient?

This would be a hard question to answer by means of general reasoning about the nature of context and universes of discourse. But fortunately I think there is an empirical argument to hand. Recall that genitival definite descriptions do not seem to be able to host indices, to judge by their inability to be bound. Thus we have the contrast in (92), repeated here as (104).

(104) a.   John fed no cat of Mary's before the cat of Mary's was
               bathed.
         b.   *John fed no cat of Mary's before Mary's cat was bathed.

We have to conclude, then, that the semantics of *Mary's cat* really is just something like "the unique x such that x is a cat of Mary's," with no invocation of variable assignments via indices. Now if it were indeed possible to obtain the no uniqueness reading of (101) by means of a semantics like this, and a narrow universe of discourse that did not include Trent Lott, we would also expect a variant of the sentence with a genitival definite description in the place of *the Mississippi Republican* to have a no uniqueness reading. That is, we would expect (105) to have a no uniqueness reading.

(105) Thad Cochran, Mississippi's Republican senator, announced
            today that . . .

It is a sharp judgment, however, that (105) does *not* have a no uniqueness reading. This sentence can only be taken to imply that Mississippi has only one Republican senator.[27] To sum up: the alternative to supposing a pair of representations like (102) and (103) is to suppose that the no uniqueness reading can be obtained without indices, merely through narrowing down the universe of discourse in a particular way; but this alternative predicts falsely that (105) will have a no uniqueness reading; so we are left with the representations in (102) and (103), and a vindication of Donnellan's referential-attributive distinction.[28]

Trace Conversion   If we adopt the copy theory of movement (Chomsky 1993), we must admit some mechanism for altering lower copies to make them interpretable, since (107), the result of applying QR to (106), is uninterpretable as it stands.

(106) A girl talked to every boy.

(107) [every boy][a girl talked to every boy]

The simplest method I know of is Fox's (2002) "trace conversion":

(108) *Trace Conversion*
            1. Variable Insertion: Det Pred $\Rightarrow$ Det [Pred $\lambda y. y = x$]
            2. Determiner Replacement: Det [Pred $\lambda y. y = x$] $\Rightarrow$ THE [Pred $\lambda y. y = x$]

This means that instead of (107) we will have (109).

(109) [every boy][λx [a girl talked to [THE [boy $\lambda y. y = x$]]]]

In the light of the foregoing discussion, we can see that the combination of $\lambda y. y = x$ and THE introduced by Fox is now independently motivated. It is how *the* works in overt bound definite descriptions.

I propose, therefore, the following simplified theory of trace conversion: when moving an NP, we just replace the lower determiner with [THE i], for some index i, and adjoin λ_i to the target of movement. So instead of (109) we end up with (110); our earlier example (77) will have the LF (111).

(110) [every boy][λ_2 [a girl talked to [[THE 2] boy]]]

(111) [no senator] [λ_2 [Mary talked to [[THE 2] senator] before [[the 2] senator] was lobbied]]

Note how the trace (underlined) in (111) is identical to the overt bound definite description. This is appropriate, since they seem to have identical semantics.

In addition to the original discussion involving bound definite descriptions, we have now seen two considerations that favor the hypothesis that *the* takes two arguments, an index and a normal NP: we can account for occasions when non-bound definite descriptions like *the Mississippi Republican* have no uniqueness presupposition; and we have a simple account of trace conversion, using independently justified resources.

3.4   Pronoun Plus Relative Clause

Recall that during the course of the argumentation about the referential-attributive debate in section 3.3.3 I introduced a special new index, 0, with the interpretation $[\lambda x : x \in D_e . x \in D_e]$. This was necessary in order for the index on *the* in (96), repeated here as (112), not to cause the sentence to crash.

(112) Every man who owns a donkey beats the donkey.

In this section we will see the index 0 used in other contexts, with pronouns and demonstrative determiners. The argumentation will hopefully lend support to the postulation of this element, and at the same time introduce a powerful new piece of evidence in favor of analyzing English pronouns as definite articles.

Consider examples like (113) and (114).

(113) He who hesitates is lost.

(114) She who must be obeyed has made her entrance.

It looks as if it is possible to combine a pronoun in English directly with a restrictive relative clause. The construction seems to be productive, subject to a restriction to high register. The examples that it is possible to construct all have a rather grandiose or epic feel to them, as we see further in (115).

(115) a. He who finds the Grail shall find also great honor.
      b. !He who spills my cup of coffee will be in trouble.
      c. He who has found the Grail shall find also great honor.
      d. !He who has spilt my cup of coffee will be in trouble.

In examples like (114), of course, this portentous quality has an effect more jocular than sublime.

    Another restriction is that it seems to be impossible to use *it* in this construction, as we see in (116). Note, at the same time, that we can have relative clauses seemingly taken directly by demonstratives.

(116) a. *It that rolls fastest gathers no moss.
      b. *It which rolls fastest gathers no moss.
      c. That which rolls fastest gathers no moss.
      d. Those who hesitate are lost.

I will not attempt to investigate the impossibility of *it* here, though one suspects it may be related to the inability of this word to figure in contexts where one expects demonstratives:

(117) a. Look at that!
      b. Look at him!
      c. Look at her!
      d. *Look at it!

Let us concentrate on the analysis of (113), (114) and (115).

    The question which is naturally raised is whether the pronouns combine directly with the relative clauses in these cases, as one might think on the basis of the overt material, or whether some phonologically null noun combines with the relative clause and then the definite article combines with this complex. The latter option is made available to us because we have proposed that indices are phonologically null nouns. The choice, then, is between the analysis in (118) and the one in (119).

(118) a. [he [who hesitates is lost]]
      b. [she [who must be obeyed]]

(119) a. [he [0 [who hesitates]]]
      b. [she [2 [who must be obeyed]]]

Note that the index 0 is necessary in (119a), since we are dealing with a generic statement, and no particular person can be meant by *he who hesitates*.[29] In (119b), a particular person is evidently meant, and a normal index can be used.

How to choose between these two analyses? I think we can be helped by the observation that it is not possible to use the normal definite article *the* in one of these constructions, as we see in (120b).

(120) a.   The one who hesitates is lost.
      b.   *The who hesitates is lost.

Recall from section 2.1.3 that *the* does not allow a phonologically null complement. An attractively economical approach to the ungrammaticality of (120b) uses this observation in a modified form: although the relative clause is phonologically realized, there is no phonologically realized head noun (or inner NP, assuming relative clauses to be adjoined), and this violates the selectional requirements of *the*. So a relative clause by itself cannot form a full NP. We can assume that pronominal definite articles subcategorize for full NPs; and this means that (119), not (118), must be the correct analysis of (113) and (114).[30]

Before we leave these examples, one more should be added to the paradigm. In (121), we see a relative clause as part of the complement of a pronoun which must be D-type.

(121)   Every man who met a woman who had to be obeyed said that she who had to be obeyed told him to make himself scarce.

Since there is an antecedent for NP-deletion in the word *woman*, the phrase *she who had to be obeyed* in this example is actually ambiguous. It could be analyzed as in (122), along the lines we have just been exploring; or it could have the structure in (123), where the inner NP *woman* will be deleted in the phonological component.

(122)   [she [0 [who had to be obeyed]]]

(123)   [she [$_{NP_2}$ [$_{NP_1}$ woman] [who had to be obeyed]]]

This and the other examples in this section are particularly clear and visible demonstrations of the utility of analyzing pronouns as definite articles. Contrast the theories of dynamic binding and variable-free semantics explored in chapter 1: they both say that pronouns are of type e and take no complements, and would presumably therefore face difficulty in accounting for the data adduced here.

3.5   Pronouns Revisited

3.5.1   The Case for Two Arguments for Pronouns
As things stand at the moment, then, we have two types of definite article. There are definite articles proper, which take an index and a normal NP,

as shown in (124a). And there are pronouns, which take just one argument, either an index or a normal NP, as shown in (124b). Recall that, in order to make the syntactic requirements of pronouns uniform, indices were claimed to be a kind of NP in section 3.2.2.

(124) a. [[the i] NP]
      b. [it NP]
         [it i]

A natural question to ask now is whether pronouns should really be thought to take just one argument and not two, like overt definite articles. The latter position, it might seem, would be attractive if sustainable, since then the hypothesis behind this whole work would hold in a particularly strong form: there really would be just one syntax and semantics for pronouns and definite descriptions (and proper names, I will argue later), and the language learning task would accordingly be simplified more than if we had to posit two related structures.

If pronouns were always to have slots for both indices and (other) NPs, there would be a question of whether the NP slot would always be filled by a regular lexical NP like *donkey* or *Queen of Siam*. Since there would have to be NP-deletion every time a pronoun was used, according to such a theory, this position might appear to run into difficulties with occasions where there is no NP in preceding discourse that could serve as antecedent. Suppose, for example, that we are walking along silently and someone passes us, and I say (125).

(125) He looks happy!

It might appear that no regular NP could be in the putative second argument slot of *he* in this example. The question is complicated, however, by the observation made in section 2.1.3. To repeat, a visitor being enthusiastically leapt upon by his host's dog might nod at it and say (126).

(126) Mine does just the same.

There is no difficulty here in interpreting the utterance as claiming that the speaker's *dog* does just the same. Would it be possible to claim, then, in the framework envisaged, that regular lexical NPs are always supplied in the second argument slot, by whatever process allows us (presumably) to supply *dog* in (126) without a linguistic antecedent?

I think there are difficulties with such a theory. Imagine the following scenario. We are walking through Boston, and come across someone with the following characteristics: early twenties, male, skateboarding, wearing a Red Sox cap, smiling broadly. Imagine that under these circumstances I gesture and say (127).

(127) Most look more depressed than that.

I would, I think, produce a feeling of some confusion. Do I mean that most young men in Boston look more depressed than that? Or most skateboarders? Most Red Sox fans? Most wearers of baseball caps? It is not at all clear how the NP-deletion is to be resolved in this example, and the hearer is left casting around for the intended NP. Now, on the other hand, suppose that in exactly the same scenario I did not say (127) but instead said (125). This time there is no feeling of confusion and casting around. But if it were necessary to supply a regular lexical NP after *he* in (125), there would surely be just as much confusion produced by (125) in the given scenario as there would by (127); for the description under which I am thinking of the young man, or under which I expect my audience to think of him, is no clearer in the one case than it is in the other.

I conclude that any theory according to which pronouns take two arguments, just like overt definite articles, will have to allow the second argument to be a kind of default item which is always available and does not need to be recovered by means of a linguistic antecedent or overwhelming contextual salience (as, presumably, in the dog case, (126)). We will have to suppose that there is a functional item that serves this purpose: let ONE be a phonologically null noun with interpretation $[\lambda x : x \in D_e. x \in D_e]$, which can appear in the argument slot for a (non-index) NP provided by a pronoun. So in the case of our example (125), repeated as (128a), which by stipulation has no previous linguistic context, the pronoun would have an LF like the one in (128b).

(128) a. He looks happy!
      b. [[he 2] ONE]

The meaning of ONE, of course, makes it applicable to all entities of type e; this, as well as its being a functional as opposed to a lexical item, makes it plausible that it would always be available, without being subject to the normal strictures of NP-deletion.

There is a question, of course, as to whether this null noun ONE would be available in other places too, not just as the complement of pronouns. I do not propose to investigate this question exhaustively here, but it seems to me that it would probably be possible to maintain the most desirable position, namely that ONE is generally available, with its occurrence restricted only by independently motivated factors. It is plausible, for example, that ONE can be invoked to explain the alternation shown in (129) and (130) between *this* and *that* occurring "bare" and these words occurring with overt NP complements.

(129) a. This cap is red.
      b. This is red.

(130) a. That cap is red.
      b. That is red.

This kind of alternation with demonstratives is very common crosslinguistically, of course.[31] On the view put forward here, it is to be accounted for by positing structures like those in (131).

(131) a. [[this 2] cap]
      b. [[this 2] ONE]

The lexical entries of *this* and *that* will presumably look rather like the entry given in (95) for *the*, the difference being that *this* and *that* will have to have the appropriate proximal and distal features specified.[32]

What about other determiners, like *all*, *some* and *most*? Would the posited null noun ONE cause any problems in connection with these? To begin addressing this question, let us consider whether positing ONE leads us to expect (127), repeated here as (132), to be felicitous in the circumstances described above.

(132) Most look more depressed than that.

We are now supposing that we could have ONE be the complement of *most*, which would produce a meaning, "Most individuals (in the technical sense: entities of type e) look more depressed than that." In this case, at least, I think that it is clear that we can allow that this meaning is made available by the grammar without thereby being forced to conclude that the utterance should be felicitous. The reason is that the utterance in question is obviously provoked by the sight of the young man of our scenario, and there is therefore a natural expectation that the speaker will be saying that most individuals who have one of *his* qualities look more depressed than that.

Moving beyond this example, I think it can readily be appreciated that there will be few if any circumstances under which quantification will be felicitous if the restrictor designates the entire domain of entities of type e, and thus fails to restrict at all. Generally speaking, people's concerns are not so catholic that the whole of D_e would form a natural subject of discussion: there is an irresistible urge to tacitly narrow down the domain of quantification to something that people might plausibly be talking about. Particular obstacles, moreover, arise in particular cases. In the case of existential quantifiers (*some, few, at least three*), Gricean maxims presumably come into play: the speaker would be making a weaker claim if the implicit domain were all of D_e than if the domain were narrower, and the Gricean maxim enjoining informativeness would therefore tend to make speakers select and audiences assume narrower domains. If the quantification is universal and the domain is D_e, it is difficult to think of any VP predicate that would make the utterance true, and impossible, as far as I can see, to think of such a predicate that would be in common use among nonphilosophers. (The only possible examples I can think of are things like *are identical to themselves* and *are either prime numbers or not prime numbers*.) And quantifiers like *most* would presumably suffer from the fact that the domain of entities of type e is very, very large, perhaps infinite:[33] it is difficult to see how one could possibly go about calculating what would count as *most* entities of type e, or how one would ever be in a position to make a claim about most such entities. I tentatively conclude, therefore, that the hypothesis that ONE exists is not open to the objection that it leads us to overgeneralize and predict that lots of apparent NP-deletion examples are good that are not. Pragmatic factors will tend to make the interpretation with ONE hard, if not impossible, to obtain.

Returning to the question of the argument structure of pronouns, it does now seem possible to maintain that they have the same argument structure as *the*. We are left with the picture in (133).

(133) a. [[the i] NP]
      b. [[it i] NP]

Note that if we adopt this hypothesis it will no longer be necessary to assume that indices are NPs, since they no longer occupy the same slot as regular NPs. The defender of (133) can maintain that indices are not NPs, although they will still be of type $\langle e, t \rangle$.[34]

The revised theory in (133) is attractive because of the unity it brings to overt definite descriptions and pronouns. Ideally, of course, we would find empirical arguments for it too. I know of two such arguments, one concerning resumptive pronouns, and the other concerning focused bound pronouns.

3.5.2 Focused Bound Pronouns

One argument in favor of pronouns taking two arguments is to be found in work by Uli Sauerland (2000, 2002). Sauerland points to occasions when bound pronouns are focused, as in (134).

(134) On Monday, every boy called his mother. On TUESday, every TEAcher called HIS mother.

How can the focus on the second *his* be justified? Only by its denotation contrasting appropriately with that of some previous constituent, according to contemporary theories of focus (Rooth 1992a; Schwarzschild 1999, and much other work). At this point, it is natural to suggest that difference in indices between the first *his* and the second will be sufficient to bring about the necessary contrast. Let us follow Sauerland in using the following corollary of the focus-licensing theory of Schwarzschild 1999:

(135) A focus on an XP that is asymmetrically dominated by a non-focused phrase is licensed only if there is a Focus Domain FD asymmetrically dominating XP such that for a Focus Antecedent FA in the preceding discourse (or entailed by it) the following two conditions are satisfied:
   a. *Givenness*: $[\![FA]\!] \in [\![FD]\!]_f$ (i.e., there is a Focus Alternative FD′ of FD with $[\![FA]\!] = [\![FD']\!]$).
   b. *Contrastiveness*: $[\![FA]\!] \notin [\![FD^-]\!]_f$, where FD⁻ is identical to FD, except that XP is not focused in FD⁻.

One might now attempt to use indices in order to explain the focus in (134) by assuming the indexing in (136) and taking the choices of FA, FD, FD′ and FD⁻ in (137).

(136) On Monday, every boy λ_1 t_1 called his$_1$ mother. On Tuesday, every TEAcher λ_2 t_2 called HIS$_2$ mother.

(137) a. FA $=$ his$_1$ mother
   b. FD $= [HIS_2]_F$ mother
   c. FD′ $=$ his$_1$ mother
   d. FD⁻ $=$ his$_2$ mother

Given these choices, the Givenness condition of (135) is satisfied because one of the focus alternatives of $[[HIS_2]_F$ mother] is [his$_1$ mother], as required. And the Contrastiveness condition is arguably satisfied because the set of focus alternatives of FD⁻, [his$_2$ mother], contains only the semantic value of [his$_2$ mother], since nothing in this phrase is focused; and the semantic value of FA, [his$_1$ mother], is not identical to this, since there are assignments in which 1 is not treated the same way as 2.

Thus one way of spelling out an attempt to explain the focus in (134) by means of contrasting indices. Sauerland, however, has the following ingenious argument against this. Consider *however*, as it is used when it appears between subject and VP:

(138) Carl called Mary ...
    a.   ... John, however, wrote Mary.
    b.   ... John, however, called Berta.
    c. *... John, however, called Mary.
    d. *... Carl, however, called Berta.

For *however* in this position to be allowed, it seems as if both the subject NP and the following VP (or T′) must differ in meaning from those in some sentence in the preceding discourse. Now consider the following example.[35]

(139) Every TEAcher λ_1 t_1 believes that SHE$_1$ will win.
    a.   Every GIRL, however, λ_2 t_2 believes that SHE$_2$ will win.
    b. *Every GIRL, however, believes that she'll win.

Even if we could explain the focus on *she* in both sentences by means of contrasting indices, says Sauerland, this will still not enable us to explain the felicity of *however* in (139a). For *however* requires that there be some contrast between VP meanings as a whole, and when we come to consider the VP meanings as a whole in each sentence, the index on *she* is bound by the higher lambda. We end up with mere alphabetic variants, then, which must, by one of the most basic conventions about logical languages, represent the same function. So difference in indices on *she* is not enough to explain the felicity of *however* in (139a). More is required.

A defender of the view that difference in indices is able to explain the relevant contrasts might argue at this point that we do not know for sure that *however* requires a difference in the VP/T′ meanings *as a whole*. Perhaps *however* is licensed if there is just some constituent within the VP/T′ that differs in meaning from a constituent that is in some sense parallel in the previous discourse. For example, *however* could be justified in (138a) above not because *wrote Mary* differs in meaning from *called Mary*, but simply because *wrote* differs in meaning from *called*. It would be necessary, of course, in spelling out this rival view to provide an account of which pairs of lexical items are able to figure like this in the licensing of *however*: we would not want this word to be licensed just because *Mary* differs in meaning from *called* in examples like those above. But suppose such an account were successfully given. I think that there is still an insuperable problem facing the rival view. That is that it seems to predict incorrectly that *however* will be licensed in a discourse like the following.

(140) Carl called Mary. *John, however, called her$_2$.

Suppose that the index 2 is mapped to Mary. It is clear, then, that the second sentence here is deviant. But recall that a defender of the view that difference in indices can account for the focus phenomena we are examining is committed to the view that pronouns with different indices differ in meaning because there are assignments which do not treat the two indices alike; this was essential in the argumentation above. Given this, we can surely argue here that *Mary* and *her* differ in meaning in the current example, because there are assignments in which 2 is not mapped to Mary. So the view that *however* is licensed just by *parts* of the relevant surrounding constituents differing in meaning predicts that the second sentence in (140) will be grammatical, contrary to fact.[36]

We can take it, then, that difference in indices is not sufficient to explain the focused pronoun in our original example (134), repeated here.

(141) On Monday, every boy called his mother. On TUESday, every TEAcher called HIS mother.

With this possibility gone, the only other possibility seems to be that the two occurrences of *his* differ in more substantive descriptive content. In his 2000 paper, Sauerland concludes that the two pronouns incorporate NPs at LF, so that the first *his* is represented as [the$_i$ boy's] and the second one as [the$_i$ teacher's]. Indices are necessary because the pronouns are evidently bound by c-commanding antecedents; normal NPs are necessary in order to provide contrasting descriptive content to enable focus to be placed on the second pronoun. This, of course, would be evidence of precisely the kind of tripartite structure for pronouns that is currently under discussion.

Sauerland 2002, however, offers two arguments against this earlier position and in favor of a new one whereby the pronouns in (141) are analyzed as consisting of an indexed definite article plus a variable over properties, as in (142) (= (42) in Sauerland 2002).

(142) [the$_i$ P]

The property index, of course, would pick up the property of being a boy in the case of the first pronoun in our example, and the property of being a teacher in the case of the second pronoun.

The first argument against the earlier position appeals to Schwarzschild's (1999) claim that focus must be placed on the smallest constituent possible (Sauerland 2002, 41–43). The idea in the present case, then, would be that when we have two structures of the form [the NP], with only the NPs contrasting, focus would have to go on the NP and would not be allowed to go on the definite article. But in our example we do have focus on *his*, which is taken to be the spell-out of the definite article; so there cannot be any NP syntactically present, since if there was focus would have to be restricted to this and could not be phonetically realized.

The problem that I see with this argument for Sauerland's purposes is that it seems to affect his currently favored proposal just as much as it affects the earlier one. In his current proposal too there is a syntactically realized item present after the definite article, namely the property vari-. able, and it is hard to see why this should be exempt from the argument just raised while normal NPs are not. It is more likely that some minor adjustment needs to be made to Schwarzschild's theory of focus placement, a possibility that Sauerland himself acknowledges.

The second argument that Sauerland (2002, 43–44) levels against his own earlier view concerns example (143), which is attributed to Pauline Jacobson. (See also Jacobson 2000b, 74.)

(143) Every man who loves his mother talked to every man who
       HATES HIS mother.

Sauerland points out that this example seems to raise the problem of antecedent-containment. We can easily find NPs which distinguish the two sets of men and might look like suitable candidates for antecedents to NP content in the pronouns on an ellipsis-based account: *man who loves his mother* and *man who hates his mother*. But these NPs contain the very pronouns that we are looking for content for. None of the remedies for analyzing antecedent containment in the case of antecedent-contained VP-ellipsis seem applicable here. It must be concluded, then, says Sauerland, that we cannot find any suitable antecedents for NP-deletion in this example, and that a property variable is needed to do the job of filling in suitable content to license the focus.

I think, however, that the earlier position can survive these considerations too. As for finding an antecedent for NP-deletion, we can suppose that the antecedent is *man* in each case, and the problem of antecedent containment disappears. We are left, of course, with the necessity of explaining the contrast, which is difficult if the syntactically present descriptive material on the pronouns is the same in each case. To do this, we could say that we tacitly supply extra descriptive content, differing in the two cases, and that this is taken into account when the availability of focus is calculated. It is plausible anyway to suppose that we are capable of narrowing the domain of discourse in different ways when we make sense of different definite descriptions—see section 4.4.1 for further discussion.

And some proposals about the mechanics of this domain-narrowing (for example, von Fintel 1994) actually have extra descriptive content present within DP, picked up by a variable. If we do this here, then, we could claim that in effect we interpret the first pronoun as, for example, 'the loving man's' and the second as "the malevolent man's"; this extra descriptive content is then taken into account in the calculation of focus, and we arrive at the right results.

I do not think, then, that Sauerland has put forward a convincing case for rejecting his own earlier view that in his contrastively focused bound pronouns we have NP content. But is there any positive reason actually to prefer the earlier view over the later one? I think there is. Sauerland's later view says that the descriptive content of D-type pronouns (which is effectively what these pronouns are, as Sauerland points out) can be provided solely by a property variable. No syntactic NP antecedent is necessary. This, then, plunges us straight back into the problem of the formal link, discussed in section 2.4. If pronouns can pick up descriptive content solely by property variables, as Sauerland maintains, why can we not say (144)?

(144) *Every married man is sitting next to her.

It seems that the best overall solution is the one which makes an NP antecedent for descriptive content in pronouns obligatory. This does not of course make it necessary that all the descriptive content we understand in pronouns should come from the NP; we need a little extra flexibility to deal with (143).

In other words, the best way of dealing with Sauerland's data concerning contrastively focused pronouns while simultaneously avoiding the problem of the formal link is to follow Sauerland 2000 and suppose that pronouns incorporate both an index and an NP. This is empirical support, then, for the tripartite view of pronouns currently under discussion.

3.5.3   Resumptive Pronouns

Another possible source of empirical evidence on this matter comes from resumptive pronouns. Yael Sharvit (personal communication) has pointed out that if the theory of trace conversion described in section 3.3.3 is on the right lines, then we have reason to believe that pronouns take two arguments, as just suggested, because this would give us a very neat theory of certain resumptive pronouns. There are some environments where resumptive pronouns appear to alternate freely with gaps (traces), as we see in the following data from Suñer's (1998) study of relative clauses.

(145) *Spanish*
    a. una cierta   senadora que Luis llamó
       a   certain senator   that Luis called
       'a certain senator that Luis called'
    b. una cierta   senadora que Luis **la**   llamó
       a   certain senator   that Luis her called
       'a certain senator that Luis called'

(146) *Hebrew*
    a. ha- ʔiš   še- raʔiti
       the man that saw.1s
       'the man I saw'
    b. ha- ʔiš   še- raʔiti **ʔoto**
       the man that saw.1s him
       'the man I saw'

(147) *Irish*
    a. an fear al bhuail tú
       the man C struck you
       'the man you struck'
    b. an fear an bhuail tú   é
       the man C struck you him
       'the man you struck'

Recall that the theory in section 3.3.3 had traces looking like (148), after the determiner originally in the lower copy had been replaced with [THE i] (where i is the index used on the λ inserted just below the target of movement).

(148) [[THE i] NP]

This, of course, is also the structure supposed for pronouns under the theory that they take two arguments. Sharvit's suggestion is that the hypothesis that pronouns take two arguments will allow us to view certain resumptive pronouns as directly spelling out traces. The phonological reflex is exactly what we would expect given the lexical material present, provided that pronouns take both an index and an NP. This is an attractive account of data like that given above: we simply say that in Spanish, Hebrew, and Irish (in certain environments), traces can optionally receive phonological content, contrary to their behavior in English.[37]

    The apparently free alternation between pronouns and gaps just exemplified is a prima facie argument that resumptive pronouns should be assimilated to traces in at least the above contexts. Furthermore, Aoun and Benmamoun (1998) have shown that the sites of some resumptive pronouns are linked to their antecedents by movement in Lebanese Arabic clitic left-dislocation constructions. In clitic left-dislocation, a lexical NP shows up clause-initially and is related to a clitic inside the clause. A simple Lebanese Arabic example is (149). (I follow Aoun and Benmamoun in their convention of writing clitic left-dislocated NP and related clitic in boldface.)

(149) **Naadya ʃeef-a**   Kariim mbeeriʕ.
      Nadia   saw.3SM-her Karim yesterday
      'Nadia, Karim saw her yesterday.'

The relation between left-dislocated NP and clitic can violate island conditions, as shown by means of an adjunct island in (150). As we expect, it is not possible to relate a topicalized NP to a gap in such a position, as shown in (151).

(150) Smaʕt   ʔənno **Naadya** raʕt   mən duun ma   taʕke
      heard.1s that   Nadia left.2SM without   COMP talking.2s
      maʕ-**a**.
      with-her
      'I heard that Nadia, you left without talking to her.'

(151) *Smaʕt   ʔənno **Naadya** raʕt   mən duun ma   tʃuufe.
      heard.1s that   Nadia left.2SM without   COMP see.2SF
      'I heard that Nadia, you left without seeing.'

This insensitivity to islands on the part of the NP-clitic relationship indicates that some clitic left-dislocation examples must have the NP generated in situ (or at least not within the island), with the clitic not a trace (or at the site of a trace) but merely an ordinary pronoun coreferential with the NP.[38] This is an option that is to be expected, of course. But there are other examples adduced by Aoun and Benmamoun (1998) that show that the NP must reconstruct to a position at or near the site of the clitic. Consider the examples in (152).

(152) a. **Təlmiiz-a   ʃʃitaan**   btaʕrfo ʔənno kəll mʕallme
         student-her the-naughty.MS know.2P that   every teacher.F
         ʔaaṣaṣət-**o**.
         punished.3SF-him
         'Her naughty student, you know that every teacher punished him.'

b. *Təlmiiz-a ʃʃitaan   fallayto ʔablma kəll mʕallme
student-her the-naughty.MS left.2P before every teacher.F
tʔaaṣəṣ-o.
punished.3SF-him
'Her naughty student, you left before every teacher punished
him.'

In (152a), a reading is available on which the **a** 'her' in **Təlmiiz-a ʃʃitaan**
'her naughty student' is bound by *kəll mʕallme* 'every teacher'. No such
reading is available in (152b), where **Təlmiiz-a ʃʃitaan** is separated from
any position c-commanded by *kəll mʕallme* by an adjunct island. The
bound reading in (152a) can only be obtained by **Təlmiiz-a ʃʃitaan** being
interpreted in a position below *kəll mʕallme*; in other words, it must *reconstruct*, and reconstruction is a property of movement. The fact that
the interpretation is blocked by an island in (152b) confirms the hypothesis that it relies on movement. So we have evidence that the relation between the clitic left-dislocated NP and the site of the resumptive pronoun
is one of movement.

I have carefully talked about the site of the resumptive pronoun and
not the resumptive pronoun itself because this evidence does not in itself
show that the resumptive pronoun must be the spell-out of a trace—
Aoun and Benmamoun (1998) themselves assume that in these cases the
clitic pronoun is originally cliticized onto the left-dislocated NP, and remains behind when the latter moves. Is there any way in which one can
distinguish between the resumptive pronoun being the trace and its being
a clitic?

One problem for the view that the resumptive pronoun is a clitic is that
it is unclear how semantic interpretation could take place if this were the
case. The clitic ends up being the sister of the (trace of the) left-dislocated
NP; so the analysis has two items of type e be sisters, meaning that semantic composition will not be able to take place. The only reply that I
can think of making on Aoun and Benmamoun's behalf is that it must
be possible to have semantic composition of some kind take place between two items of type e because it is possible to put two such items in
apposition, as in (153).[39]

(153) Amundsen, the greatest explorer of the age, is setting out for the
Pole.

But this idea runs into difficulty for a very simple reason: in Lebanese Arabic it is impossible on the surface to have weak pronouns cliticized onto

DPs and interpreted as being in apposition to them (Abbas Benmamoun and Lina Choueiri, personal communications). There is no reason to think that being unpronounced would make a configuration like this any better, in either syntactic or semantic terms, and therefore I conclude that Lebanese Arabic cannot have it in phonologically null material either. But this means that there is no way for the structures posited by Aoun and Benmamoun to be interpreted, and that we are only left with the possibility that Lebanese Arabic resumptive pronouns separated from left-dislocated NPs by movement are spelled-out traces.[40]

Overall, I think it is clear that the simplest explanation of resumptive pronouns that appear where we expect traces, crosslinguistically, is that they *are* traces. This hypothesis avoids the messy situation of having separate traces and pronouns at the relevant places, when only one argument is needed. And if these resumptive pronouns are spell-outs of traces, we have a reason to prefer the hypothesis that pronouns have two arguments, since that would make them identical to traces anyway according to the independently motivated theory of trace conversion.

3.6 Conclusion

To summarize briefly, we have seen in section 3.2 that it is possible to give a unified theory of the semantics of D-type, referential and bound pronouns by having indices be NPs, of type $\langle e, t \rangle$, and saying that pronouns take either normal NPs or these new NPs, as in (154).

(154) a. [it donkey]
       b. [it 2]

In section 3.3, however, we then saw that the existence of bound definite descriptions implied that the overt definite article *the* takes two arguments, an index and a normal NP. This position was shown in section 3.3.3 to have interesting and beneficial consequences for two intellectually disparate areas, the referential-attributive distinction and trace-conversion. It was then asked (in section 3.5) whether it would be possible to say that pronouns too take two arguments, just like overt definite articles, in order to have a more unified theory of the two types of definite description being posited. This would give us the scheme in (155) (where indices need no longer be considered NPs) and the basic semantics in (156) for overt definite articles and pronouns.

(155) a. [[the i] NP]
      b. [[it i] NP]

(156) $\lambda f_{\langle e,t \rangle}. \lambda g : g \in D_{\langle e,t \rangle}$ & $\exists! x (f(x) = 1$ & $g(x) = 1). \iota x(f(x) = 1$ & $g(x) = 1)$

The evidence presented concerning focused bound pronouns and resumptive pronouns suggests that (155) is indeed preferable to (154). This means that pronouns have the same structure as overt definite descriptions.

Chapter 4

Indistinguishable Participants

The Hitchhiker's Guide to the Galaxy has a few things to say on the subject of towels.

A towel, it says, is about the most massively useful thing an interstellar hitchhiker can have. Partly it has great practical value. You can ... wrap it around your head to ward off noxious fumes or avoid the gaze of the Ravenous Bugblatter Beast of Traal (a mind-bogglingly stupid animal, it assumes that if you can't see it, it can't see you).

—Douglas Adams, *The Hitchhiker's Guide to the Galaxy*

4.1 The Nature of the Problem

In the previous two chapters, we have seen how a revised version of the D-type analysis can deal with two of the problems for this approach described in section 1.3.2: the problem of the formal link (section 2.4) and the problem of pronominal ambiguity (chapter 3). It remains to be seen if any solution can be given to the third problem for the D-type analysis mentioned in section 1.3.2, namely, the problem of indistinguishable participants.

To recapitulate, Hans Kamp has drawn attention to sentences such as (1) (Heim 1990).

(1) If a bishop meets a bishop, he blesses him.

If we try to analyze this example using situation semantics and D-type pronouns, the objection goes, there are no suitable functions that could be used to interpret the pronouns *he* and *him*. Suppose we use the situation variable s for the minimal situations specified by the antecedent, and s' for the extended situations specified by the consequent. If we try to interpret either pronoun as a definite description whose descriptive content is "bishop in s," we do not achieve the right results, because we end up with "the unique bishop in s" when in fact there are two bishops in each situation s. The same happens if we try "bishop who meets a bishop in s"; since meeting is a symmetrical relation, it is alleged that in any situation in which a bishop meets a bishop there are two bishops of whom it can be said that they meet a bishop, and hence no sense can be made of "the unique bishop who meets a bishop in *s*."

One might be tempted to object at this point that meeting is not in fact a symmetrical relation. After all, the verb often seems to mean just "come across"—I can meet a brick wall or an impasse without these things thereby meeting me, and one might argue that the reciprocity we understand when the word is used of social situations is based merely on world knowledge and not on the semantics of the verb. But the example could be changed to something like (2).

(2) If a bishop is in the same room as another bishop, he blesses him.

This example, although perhaps slightly more awkward than (1), is also grammatical. And there seems to be no way of getting round the fact that being in the same room is necessarily a symmetrical relation.[1] The problem remains, therefore; for the sake of brevity, I will continue to use the verb *meet*.

While the D-type approach seems to founder on these examples, dynamic theories have no trouble. They obtain truth conditions for (1) equivalent to, "For all x, for all y, if x is a bishop and y is a bishop and x meets y, then x blesses y." To see this in detail for the example of Dynamic Predicate Logic, return to appendix A.1 and interpret Mx as "x is a bishop," Dy as "y is a bishop," Oxy as "x meets y," and Bxy as "x blesses y."

Conventional wisdom, then, says that the problem of indistinguishable participants is a powerful empirical argument in favor of dynamic theories over D-type theories. In this chapter, however, I will argue exactly the opposite: the relevant data constitute a powerful empirical argument in favor of D-type theories over dynamic theories. In section 4.3 I will argue that when we examine some previously neglected data it becomes clear that dynamic theories make incorrect predictions in this area, and in section 4.4 I will present a new D-type solution that deals with both the old and the new facts. First, however, I wish to examine the three previous attempts that I know of to solve the problem in a D-type framework.

4.2 Previous D-Type Solutions

4.2.1 Neale 1990

As we have seen in section 2.4, Neale translates sentences into a formal language RQ, a modification of first-order logic which includes restricted

quantifiers, and then calculates the truth conditions of these RQ translations. To repeat, the crucial rule he uses for donkey sentences is (3) (Neale
1990, 182–183).

(3) If x is a pronoun that is anaphoric on, but not c-commanded by, a
nonmaximal quantifier[2] "$[Dx : Fx]$" that occurs in an antecedent
clause "$[Dx : Fx](Gx)$," then x is interpreted as "$[\text{the } x : Fx \ \& \ Gx]$."

Now consider the following, slightly more natural, variant of (1).

(4) If a bishop meets another bishop, he blesses him.

Neale (1990, 245–247) obtains the right truth conditions for examples
like this by translating the D-type pronouns as restricted quantifiers
of the form $[\text{whe } x : Fx]$, where F is constructed by his normal rules,
especially (3), and the semantics for the new quantifier is as follows:
$[\text{whe } x : Fx](Gx)$ is true iff $|\mathbf{F} - \mathbf{G}| = 0$ and $|\mathbf{F}| \geq 1$. So the consequent in
(4) would receive the RQ translation in (5).

(5) $[\text{whe } x\text{: bishop } x \ \& \ [\text{a } y\text{: bishop } y \ \& \ y \neq x](x \text{ meets } y)]$ $([\text{whe } y\text{:}$
$\text{bishop } y \ \& \ y \neq x \ \& \ x \text{ meets } y](x \text{ blesses } y))$

To paraphrase: for every x such that x is a bishop and there a y such that
y is a bishop and x is not identical to y and x meets y, and for every z
such that z is a bishop and z is not identical to x and x meets z, x blesses
z. This certainly seems to capture the truth conditions of the above example. One is left feeling a bit uneasy, however. The essential move here
is to make pronouns numberless, standing for quantifiers meaning "every
z such that Fz" or "whatever x were F." We might ask whether this is not
just doing violence to the facts. The pronouns in question *do* have number
features, whose distinctive content we intuitively recognize quite plainly.

To sharpen this criticism, let us consider how Neale could possibly account for the presence and value of number features on these pronoun
quantifiers. (He does not tell us himself.) Since these items no longer
have semantically significant number, the number features (and other ϕ-
features) on each pronoun must presumably be present by mechanical,
syntactic agreement with its antecedent. It is difficult to see where else
they could come from, since in the syntax on Neale's account a donkey
pronoun does not have an NP sister. (Contrast the NP-deletion theory.)
But then we would expect, for example, (6a) to be grammatical.

(6) a. *If a bishop meets more than one parishioner at once, he blesses
him.
b. If a bishop meets more than one parishioner at once, he blesses
them.

The pronoun *him* in (6a) has the same number feature as its antecedent *more than one parishioner*, and yet the sentence is ungrammatical. It is unclear how Neale can account for this. (The semantics surely cannot help, since (6a) and (6b) will receive exactly the same RQ translation on this theory.) Likewise, it is unclear how the grammatical (6b), with its clash of formal number features, is to be dealt with. On the NP-deletion theory, on the other hand, the contrast in (6) falls out naturally: the ϕ-features on the pronouns are derived by agreement with their phonologically null NP sisters; and the singular [him ~~parishioner~~] in (6a) is ruled out because it incorrectly implies that there is just one parishioner in each of the situations s defined in the protasis. This distinction seems to be collapsed in Neale's theory, however.[3]

I am not inclined to adopt Neale's solution, therefore.

4.2.2   Heim 1990

Heim (1990, 157–158) presents a solution which she herself immediately criticizes, but since certainty is hard to find in this area, I present a summary of it here in case it contains some insight that might unjustly be forgotten.

The beginning of Heim's discussion is the problem of what quantificational adverbs like *always* and *usually* quantify over.[4] In (7), we get the impression that it is donkey-owning farmers that are being quantified over: most donkey-owning farmers are rich.

(7) If a farmer owns a donkey, he's usually rich.

In (8), however, it seems to be farmer-donkey pairs that are being quantified over: most pairs of a farmer and donkey he owns are such that the farmer in that pair deducts the donkey in that pair from his taxes.

(8) If a farmer owns a donkey, he usually deducts it from his taxes.

The kind of situation semantics we have seen so far makes the right prediction for (8): we quantify over minimal situations, and say that the sentence claims that most minimal situations in which a farmer owns a donkey can be extended to situations where the farmer deducts the donkey from his taxes. This is obviously equivalent to quantifying over farmer-donkey pairs.

For (7), however, something else has to be said. To get the reading in which there is quantification over farmers, Heim, adapting an idea from Kadmon 1987, introduces an optional operation of prefixing situation variables to S nodes at LF. The semantics for such structures is that given in (9).[5]

(9) $[\![{}_s\phi]\!]^g = 1$ iff $\exists \mathbf{s}'[g(s) \le \mathbf{s}' \ \& \ [\![\phi]\!]^{g^{\mathbf{s}'/s}} = 1]$

In other words, $[\![{}_s\phi]\!]^g = 1$ if and only if $g(s)$ can be extended to a situation in which ϕ is true. For (7), we now posit an LF (10).

(10) usually$_{s_1}$
    if $[[a_x \ \text{farmer}(s_1)(x)] \ {}_{s_1}[[a_y \ \text{donkey}(s_1)(y)][x \ \text{owns}(s_1) \ y]]]$
    $_{s_2}[f_1^1(s_1) \ \text{is-rich}(s_2)]$

Roughly, the truth conditions for this are that most minimal situations $\mathbf{s_1}$ such that there is an individual x such that x is a farmer in $\mathbf{s_1}$, and there is *an extension of* $\mathbf{s_1}$ such that x owns a donkey *in this extension*, can be extended to situations $\mathbf{s_2}$ such that the unique farmer in $\mathbf{s_1}$ is rich in $\mathbf{s_2}$. So the quantification is just over small situations containing just one farmer each, and the desired reading is captured.

Heim then goes on to use the special prefixation operation to analyze indistinguishable participant sentences. (11) would have an LF (12).

(11) If a man lives with another man, he always shares the rent with him.

(12) always$_{s_1}$
    if $[[a_x \ \text{man}(s_1)(x)] \ {}_{s_1}[[a_y \ \text{man}(s_1)(y)][x \ \text{lives-with}(s_1) \ y]]]$
    $_{s_2}[f^1(s_1) \ \text{shares-rent-with}(s_2) \ f^2(s_1)]$

We can now, it seems, find suitable values for the functions f^1 and f^2: f^1 could be a function that maps a situation $\mathbf{s}$ to the unique man in $\mathbf{s}$, and f^2 could be a function that maps a situation $\mathbf{s}$ to the unique man that the man in $\mathbf{s}$ lives with. So the truth conditions for (12) are roughly that every minimal situation $\mathbf{s_1}$ such that there is an individual x such that x is a man in $\mathbf{s_1}$, and there is an extension of $\mathbf{s_1}$ such that x lives with another man in this extension, can be extended to a situation $\mathbf{s_2}$ such that the man in $\mathbf{s_1}$ shares the rent in $\mathbf{s_2}$ with the man the man in $\mathbf{s_1}$ lives with. The problem of indistinguishable participants thus seems to be averted.

The trouble is that, as Heim observes, this analysis has the relevant sentences make presuppositions which in fact they do not make. Sentence (11), for example, is predicted to presuppose that each relevant man has at most one male roommate ("the man the man in $\mathbf{s_1}$ lives with"). This is just not the case, however. It seems to be a fairly clear intuition that (11) is falsified if Tom, Dick, and Harry share an apartment, but Tom and Harry cover the rent between them. I cannot see at the moment how to change Heim's analysis in a way that would deal with this drawback while keeping its basic character.

4.2.3 Ludlow 1994

Ludlow (1994, 170–172) suggests that the participants in our examples can be distinguished because they will be assigned different thematic roles. He suggests that no two arguments in a sentence can have the same thematic role. (We should interpret him as meaning that no two arguments of the same *event* can have the same thematic role.) For the antecedent of a sentence like (13), there will be two distinct thematic roles θ_1 and θ_2, such that the semantics is something like (14).

(13) If a bishop is in the same room as another bishop, he blesses him.

(14) There is an event e such that there is an individual x such that x is a bishop and there is an individual y such that y is a bishop and y is not identical to x, such that e is an event of being in the same room and $\theta_1(e, x)$ and $\theta_2(e, y)$.

Then the *he* of the consequent can be analyzed as a definite description involving θ_1, say, and the *him* as a definite description involving θ_2.

It seems, however, that this proposal begs the question. No specific suggestions are made concerning the identity of the distinct thematic roles θ_1 and θ_2, for (13) or any other case; and no reasons are given to make the existence of such roles seem necessary on a priori or methodological grounds. It is merely asserted that there could be such roles. We are naturally under no obligation to believe this, given that neither conceptual argumentation nor actual specimens of the beasts are provided. Indeed, it is prima facie plausible to say that symmetrical relations do by definition constitute eventualities whose arguments have identical thematic roles, if we are to maintain any relationship between thematic roles and discernible differences in the properties of entities in extralinguistic reality.[6]

The only additional consideration in favor of Ludlow's proposal that I am aware of is given by Schein (1993, 95–96). The argument goes as follows. Take the pairs of sentences in (15) and (16).

(15) a. The Carnegie Deli sits opposite Carnegie Hall.
     b. Carnegie Hall sits opposite the Carnegie Deli.

(16) a. Avery Fisher Hall is different from Alice Tully Hall.
     b. Alice Tully Hall is different from Avery Fisher Hall.

Schein gives these sentences the truth conditions shown in (17) and (18).

(17) a. $\exists e(\text{sits}(e) \wedge \text{Theme}(e, \text{CD}) \wedge \text{opposite}(e, \text{CH}))$
     b. $\exists e(\text{sits}(e) \wedge \text{Theme}(e, \text{CH}) \wedge \text{opposite}(e, \text{CD}))$

(18) a. $\exists e(\text{different}(e) \wedge \text{Theme}(e, \text{AF}) \wedge \text{from}(e, \text{AT}))$
  b. $\exists e(\text{different}(e) \wedge \text{Theme}(e, \text{AT}) \wedge \text{from}(e, \text{AF}))$

Suppose, says Schein, that Carnegie Hall sitting opposite the Carnegie Deli were indeed the same event as the Carnegie Deli sitting opposite Carnegie Hall. Then there would be one event e that would satisfy all the predicates in both (17a) and (17b). In particular, from (17) we would be able to deduce (19).

(19) a. $\exists e(\text{sits}(e) \wedge \text{Theme}(e, \text{CD}) \wedge \text{opposite}(e, \text{CD}))$
  b. The Carnegie Deli sits opposite the Carnegie Deli.

Similarly, from (18) we would be able to deduce (20).

(20) a. $\exists e(\text{different}(e) \wedge \text{Theme}(e, \text{AF}) \wedge \text{from}(e, \text{AF}))$
  b. Avery Fisher Hall is different from Avery Fisher Hall.

Since the assumption has produced an absurdity, Schein concludes, we cannot say that Carnegie Hall sitting opposite the Carnegie Deli is the same event as the Carnegie Deli sitting opposite Carnegie Hall, and similarly for other symmetric predicates. This means that we can now go back to (13), repeated here as (21), and analyze it, to a first approximation, as in (22).

(21) If a bishop is in the same room as another bishop, he blesses him.

(22) For all events e such that there is an individual x such that x is a bishop and an individual y not identical with x such that y is a bishop and e is an event of x being in the same room as y, there is a related event e' such that e' is an event of the bishop who was in the same room as another bishop in e blessing the bishop that he was in the same room as in e.

Since, for any two bishops x and y, there are indeed distinct events of x's being in the same room as y and y's being in the same room as x, it now makes sense, according to Schein, to talk about "*the* bishop who was in the same room as another bishop" in a certain event.[7]

Before we accept this argument, however, I think we should reconsider the crucial predicates used in the example sentences. Let us begin with (15), the sentences about Carnegie Hall sitting opposite the Carnegie Deli. On closer inspection, it begins to seem dubious that these sentences are really relevant. Schein needs to show that paradox results from supposing that only one event takes place when a *symmetrical* predicate holds of two entities. But the predicate from these sentences that he chooses to represent by means of an event variable in the truth conditions in (17) is *sit*, which, so far from being symmetrical, is not even a transitive verb. What Schein has shown, in fact, is that paradox results when we assume that there is only one sitting event when two things are sitting, but this, in view of the fact that *sit* is a distributive predicate, is not surprising. There is of course a symmetrical predicate lurking in these sentences, namely the predicate *(be) opposite*; but if *sits opposite* in (15) is replaced with *is opposite*, and an event variable used to represent *is opposite* in the truth conditions, it becomes impossible to run any version of Schein's argument.

Let us go on to reconsider (16), the sentences about Avery Fisher Hall being different from Alice Tully Hall. Here we must begin by asking what is the nature of the predicates *different* and *from* in the truth conditions in (18). I assume that we should interpret (18a) and (18b) as (23a) and (23b).

(23) a. There exists an event *e* such that *e* is an event of being different and a Theme of *e* is Avery Fisher Hall and a point of comparison of *e* is Alice Tully Hall.

   b. There exists an event *e* such that *e* is an event of being different and a Theme of *e* is Alice Tully Hall and a point of comparison of *e* is Avery Fisher Hall.

Schein's next move is to suppose that there is exactly one event constituted by Alice Tully Hall being different from Avery Fisher Hall and vice versa. Collating the information in (23a) and (23b), we come up with the formulation in (24) as a description of this event.

(24) There exists an event *e* such that *e* is an event of being different and Themes of *e* are Avery Fisher Hall and Alice Tully Hall, and points of comparison of *e* are Avery Fisher Hall and Alice Tully Hall.

From this, we can presumably draw paradoxical conclusions involving things being different from themselves.

However, let us take another look at the formulas in (23). They incorporate a distinction between the Theme of the event of being different and what I have called the point of comparison of that event, or the thing that the Theme is different from. I submit that this way of putting things incorporates precisely the fine-grained differentiation of events that Schein is supposedly trying to establish at this point. Someone who really thought that there was only one event involved in Avery Fisher Hall being different from Alice Tully Hall and Alice Tully Hall being different from Avery Fisher Hall would not give (18) as the truth conditions of the sentences in (16) in the first place. Rather, they would analyze both sentences in (16) as in (25).

(25) There exists an event e such that e is an event of being different and
the Themes of e are Avery Fisher Hall and Alice Tully Hall.

No version of Schein's argument can be run on this revised analysis. It
seems, then, that Schein is still faced with the task of establishing that
the two objects in question do in fact have different θ-roles.

I conclude that more work would have to be done to make Ludlow's
(1994) proposal a viable solution.

4.3   The Problem of Coordinate Subjects

Before presenting a new D-type solution to the problem of indistinguishable participants, I wish to introduce some previously neglected data that
show that dynamic theories too have trouble in this area. Consider the
contrast between (26a) and (26b), and the analogous one between (27a)
and (27b).[8]

(26) a.   If a bishop meets a bishop, he blesses him.
     b.   *If a bishop and a bishop meet, he blesses him.

(27) a.   If a bishop meets another bishop, he blesses him.
     b.   ?*If a bishop and another bishop meet, he blesses him.

In the case of (26b) and (27b), one does indeed have the intuition that
the sentences are bad because there is no way to resolve the anaphora
and satisfy the uniqueness presuppositions of *he* and *him*. In other words,
these really do seem to be cases of indistinguishable participants. It seems
that the D-type analysis stands a good chance of making the right predictions here, then, although of course we still need to account for the grammaticality of (26a) and (27a), and find some way of differentiating them
from (26b) and (27b).

But let us work out what prediction dynamic theories make about (26b)
and (27b). It is possible to see what they must say by examining the data
in (28).

(28) a. If a bishop meets a nun, he blesses her.
     b. If a bishop and a nun meet, he blesses her.

Note that (28b) is perfectly grammatical. Now it is characteristic of
dynamic theories, as opposed to D-type theories, that they do not make
use of any descriptive content in resolving donkey anaphora. Instead, as
we have seen in chapter 1, they establish variables or "discourse markers"
for each indefinite antecedent in discourse representation structures or
dynamically changing assignments; the subsequent pronouns anaphoric

to the indefinites are interpreted by means of the discourse markers and dynamic binding, as chapter 1 shows for the example of Dynamic Predicate Logic. So for the donkey pronouns in (28b) to be interpreted, it must be necessary that a conjunction of two indefinites as subject of the antecedent of a conditional can establish discourse markers that can be used for the interpretation of pronouns in the consequent. But then it is evident that dynamic theories predict (26b) and (27b) to be grammatical too, since precisely the same configuration is involved.

We must conclude, then, that dynamic theories too face a problem of indistinguishable participants. They predict the ungrammatical (26b) and (27b) to be good. D-type theories, on the other hand, can distinguish between these sentences and (28b), since they use descriptive content, which is precisely where the ungrammatical sentences and (28b) differ.

4.4   A New D-Type Solution

The task facing a theory of indistinguishable participant sentences, then, is to allow (29a) to be good while predicting (29b) to be bad.

(29) a.   If a bishop meets a bishop, he blesses him.
      b.   *If a bishop and a bishop meet, he blesses him.

I will first show how to deal with (29a) using a D-type strategy, before returning to (29b). The basic idea is that the two participants in (29a) are distinguished in terms of the structure of the situations that the semantics assigns to the antecedent of the conditional, whereas in (29b) this is not the case. I will call sentences like (29a) "transitive cases," and sentences like (29b) "intransitive cases."

4.4.1   Transitive Cases
I assume that (30), the core of the antecedent in (29a), has an LF essentially isomorphic to (31).[9]

(30) a bishop meets a bishop

(31) $[[\text{a bishop}] [\lambda_6 [[\text{a bishop}][\lambda_2[t_6 \text{ meets } t_2]]]]]$

As a straightforward calculation reveals,[10] the semantics set out in section 2.2 yields the denotation (32) for (31).

(32) λs_1. there is an individual x and a situation s_2 such that s_2 is a minimal situation such that $s_2 \leq s_1$ and x is a bishop in s_2, such that there is a situation s_3 such that $s_3 \leq s_1$ and s_3 is a minimal

situation such that $s_2 \leq s_3$ and: there is an individual y and a situation s_4, such that s_4 is a minimal situation such that $s_4 \leq s_3$ and y is a bishop in s_4, such that there is a situation s_5 such that $s_5 \leq s_3$ and s_5 is a minimal situation such that $s_4 \leq s_5$ and x meets y in s_5.

The precise structure of the various situations specified by these truth conditions may be hard to keep in one's head while reading them, so it is suggested that (32) be read while looking at the diagram in (33). It should be emphasized, however, that (33) is meant as an *aide-mémoire* only, and should not be assigned any theoretical import.

(33)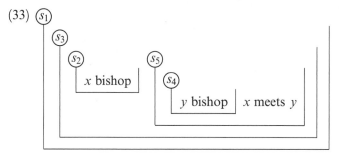

Diagram (33) does, however, enable one to appreciate a fact about the situation semantics we have been using: the inclusion relations among the situations specified in the truth conditions of a sentence very closely mirror the inclusion relations among the syntactic constituents of the sentence. To see this even more clearly, consider (34a), an alternative notation for displaying the structure of situations, and compare it to the LF syntactic structure (31), repeated as (34b).

(34) a. $[_{s_3}[_{s_2}$ x bishop] $[_{s_5}[_{s_4}$ y bishop] x meets $y]]$

b. [[a bishop] $[\lambda_6$ [[a bishop] $[\lambda_2$ [t_6 meets t_2]]]]]

This parallelism is to be expected, of course, given that we have been using the notions of situations and extended situations as devices to give the truth conditions for quantificational structures, and the LF structure of a sentence in any grammar that uses QR will also directly display quantificational structure.

Returning to our main theme, it also evident that, for any two individuals x and y, the situation structure described in (32) and displayed in (33) treats x and y differently. Note that s_5 is defined as a *minimal* situation that contains s_4 and x meeting y. (In fact in this case we could say *the* minimal situation—there is only one minimal situation with these properties.) This ensures that s_2 (x's being a bishop) cannot be part of s_5,[11] so that x is distinguished structurally from y within the situation structure in (33).

It is important to clarify the nature of this distinction as much as possible. If we just look at (33), it is intuitively obvious that x and y are not treated symmetrically, since y's being a bishop but not x's being a bishop is part of the large situation s_5, and x but not y is part of the small situation s_2. If we start to think about what this means for particular actual cases of a bishop meeting a bishop, however, things start to become unclear. In any particular case, there will be no such obvious asymmetry between the bishophood of one bishop and the bishophood of the other. There is no reason why, on observing a meeting of two bishops, we should analyze it in terms of the nonsymmetrical situation structure in (33), rather than a perfectly symmetrical situation structure. So what is the status of the asymmetry in (33)?

It might be helpful at this point to review some of the underlying metaphysics of situations on which the semantics used here is based. Recall from section 2.2.1 that situations are the natural language metaphysics equivalent of the *states of affairs* of Armstrong 1978, where, within Armstrong's realist ontology, a state of affairs is one or more "thin" particulars having one or more properties or standing in one or more relations. So the situations s_2 in (33) are states of affairs because they each consist of a thin particular x instantiating the bishop property. Note now that, as Armstrong says (1978, 115), the state of affairs of an actual thin particular instantiating a property is not repeatable in the way that universals are, and so is itself a particular: "Particularity taken along with universality yields particularity again" (Armstrong 1978, 115). Let us apply this principle too to the case of (33). It means that there are particulars s_2 consisting of thin particulars x instantiating the bishop property, and particulars s_5 consisting of thin particulars x and y jointly instantiating the meeting relation while y instantiates the bishop property (but x does not). According to the metaphysics we are working with, these particulars are on a level with any other thick particulars, even ones that might seem more intuitively natural (such as thin particulars with all their nonrelational properties). Importantly for our present purposes, the particulars s_2 and the particulars s_5 are just as impeccable in their thick particularity as any particulars that would result from taking the same incidents of bishops meeting and dividing them up, as it were, according to a symmetrical pattern.

I hope it is now clear that the situation structure in (33) cannot be impugned, within the context of the metaphysics out of which it grew, on the grounds that it gives a nonsymmetric structure to incidents that are "really" symmetrical in their characteristics. The most that can be said against it is that, given a number of incidents of two bishops meeting, there is no *need* to conceive of them as consisting of particulars s_2 and s_5. But to this it can be replied that there is no *need* to conceive of them as consisting of the particulars we would get from a symmetric pattern, either. According to the current metaphysics, they *do* consist of particulars s_2 and s_5, and at the same time they *do* consist of symmetric particulars. The semantics is quite free to manipulate any of these objects and more.[12]

This opens the way, then, for an explanation of the differentiation of the bishops that is necessary for the D-type strategy to analyze this kind of example. For any situation containing two particulars s_2 and s_5, defined as above, call the bishop whose bishophood is not a constituent of s_5 the "distinguished" bishop. Suppose, at first, that the descriptive content of D-type pronouns could be any property or relation recoverable from the context. Then we could give (35) the semantics in (36).

(35) If a bishop meets a bishop, he blesses him.

(36) λs_6. for every minimal situation s_7 such that $s_7 \leq s_6$ and $[32](s_7) = 1$, there is a situation s_8 such that $s_8 \leq s_6$ and s_8 is a minimal situation such that $s_7 \leq s_8$ and the distinguished bishop in s_8 blesses in s_8 the nondistinguished bishop in s_8.

The diagram showing the structure of the situations for the whole sentence is in (37). Let us take it for granted that our standard example (35) has truth conditions which amount to the claim that when two bishops

(37)

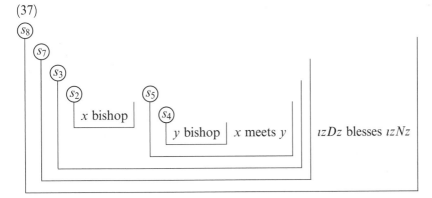

meet they bless each other. To see that the semantics in (36) is correct, it is necessary to appreciate the following fact about the kind of division into situations s_2 and s_5 that we are dealing with. Given the thin particulars, bishop properties, and meeting relation of any actual pair of bishops meeting, there are two ways of dividing these entities up into thick particulars s_2 and s_5: one way would have one bishop in the thick particular s_2 (and thus distinguished), and another way would have the other bishop in that particular. Besides (37), that is, we could also have (38), for any pair of bishops x and y.

(38)

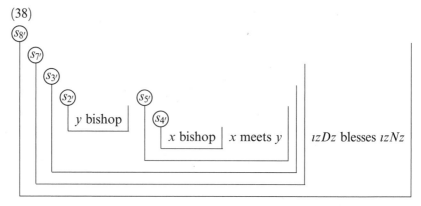

Now the situations s_7 are defined as having the situations s_2 and s_5 as parts; and since there are two distinct pairs of situations s_2 and s_5 for each pair of meeting bishops (written $\langle s_2, s_5 \rangle$ and $\langle s_{2'}, s_{5'} \rangle$ in the diagrams above), there are two distinct situations s_7 too (written s_7 and $s_{7'}$ above). This must be the case, since two things cannot be the same if they are composed of different parts. Furthermore, given any actual pair of bishops meeting, one bishop will be distinguished in one of the resulting situations s_7 (and in the situation s_8 built on top of it), and the other bishop will be distinguished in the other resulting situation s_7 (and corresponding situation s_8). Thus x is distinguished in s_7 and s_8 in (37), and y is distinguished in $s_{7'}$ and $s_{8'}$ in (38). Now the claim in (36) is that for each situation s_7, there is an extended situation s_8 such that the distinguished bishop in s_8 blesses the nondistinguished bishop in s_8. Thus, in (37), since x is distinguished in s_8, x has to bless y in s_8; and in (38), since y is distinguished in $s_{8'}$, y has to bless x in $s_{8'}$. So both bishops end up having to bless the other one. It seems, then, that the semantics in (36) is correct.

It is necessary, for this solution to work, that the nonsymmetric division of the bishop-meeting incidents into situations s_2 and s_5 be maintained, as shown in (37), when the interpretation of *he* and *him* is being worked out. If the nonsymmetric structure is no longer available when we come to try to locate "the distinguished bishop in s_8" and "the nondistinguished bishop in s_8," we will of course be at a loss. But I see no difficulty in the hypothesis that this structure is still available; indeed it seems to me to be the default position.[13]

Native speakers consistently report that the sentence under discussion entails that when two bishops meet, each will bless the other, as we have assumed. This judgment seems, however, to have an odd status—some informants are inclined at first to say that a scenario in which only one bishop blesses the other is not a counterexample to the claim, and only say that the second also has to bless the first when they are explicitly invited to consider whether this is necessary. Interestingly, it seems that the analysis just given is fully consistent with this hesitancy. Let us suppose that the truth conditions produced by the language faculty are indeed those given in (36). Then the chain of reasoning outlined above (about the existence of two situations s_7 for every pair of meeting bishops) is not given automatically by the language faculty, and it is understandable that some speakers do not at first realize that every actual pair of bishops meeting contributes two situations s_7; this explains the willingness that some speakers initially show to accept a scenario in which only one blessing takes place as conforming to the generalization made by the sentence.

If we could sustain the position that the descriptive content of D-type pronouns was obtained by simply taking any property or relation recoverable from the context, I think that we would have a solution here for the D-type analysis of the transitive cases. But this is not consistent with the theory advocated earlier in this book, that D-type anaphora is NP-deletion (chapter 2). I think, however, that the basic solution just outlined can still be maintained under this latter theory. It is well known, in fact, that the overt descriptive content of definite descriptions with *the* is regularly supplemented by speaker and hearer, in order to enable something to be uniquely picked out when we say things like *the table* and *the office*, as opposed to *the President of the U.S. in 2002*: this is what goes under the rubric of the problem of "incomplete" or "improper" definite descriptions (Heim 1991, 505–506; Larson and Segal 1995, 329–334, 336–337). It is, I think, generally acknowledged that the exact mechanisms by which this supplementation is achieved remain obscure: there is perhaps a consensus that the right answer is to be found along the lines of "narrowing down the domain" with respect to which the definite descriptions are interpreted, but this idea is vague and in need of being spelled out in detail, as Heim (1991, 506) emphasizes, and I do not know of any explicit, promising attempt to do this. Given this situation, it is not unreasonable to suggest that the consequent of (35) has the LF [[he bishop] [blesses [him bishop]]], as required by the NP-deletion theory of D-type anaphora, but is interpreted as in (36), with "distinguished" and "nondistinguished" supplied by whatever mechanism or mechanisms enable us to narrow down the extension of the syntactically present descriptive material in other improper definite descriptions.

Note that the solution (or outline of a solution) suggested here relies on our being able to make a swift change from understanding [he bishop] one way to understanding [him bishop] another, despite the fact that the latter phrase seems like it should be synonymous with the former. I do not think that there is a problem here, however, since there are already examples of this phenomenon in the literature, admittedly in milder versions. One relevant example is the following (Heim 1991, 505).

(39) The table is wobbly. We should have kept Aunt Lida's oak table.

One strategy for dealing with this would say that during the first sentence Aunt Lida's oak table is not salient enough to be the referent of *the table*, which picks out the most salient table, presumably the one at which the speaker is sitting. The mention of Aunt Lida's oak table makes that table salient during the second sentence, but by that time the phrase *the table* of the first sentence has already done its job, and the sudden salience of this second table cannot disrupt the anaphora resolution that has already happened. In the bishop sentence, the situation is more radical, since both bishops (for each situation) have been mentioned by the time we get round to dealing with [he bishop] and [him bishop]. But there is a basis for differentiating the two bishops, as already pointed out, and there is a some intuitive reason to suppose that what I have been calling the "distinguished" bishop in each case is more salient than the other one, since he is the odd one out, the one whose properties are partially barred from the large situations s_5, where everything else goes on. So something very like the strategy suggested for (39) can probably go on: [he bishop] (the first definite description with descriptive content *bishop*) is interpreted as being the distinguished bishop in each situation, since these are the most salient bishops; and then [him bishop] is necessarily interpreted as picking out the nondistinguished bishops, since it has to pick out others. (We do not have a reflexive *himself*.)

It has to be admitted that the difference in salience here is rather small, especially when compared with that which obtains in robust examples like (39). But this seems entirely appropriate for the status of the anaphora resolution in bishop sentences, because native speakers report that it is in fact possible to understand *he* in (35) to be the "the second bishop" and *him* to be "the first bishop," even though the converse assignment is the most natural way of understanding things. (Unfortunately, informants are seldom able to offer anything further in explication of this intuition!) I would appeal to the illuminating discussion of relative salience by David Lewis in *Counterfactuals* (1973, 116), where, considering the idea that two things might be equally salient (in the context of an utterance that we need not examine), he says the following: "Consider that comparative salience is shifty in the extreme. Nothing is easier than to break the tie; and if it were broken *either way* the sentence would be true. Recognizing the inevitable vagueness of comparative salience, we see that we almost never will simply have a tie. What we will have is indeterminacy between many reasonable ways to resolve the vagueness." This, I submit, is an excellent description of the situation we have in bishop sentences under the current analysis: the difference in salience is small, and both resolutions are possible, though one is favored. It does, then, seem possible to analyze the transitive bishop sentences in the present theory of D-type anaphora.[14]

4.4.2   Intransitive Cases

We can, then, give a D-type account of the grammaticality of the transitive cases. It remains to be shown, however, that the devices of which we have availed ourselves do not incorrectly end up predicting that the intransitive cases will also be grammatical.

Consider our example (40).

(40) *If a bishop and a bishop meet, he blesses him.

A potential worry, which should be dismissed, is that at LF the two DPs in the subject of the protasis could QR and form a quantifier structure like that which we saw earlier in (34b), which enabled the two bishops to be distinguished in the transitive cases. We should, in other words, be able to rule out an LF like (41) for the IP of the protasis.[15]

(41) [[a bishop] [λ_6 [[a bishop] [λ_2 [t_6 and t_2 meet]]]]]

Fortunately, we have independent reasons to suppose that such an LF is impossible, since the Coordinate Structure Constraint generally rules out movement from a coordinate structure even at LF, as we saw in section 2.5.3. (The present case does not fall under the exceptions mentioned there.) We can confirm that such movement is impossible by examining examples like (42).

(42) Every bishop and one nun carried a piano upstairs.

Let us suppose that this example could have an LF like (43), ignoring the necessity for QRing *a piano*.

(43) [[every bishop] [λ_6 [[one nun] [λ_2 [t$_6$ and t$_2$ carried a piano upstairs]]]]]

We would then expect that the sentence could mean, "For every bishop x, there is one nun y such that the group consisting of x and y (jointly) carried a piano upstairs." It is clear that the sentence can have no such reading, however. So the type of QR from a coordinate structure that would enable the bishops to be distinguished in (40) is not possible.

There is still the question, however, of what exactly the LFs and denotations are for examples like those in (44).

(44) a. A bishop and a bishop meet.
     b. Every bishop and one nun carried a piano upstairs.

If we are unable to provide a plausible account of such structures, then we are still open to the not exactly cogent but still not negligible criticism that the correct account, when it is revealed, might somehow differentiate between the bishops in (44a).

I begin to address this question by considering (44b), which, as we have already seen, is more revealing of its LF structure than (44a). As we expect with an ambiguous predicate like *carried a piano upstairs*, (44b) is ambiguous (or at least vague) between a distributive and a collective reading. The distributive reading says that every contextually salient bishop carried a piano upstairs (alone, unaided), and one nun did too. The collective reading says that a group of people carried a piano upstairs between them, and the group consisted of every contextually salient bishop plus one nun. I will follow Link (1983, 309) and Landman (1989, 564) and assume that the collective reading is basic, and that the distributive reading is obtained by recognizing that the predicate has a lexical property of distributivity (Link) or applying a distributivity operator (Landman). The problem, then, is to arrive at this collective interpretation.

In order to arrive at the collective interpretation, it will obviously be necessary to have an appropriate denotation for *and*. I have not seen any definition of *and* that will take two QPs as its arguments and give as output a group, or plural individual, whose members will be determined by the arguments—the definition of *and* in Partee and Rooth 1983, for example, seems to predict only readings where the VP predicate distributes down at least to the denotations of the arguments—but it does not seem too hard to write such a thing down. For plurality, I will adopt the lattice-theoretic analysis of Link 1983, and the terminology to be found in that article. In particular, then, $a \oplus b$ is the individual sum of a and b, in Link's sense, and $\leq_i$ is the individual part relation, whereby $a \leq_i a \oplus b$. Given this theoretical background, we can suppose the following possible lexical entries for the *and* we have here, where (45a) is just an extensional version of (45b).

(45) a. $\lambda f_{\langle et, t\rangle}. \lambda g_{\langle et, t\rangle}. \lambda P_{\langle e, t\rangle}. \exists x \, (f(\lambda y. y \leq_i x) = 1 \, \& \, g(\lambda y. y \leq_i x)$
$= 1 \, \& \, Px)$

   b. $\lambda \mathcal{F}_{\langle\langle se, st\rangle, \langle s, t\rangle\rangle}. \lambda \mathcal{G}_{\langle\langle se, st\rangle, \langle s, t\rangle\rangle}. \lambda \mathcal{P}_{\langle se, st\rangle}. \lambda s.$ there is an individual x
   and a situation s' such that s' is a minimal situation such that
   $s' \leq s$ and $\mathcal{F}(\lambda u_{\langle s, e\rangle}. \lambda s'''. u(s''') \leq_i x$ in $s''')(s') = 1$ and
   $\mathcal{G}(\lambda u_{\langle s, e\rangle}. \lambda s'''. u(s''') \leq_i x$ in $s''')(s') = 1$, such that there is a
   situation s'' such that $s'' \leq s$ and s'' is a minimal situation such
   that $s' \leq s''$ and $\mathcal{P}(\lambda s'''. x)(s'') = 1$

Example (45b) is basically an existential quantifier of a certain sort, and it is based closely on the denotation for *a* that we saw in section 2.2, repeated in (46a).[16] I also give in (46) the denotations of *bishop* and *meet* that fall out naturally from the semantics in section 2.2. Note that intransitive *meet* is constrained to take only individual sums (plural individuals) as its arguments.

(46) a. $[\![a]\!]^g = \lambda \mathcal{P}_{\langle\langle s, e\rangle, \langle s, t\rangle\rangle}. \lambda \mathcal{Q}_{\langle\langle s, e\rangle, \langle s, t\rangle\rangle}. \lambda s.$ there is an individual x
   and a situation s' such that s' is a minimal situation such that
   $s' \leq s$ and $\mathcal{P}(\lambda s. x)(s') = 1$, such that there is a situation s'' such
   that $s'' \leq s$ and s'' is a minimal situation such that $s' \leq s''$ and
   $\mathcal{Q}(\lambda s. x)(s'') = 1$

   b. $[\![bishop]\!]^g = \lambda u_{\langle s, e\rangle}. \lambda s. u(s)$ is a bishop in s

   c. $[\![meet]\!]^g = \lambda u_{\langle s, e\rangle}. \lambda s : \exists x \exists y (x \leq_i u(s)$ in $s \, \& \, y \leq_i u(s)$ in s
   $\& \, x \neq y$ in $s). u(s)$ meet in s

It is easy to calculate, then, that the denotation of (44a), repeated as (47), is (48).[17]

(47) A bishop and a bishop meet.

(48) $\lambda s_7.$ there is an individual z and a situation s_8 such that s_8 is a
   minimal situation such that $s_8 \leq s_7$ and [there is an individual x and

a situation s_2 such that s_2 is a minimal situation such that $s_2 \leq s_8$ and x is a bishop in s_2, such that there is a situation s_3 such that $s_3 \leq s_8$ and s_3 is a minimal situation such that $s_2 \leq s_3$ and $x \leq_i z$ in s_3] and [there is an individual y and a situation s_5 such that s_5 is a minimal situation such that $s_5 \leq s_8$ and y is a bishop in s_5, such that there is a situation s_6 such that $s_6 \leq s_8$ and s_6 is a minimal situation such that $s_5 \leq s_6$ and $y \leq_i z$ in s_6], such that there is a situation s_9 such that $s_9 \leq s_7$ and s_9 is a minimal situation such that $s_8 \leq s_9$ and z meet in s_9

Once again, this is virtually incomprehensible without some form of mnemonic assistance, so it is suggested that the reader read through it while glancing at the diagram in (49), which represents the structure of the situations. It is evident that there is a significant difference between

(49)

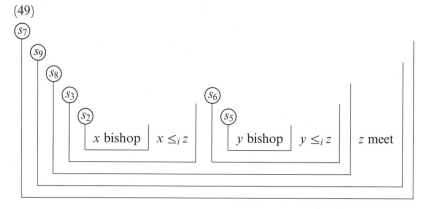

(49) and (33). In (49), there genuinely seems to be no difference between the two bishops in terms of the situation structure that they are embedded in, as it were, and the properties that they instantiate in various situations. In other words, this is a genuine case of indistinguishable participants, and we thus predict that there is indeed no way to construct a definite description which can pick out one of these bishops without being applicable to the other; thus the corresponding donkey sentence (40) is correctly predicted to be unacceptable by the current approach.

4.5 Conclusion

We have seen that dynamic semantics makes incorrect predictions about the data we have examined in this chapter, while the current variant of the D-type approach makes the correct predictions. Thus the problem of indistinguishable participants is a clear empirical argument favoring the D-type approach over dynamic semantics.

It is also worth noting that, if the analysis presented in this chapter is along the right lines, we have come across a rather interesting trait of the human cognitive system. We find it amusing to contemplate an imaginary creature like Douglas Adams's Ravenous Bugblatter Beast of Traal, which, you will recall, assumes that if you can't see it, it can't see you; in other words, it mysteriously treats nonsymmetric relations as symmetric. But we now have reason to believe that human beings have cognitive capacities, namely syntactic representation and situation semantics, which conspire to take essentially symmetric relations and treat them as non-symmetric. I will not attempt in the present work to go into the related question of whether this makes us "mind-bogglingly stupid."

Chapter 5

Japanese *kare* and *kanozyo*

5.1 Introduction

In this chapter, I propose to investigate a fundamental claim of dynamic semantics, namely that donkey pronouns are interpreted as bound variables. My claim, in brief, will be that the Japanese pronouns *kare* 'he' and *kanozyo* 'she' can be donkey pronouns but cannot be bound variables, a state of affairs which would be impossible if dynamic semantics accounts of donkey anaphora were correct. At the same time, I also develop a new account of the behavior of these pronouns, which have been the focus of a fair amount of scholarly energy. My account makes crucial use of Reinhart's Rule I, applied to a novel context, and thus provides new evidence in favor of the presence of this rule in the grammar.

5.2 The Basic Data

It is well known that Japanese *kare* 'he' and *kanozyo* 'she' can be referential but not bound (Noguchi 1997 and much previous literature), as we see in the following examples.

Although I am not aware that this has been noted before in the literature, there seem to be two dialects of Japanese, as far as these words are concerned. The first places no restrictions on where *kare* and *kanozyo* may be placed with respect to coreferential terms; it is exemplified in (1) and (2).

(1) a. John$_i$-ga [kare$_i$-ga atama-ga ii to] omotte-iru.
   John-NOM he-NOM head-NOM good COMP think-PRES
   'John$_i$ thinks that he$_i$ is intelligent.'

   b. Mary$_i$-ga [kanozyo$_i$-ga atama-ga ii to] omotte-iru.
   Mary-NOM she-NOM head-NOM good COMP think-PRES
   'Mary$_i$ thinks that she$_i$ is intelligent.'

    c. Mary$_i$-ga [pro_i atama-ga ii   to]   omotte-iru.
        Mary-NOM   head-NOM good COMP think-PRES
        'Mary$_i$ thinks that she$_i$ is intelligent.'

(2) a. *Daremo$_i$-ga [kare$_i$-ga atama-ga ii   to]   omotte-iru.
        everyone-NOM he-NOM   head-NOM good COMP think-PRES
        'Everone$_i$ thinks that he$_i$ is intelligent.'

    b. *Daremo-ga$_i$ [kanozyo$_i$-ga atama-ga ii   to]   omotte-iru.
        everyone-NOM she-NOM   head-NOM good COMP think-PRES
        'Everyone$_i$ thinks that she$_i$ is intelligent.'

    c. Daremo-ga$_i$ [pro_i atama-ga ii   to]   omotte-iru.
        everyone-NOM   head-NOM good COMP think-PRES
        'Everyone$_i$ thinks they$_i$'re intelligent.'

Note that (2a) and (2b) are bad on the reading where the pronouns are interpreted as bound.[1]

The second dialect consists of speakers who also find (1a) and (1b) ungrammatical, in addition to (2a) and (2b). When the pronouns are more deeply embedded, however, exactly the same pattern emerges with respect to the grammaticality of bound and referential readings, as we see in (3) and (4).

(3) a. John$_i$-ga kare$_i$-no musume-no atarasii syasin-o   motteiru.
        John-NOM he-GEN daughter-GEN new   photo-ACC has
        'John$_i$ has a new photo of his$_i$ daughter.'

    b. Mary$_i$-ga kanozyo$_i$-no musume-no atarasii syasin-o
        Mary-NOM she-GEN   daughter-GEN new   photo-ACC
        motteiru.
        has
        'Mary$_i$ has a new photo of her$_i$ daughter.'

(4) a. *Dono titioya-mo$_i$ kare$_i$-no musume-no atarasii syasin-o
        which father-even he-GEN daughter-GEN new   photo-ACC
        motteiru.
        has
        'Every father$_i$ has a new photo of his$_i$ daughter.'

    b. *Dono hahaoya-mo$_i$ kanozyo$_i$-no musume-no atarasii
        which mother-even she-GEN   daughter-GEN new
        syasin-o   motteiru.
        photo-ACC has
        'Every mother$_i$ has a new photo of her$_i$ daughter.'

I do not know why there should be the dialectal difference, or exactly what is going on in the second dialect to make (1a) and (1b) ungrammatical. I will leave these questions aside, however, since the second dialect clearly maintains the basic pattern found in the first one: *kare* and *kanozyo* cannot be bound, even though minimally different sentences where they corefer with a type e lexical item in the place of the QP in the bad sentences are fine.

5.3 Previous Accounts

The bulk of my review and criticism of previous accounts of *kare* and *kanozyo* is based on the review carried out in Noguchi 1997, to which readers are referred for more details.

Some syntactic treatments of these facts amount only to restatements of the problem. I would include here Katada's (1991) proposal that *kare* must be operator-free and Aoun and Hornstein's (1992, 5) proposal that, "*Kare* must be A'-free." These statements may well be true, but from them we have learned nothing about the nature of *kare*; we are left wondering what about it is such that it has to be operator-free or A'-free. The same can be said about Montalbetti's (1984, 187) treatment of *kare*, which was to state that "overt pronouns cannot have formal variables as antecedents." A formal variable (the term is Higginbotham's) is a trace left by a QR'd QP or *wh*-operator. Again, this is just a restatement of the problem.

Huang (1991) suggested that *kare* and *kanozyo* cannot be bound because of competition from the reflexive pronoun: when the reflexive pronoun is possible, *kare* and *kanozyo* will not be possible. But, as Noguchi (1997, 774–775) points out, the reflexive pronoun *zibun* is subject oriented, and therefore cannot be used, for example, with a dative antecedent:

(5) a. Mary-ga   John$_i$-ni [kare$_i$-ga tensai-da   to]   it-ta.
        Mary-NOM John-DAT he-NOM   genius-COP COMP say-PAST
        'Mary told John$_i$ he$_i$ was a genius.'
    b. *Mary-ga   John$_i$-ni [zibun$_i$-ga tensai-da   to]   it-ta.
        Mary-NOM John-DAT self-NOM   genius-COP COMP say-PAST
        'Mary told John$_i$ he$_i$ was a genius.'

Since *zibun* cannot be used in this configuration, it cannot provide competition for *kare*. So on Huang's account, we predict the following to be good (Noguchi 1997, 774–775):

(6) *Mary-ga   dono hito$_i$-ni-mo   [kare$_i$-ga tensai-da   to]
    Mary-NOM which person-DAT-even he-NOM   genius-COP COMP
    it-ta.
    say-PAST
    'Mary told every person$_i$ he$_i$ was genius.'

The example is bad, however, meaning that Huang's account cannot be correct.[2]

Hoji (1991) proposes that *kare* cannot be bound because it is a demonstrative. But there are examples that show that demonstratives can in fact be bound. One such is (7), where *no senator* raises at LF and binds *that senator*.

(7) Mary talked to no senator before that senator was lobbied.

More would need to be said to make this a viable explanation.[3]

Noguchi (1997, 777) says that *kare* and *kanozyo* are nouns, citing the evidence in (8)–(10).

(8) a. tiisai kare
       small he
       (See discussion below.)
    b. sinsetuna kanozyo
       kind   she
       (See discussion below.)

(9) a. watasi-no kare
       I-GEN   he
       'my boyfriend'
    b. anato-no kanozyo
       you-GEN she
       'your girlfriend'

(10) a. kono kare
        this he
        'this male person'
     b. ano kanozyo
        that she
        'that female person'

If something can be modified by an adjective (8) or a determiner (10) and sometimes mean "boyfriend" (9), Noguchi says, we have good reason to believe that it is a noun. He further maintains the following two theses: nouns cannot be functional items; and "Binding applies only to functional items" (1997, 783). Thus is explained the inability of our words to be bound.

However, this is open to challenge on three counts. First, it is in fact dubious to say that *kare* and *kanozyo* are nouns, or at least nouns in any normal sense of the word. To start with, my informants tell me that, for example, *tiisai kare* (which Noguchi does not translate into grammatical English) means something like "he, who is small." It has the flavor, then, of a normal pronoun being modified by a nonrestrictive relative clause, and is thus not evidence for *kare* being a noun at all.[4] As for the alleged ability of our words to be the arguments of determiners, this seems to be highly restricted: no native speaker I have consulted allows *subete-no* ('all') *kare* or *futari-no* ('two') *kare*, and judgments differ sharply about *dono kare-ga* ('which ...') and *dono kare-mo* ('every ...'). Furthermore, Japanese nouns can quite generally be used with no overt determiner and receive an indefinite interpretation ('an N'), but this is completely impossible with *kare*. Rather than say that they are nouns, then, it seems more plausible to say that *kare* and *kanozyo* are basically pronouns that can be coerced into behaving like nouns in an idiosyncratic fashion, as in English locutions like *the real me* and *Is it a he or a she?*. Second, even if our words were nouns, it is simply arbitrary to assert, as Noguchi does, that nouns cannot be functional items. The lexical-functional distinction is left vague, and Noguchi needs to provide a principled account of it that clearly puts all nouns on the lexical side, even nouns that are used as pronouns and that thus seem rather "functional." Third, since binding does not apply to all functional items (e.g., not to auxiliaries or complementizers!), we still have to appeal to properties of individual functional items to determine whether or not they can be bound. So the appeal to the lexical-functional distinction looks as if it would end up being irrelevant anyway—the individual properties in question, which only some functional items possess, could very well account for the differences in bindability between words without any mention of the lexical-functional distinction being made. I am far from being convinced, then, by the account of Noguchi.

5.4 A New Account

I present here an outline of a new account. There is one type of expression in the standard logical languages we use which could be referential, could be applied to many people indiscriminately like a pronoun, and yet would not be capable of being bound, and that is a bland definite description. I suppose, then, that $[\![kare]\!] = \iota x \, male(x)$, and $[\![kanozyo]\!] = \iota x \, female(x)$.[5]

It might be tempting to object to this idea by pointing out that some definite descriptions in natural language *can* be bound, as we have seen in (7), and as most speakers find in (11).

(11) Mary talked to no senator before the senator was lobbied.

But such an objection would be misguided. My proposal is not that *kare* and *kanozyo* have the same semantics as, say, English *the male person* and *the female person*, but that they mean just something like "ιx male(x)" and "ιx female(x)." These latter expressions cannot be bound, because there are no free variables in them. Those natural language definite descriptions that can be bound *cannot* have meanings like "ιx male(x)." There must also be a (locally) free individual variable that can be bound, as we have seen in section 3.3.2.

This account, combined with the view of donkey anaphora defended in chapter 2, makes a prediction. If I am right to say that *kare* and *kanozyo* are bland definite descriptions containing no bindable individual variables, and that donkey pronouns (and donkey-anaphoric definite descriptions) covary by means of situation variables, not individual variables, then *kare* and *kanozyo* should have D-type uses. I do not know of anywhere in the previous literature on these words where this prediction has been tested. But it turns out to be correct, as we see in the following examples. The sentences in (12) are acceptable only to the speakers of the first dialect mentioned above, the one that allows (1a) and (1b). Those in (13) are acceptable to all.

(12) a. Musuko-ga iru   dono hito-mo   [kare-ga atama-ga ii
        son-NOM   exists which person-even he-NOM   head-NOM good
        to]   omotte-iru.
        COMP think-PRES
        'Every person who has a son$_i$ thinks he$_i$ is intelligent.'

    b. Musume-ga   iru   dono hito-mo   [kanozyo-ga atama-ga
       daughter-NOM exists which person-even she-NOM   head-NOM
       ii   to]   omotte-iru.
       good COMP think-PRES
       'Every person who has a daughter$_i$ thinks she$_i$ is intelligent.'

(13) a. Musuko-ga iru   dono hito-mo   kare-no atarasii syasin-o
        son-NOM   exists which person-even he-GEN   new   photo-ACC
        motteiru.
        has-PRES
        'Every person who has a son$_i$ has a new photo of him$_i$.'

b. Musume-ga iru dono hito-mo kanozyo-no atarasii
daughter-NOM exists which person-even she-GEN new
syasin-o motteiru.
photo-ACC has-PRES
'Every person who has a daughter$_i$ has a new photo of her$_i$.'

Note that in order for the situation semantics to produce the proper covariation in these examples we will have to allow the descriptive content "male person" and "female person" to be analyzed as regular situation semantics predicates, as in (14).

(14) a. $\lambda u_{\langle s,e\rangle}. \lambda s. u(s)$ is a male person in s
   b. $\lambda u_{\langle s,e\rangle}. \lambda s. u(s)$ is a female person in s

This implies that the structure of *kare* and *kanozyo* is something like [the male-person] and [the female-person].[6] From the semantics proper, we obtain for (12a) the truth conditions in (15).

(15) $\lambda s.$ for every individual x: for every minimal situation s' such that $s' \leq s$ and x is a person in s' and there is a y such that y is x's son in s', there is a situation s'' such that $s'' \leq s$ and s'' is a minimal situation such that $s' \leq s''$ and x thinks intelligent in s'' the unique male person in s''.

An issue arises here concerning the ability of the bland definite descriptions "the male person" and "the female person" to pick out the sons and the daughters, given that the parents who are also in the relevant situations may be of the same sex as their offspring. But we have already faced and dealt with an analogous issue in chapter 4, and presumably the same mechanisms that allow the incomplete definite descriptions in bishop sentences (and elsewhere) to pick out the right things can come into play in these examples too.

5.5 Consequences for Other Theories

5.5.1 A Problem for Dynamic Semantics
Dynamic semantics accounts of donkey anaphora maintain that it is accomplished via binding of individual variables, as we saw in section 1.4.1. *Kare* and *kanozyo*, however, can be donkey pronouns, as we have just seen, but cannot be, or incorporate, bound individual variables, as we saw in section 5.2. This is a counterexample to one of the most basic claims of dynamic semantics.

5.5.2   A Problem for Variable-Free Semantics

We have seen in section 1.5.1 that variable-free semantics in the style of Jacobson 2000a accounts for D-type anaphora by having pronouns have as their basic denotations the identity function over individuals $[\lambda x.\, x]$ and using the type-shifting rules **g** and **z**. If the same approach was taken to Japanese *kare* and *kanozyo*, however, we would predict that these pronouns could be bound, since, as we also saw in section 1.5.1, the variable-free semantics account of bound pronouns uses exactly the same mechanisms (basic denotation $[\lambda x.\, x]$, type-shifting rules **g** and **z**).

So variable-free semantics makes exactly the same incorrect prediction as dynamic semantics, that wherever D-type anaphora is possible, bound-variable anaphora will be possible too. Contrast the approach being advocated here, which claims that different mechanisms are at work in the two cases.

5.6   A Residual Problem

There is, however, a problem remaining for the current approach. Let us reconsider (2a), repeated here as (16).

(16) *daremo-ga $[\lambda_2$ t$_2$ [[kare-ga atama-ga ii   to]   omotte-iru]]
     everyone-NOM   he-NOM   head-NOM good COMP think-PRES
     'Everyone$_i$ thinks that he$_i$ is intelligent.'

The problem is this. Why can't *kare* in this example obtain a covarying interpretation by means of situation variables being bound? Our semantics, after all, gives us the truth conditions in (17) for (16), assuming the meaning postulated above for *kare*.

(17) $\lambda s.$ for every individual x: for every minimal situation s' such that $s' \leq s$ and x is a person in s', there is a situation s'' such that $s'' \leq s$ and s'' is a minimal situation such that $s' \leq s''$ and $\underline{x}$ (t$_2$) thinks in s'' that the unique male person in s'' (*kare*) is intelligent in s''.

Provided we happen to be quantifying over male people, there should be nothing wrong with such truth conditions. They are equivalent to, "For all x, if x is a person, x thinks x is intelligent." That is, it looks as if the sentence should be able to receive a reading indistinguishable from the bound individual variable reading by situation variables being bound. The sentence cannot have such a reading, however, as we have seen.

I believe, however, that this problem can be solved by the application of Reinhart's Rule I (Reinhart 1983; Grodzinsky and Reinhart 1993; Heim 1993; Reinhart 1997; Fox 2000, 109–137). Recall that the basic intuition behind Rule I is that bound individual variables have a kind of privileged status: in any given syntactic structure, if it is possible to replace a nonbound DP with a bound individual variable without changing the interpretation (roughly speaking), then the structure is ungrammatical. Now look at (16) and (17). It is evident that *kare* could be replaced by an individual variable with index 2 and the same interpretation would result. Rule I, therefore, will rule out the structure in (16).

There have been many versions of Rule I formulated over the years, and its exact formulation is still, I think, something on which the jury is out. In order to provide a more detailed demonstration than that just given that Rule I disallows (16), I will use the formulation in (18) (a slightly emended version of the formulation in Grodzinsky and Reinhart 1993), without any pretense that this is the last word on the subject.[7]

(18) *Rule I*

A DP α which does not consist of or contain a bound individual variable cannot be covalued with a DP β if replacing α with γ, γ an individual variable A-bound by β, yields an indistinguishable interpretation.

By two DPs being covalued, it is simply meant that their semantic values are the same. In the case of (16), *kare* is covalued with t_2: t_2 is translated in the truth conditions (17) as x and *kare* as "the unique male person in s''," and it can be seen that the unique male person in s'' will be identical to x for all situations s'', since the situations s'' contain no individuals apart from the individuals x. To apply this rule to (16), then, let $\alpha = kare$ and $\beta = t_2$. Replacing α (*kare*) with an individual variable A-bound by β (t_2) yields the structure in (2c), repeated here as (19).

(19) daremo-ga   [λ_2 t_2 [[*pro$_2$* atama-ga ii   to]   omotte-iru]]
    everyone-NOM   head-NOM good COMP think-PRES
    'Everyone$_i$ thinks they$_i$'re intelligent.'

Since the truth conditions of (19) are equivalent to those in (17), Rule I correctly prescribes that (16) is ungrammatical.

Note that the restriction on a DP α being covalued with a DP β was not put in place on the basis of any examples in which bound individual variables were covalued with items of type e that covaried by means of situation variables. Only cases of coreference and cobinding were considered, as described in note 7. It is some measure of the accuracy of the basic intuition behind Rule I that it extends without effort to this new set of circumstances.[8]

5.7   Conclusion

Examination of the Japanese pronouns *kare* and *kanozyo* has proved to be informative. In particular, it has uncovered new and seemingly fundamental problems for dynamic semantics and variable-free semantics accounts of donkey anaphora (section 5.5), and some new and unexpected corroboration of Reinhart's Rule I (section 5.6).

Chapter 6

Proper Names

6.1 Introduction

6.1.1 Extending the Analysis to Names

To recapitulate, in the preceding chapters, we have analyzed pronouns and definite descriptions as having the structure in (1).[1]

(1) [[THE i] NP]

The claim laid out in chapter 1 was that pronouns and definite descriptions were not alone in having this structure, and that proper names shared it too. If this was the case, all phrases that we intuitively take to denote individuals would have basically the same syntax and semantics. In this chapter, then, the last part of the claim will be defended: it will be argued that proper names too have the structure in (1).

The consensus among philosophers (linguists, for some reason, rarely discuss proper names) is that names are directly referential in the sense of Kaplan 1989b. That is, each name has a semantics which consists simply of the stipulation that it refers to a specified person or thing, and contributes only that object to the truth conditions of any sentence in which it occurs. If names are directly referential, they must also be rigid designators in the sense of Kripke 1972 (see section 6.2.1), and this is also widely believed.

There is already a minority view, however, that proper names have the semantics we would expect from a structure like (1). This has been most clearly and forcefully argued by Burge (1973). In section 6.1.2, then, I will set out Burge's view of proper names, and the evidence he gives in favor of it; and then in section 6.1.3 I will describe the revised version of Burge's theory advocated by Larson and Segal 1995, and set out the revised version of that which is my own view. In section 6.2, I will defend this view against some objections that have been made against related views by Kripke (1972). And in section 6.3, I will present further evidence that Burge's view not only can be sustained but must be sustained.

6.1.2   The Theory of Burge 1973

According to Burge (1973), proper names are basically predicates— nouns, in fact. A rough approximation to the semantics of a proper name NN, he says, is that it means "entity called 'NN,'" where "NN" can be spelled out with a phonological representation, and, in a literate society, I presume, an orthography. But such a formulation might be slightly misleading. According to Burge, proper names are predicates in themselves: a man called Alfred, for example, is literally an Alfred. What exactly makes one an Alfred, or a Gwendolyn or a Mary or an Aristotle, is, he says, a matter for sociology to determine: the "called" in the para- phrase "entity called 'NN'" could if necessary be spelled out in terms of a sociological account that would refer to baptisms, nicknaming, brand- naming, and many similar phenomena.[2] For the purposes of composi- tional semantics, however, such an account is not strictly necessary: in the terms in which this book has been couched, *Alfred* has the denotation $[\lambda x. x$ is an Alfred$]$, and it is no more necessary to do all the sociological (and other) groundwork about naming to use this lexical entry than it is necessary to undertake an extensive zoological project in order to use a lexical entry like $[\lambda x. x$ is a tiger$]$.

The main justification that Burge gives for this view is that proper names do indeed behave like nouns in almost all respects. They seem to contradict this hypothesis, of course, in that they occur alone in examples like (2), and therefore might be taken to denote individuals.

(2) Alfred studies at Princeton.

But abstracting away from this for a moment, we observe that they take the plural, as in (3).

(3) There are relatively few Alfreds at Princeton.

They take the indefinite and definite articles, as in (4) and (5).

(4) An Alfred Russell joined the club today.

(5) The Alfred who joined the club today was a baboon.

And they also appear seemingly productively after a wide range of other determiners:

(6) Some Alfreds are sane.

(7) Most Alfreds are crazy.

(8) Every Alfred I ever met is crazy.

(9) There are two Alfreds.

(10) Do you mean this Alfred?

(11) Which Alfred do you mean?

These uses, Burge contends, are literal uses of the name. He contrasts them with obviously metaphorical uses of names, such as (12).

(12) George Wallace is a Napoleon.

Here it is evident that George Wallace is not literally a Napoleon; rather he is being claimed to be like the most famous Napoleon in some important respect. Furthermore, if someone wanted to say that the uses of proper names in (3)–(11) were exceptional in some way, as a direct reference theorist would have to, their theory would be uneconomical, in that it would have to account for the emergence of these supposedly semantically misleading occurrences of names. Burge's theory, by contrast, faces no such problem.

Now what of unmodified uses like that in (2)? Burge (1973, 432) says that these uses of proper names "have the same semantical structure as the phrase 'that book.'" He does not explicitly mention syntactic structure, but I will take it that for our present purposes we should imagine a phonologically null determiner *that* placed before the proper name, as in (13). (This is how Larson and Segal (1995, 352) produce a syntactically explicit rendering of Burge's view.)

(13) [THAT Alfred]

The motivation behind this particular semantics, says Burge, is that the two sentences in (14) seem both to be context-dependent in the same way.

(14) a. Jim is 6 feet tall.
     b. That book is green.

The speakers and hearers of these sentences must pick out a particular book or a particular Jim in order for the sentences to express determinate propositions. Thus proper names behave like demonstratives.

Theories which do not adopt this approach to the fact that names typically denote more than one person, such as the currently popular direct reference theory, have to say that names are ambiguous. The lexicon of each speaker of English would contain several homophonous lexical items pronounced "John," for example, each one referring to a different person; and more such items will have to be added whenever the speaker gets to know more Johns. This is not a knockdown argument against theories that differ from Burge's, of course, but it is evident that Burge's theory is significantly more economical in this respect, since it needs only one lexical entry per proper name.

6.1.3 A Revised Version

I am in substantial agreement with Burge's theory as laid out in his 1973 paper, and will take it as the basis of my own view. Only one revision needs to be made, and that has already been made in essence by Larson and Segal (1995, 354–355), who propose that the null determiner understood in English before proper names is not *that* but *the*.

One consideration given by these authors, which is very powerful, is that there are languages where proper names overtly take the definite article before them, in circumstances where just the bare proper name would be used in English. This is compulsory for names of people in some dialects of German: we always have *der Hans* 'the Hans', where in English we would just expect *Hans*. The same occurred in classical Greek, for example, except that here the overt definite article was optional, so that (15a) and (15b) were equally grammatical.

(15) a. ho Sōcratēs aphīketo.
       the Socrates arrived
       'Socrates arrived.'
     b. Sōcratēs aphīketo.
        Socrates arrived
        'Socrates arrived.'

If we say that the determiner in English is a silent *the*, not a silent *that*, we automatically obtain crosslinguistic support for the idea of having a determiner there in the first place. We can simply say that English is exactly the same as German, classical Greek, and various other languages, except that in English for some reason the definite article that we see in the other languages is not pronounced.[3]

According to the view of the definite article argued for in chapter 3, proper names will look like the one in (16) when they appear to stand alone. They thus fit the schema in (17), which I have argued to be valid for definite descriptions and pronouns.[4]

(16) [[THE 2] Socrates]

(17) [[THE *i*] NP]

The index in these structures will be used, on normal occasions of use, for picking out the particular bearer of the proper name in question that we want to say something about, and will thus function exactly as Burge supposed his demonstrative did. Indeed, Burge evidently thought that a complex demonstrative *that NP* had exactly the semantics that we expect from (17): in one part of his paper he gives the semantics in (18), where *x* is a free variable to be assigned a referent by the context, for a proper name *A* (Burge 1973, 433).

(18) $\iota y (Ay \,\&\, y = x)$

It seems, then, that Burge in fact had in mind precisely the semantics that emerges from (17) given the Fregean view of the definite article I have espoused.[5]

6.2   Kripke's Objections to Descriptive Theories

In *Naming and Necessity* (Kripke 1972), Kripke puts forward three objections to theories of proper names that give them descriptive semantic content. It is important to show that the present descriptive theory is not refuted by these arguments. The present section is somewhat indebted to the corresponding section (chapter 9) of Recanati 1993, although my actual counterarguments to Kripke differ from Recanati's.[6]

6.2.1   The Modal Objection

Kripke's modal objection, adapted to the present theory, goes as follows.[7] *Socrates* cannot mean "the entity called 'Socrates,'" because if it did (19) would be analytic, and hence necessary.

(19) Socrates is the entity called Socrates.

Example (19) is not necessary, however. Socrates might not have been called Socrates. So *Socrates* cannot mean "the entity called 'Socrates.'"

The present theory of proper names, however, says that the descriptive content of *Socrates* is not exhausted by "entity called 'Socrates.'" The proper name *Socrates*, as we see in (16), is the phonological spell-out of a structure which also includes an index. In a felicitous use, the index will naturally have the value $[\lambda x. \, x = \text{Socrates}]$, and so the whole descriptive content will be "entity identical with Socrates and called 'Socrates.'" So the person Socrates is contributed by the name *Socrates* to the proposition expressed, and hence we predict that (19) will not in fact be necessary, for exactly the reason that Kripke gives: Socrates might not have been called Socrates.

It might be objected that my theory also allows for the index 0, which will not contribute Socrates to the proposition expressed. I submit, however, that it is pragmatically very difficult to have the index 0 used with a proper name: any use of a proper name in which the speaker does have some specific person in mind and intends to refer to that person is ipso facto a use that employs one of the nontrivial indices, and it is hard to construct circumstances in which a speaker might use a proper name and not intend to refer to some specific person they have in mind. They would have to be in a position to know that that name was appropriate even though they knew nothing about the person that would enable them to refer to them, and this seems contradictory.[8]

It is doubtful, then, that one could even have the index 0 on *Socrates* in (19). But for the sake of argument suppose that it were possible. It is still not clear that the actual person Socrates would not enter the proposition anyway. "The entity called 'Socrates'" in the actual world, was, of course, Socrates. So if the entity that actually uniquely satisfies a definite description whose descriptive content is purely general (in a nonmodal, non-covarying context like that of (19)) enters the proposition expressed, we still predict that (19) will not be judged necessary, even if we allow the index 0. This may well be the case, for all I know.[9]

But suppose, again for the sake of argument, that it were not the case. That is, suppose that we could have the index 0 in (19) and that the proposition literally expressed did not actually include the person Socrates; all that *Socrates* contributed was the property of being called "Socrates" and a uniqueness operator. Then Kripke would still have to demonstrate that the only thing that enters into people's judgment that (19) is not necessary is the proposition literally expressed—that is, the proposition *conveyed* could not be the thing that was judged necessary or contingent. It is such a small step from the combination of the property of being called "Socrates" and a uniqueness operator to the person Socrates that it seems inevitable that in these circumstances the proposition conveyed would be that the actual person Socrates (who could have been called something different) was called "Socrates." The step is so small, in fact, that it is doubtful whether anyone would ever be consciously aware of it, if it did happen.[10] So it would not be surprising that the sentence would be judged not to be necessary, even if its literal semantic content did not include the person Socrates.

The larger background issue here is of course Kripke's famous claim that proper names are rigid designators (Kripke 1972). According to Kripke,[11] "a designator d of an object x is rigid, if it designates x with respect to all possible worlds where x exists, and never designates an object other than x with respect to any possible world." The point is brought out by examples like those in (20), which are based on some of Kripke's original (1972) examples.

(20) a. The U.S. President in 1970 was not Nixon.
  b. Nixon was not Nixon.

Kripke invites us to consider whether there are any possible circumstances (possible worlds) in which (20a) would have been true. And the intuitive answer is that there certainly are: any circumstances in which someone else had won the relevant election would suffice. The same does not appear to hold for (20b), however: there are no possible circumstances in which Nixon was not Nixon. The conclusion is that definite descriptions like *the U.S. President in 1970* are not rigid: when evaluated with respect to different possible circumstances, they can denote different objects. Names like *Nixon*, however, are rigid: there are no possible circumstances with respect to which *Nixon* will denote anyone other than Nixon, and this accounts for the difference in status between (20a) and (20b).

It can be seen, in light of the above discussion, that the rigidity of proper names is not a problem for the current theory. It is difficult to construct examples in which proper names will not have a nontrivial index which will contribute an actual object or person to the proposition expressed, and, as Kripke (1972) has argued, we do not conceive of actual objects or people changing their identity in any relevant way when we imagine them figuring in different sets of circumstances. Furthermore, let us suppose, perhaps counterfactually, that it is possible to have the index 0 in the occurrences of *Nixon* in (20b). I think that we still predict that people will judge that there are no circumstances in which (20b) would be true. The reason is as follows. We are supposing that the semantic content of *Nixon* is just "the entity called 'Nixon.'" Then, for each circumstance of evaluation w, (20b) says that the entity called Nixon in w was not the entity called Nixon in w; if we suppose that it is indeed possible to locate a maximally salient entity called Nixon in each circumstance w, the sentence is still an obvious falsehood, then. And it will always be possible to find a suitably salient entity called Nixon: for most people, there is exactly one entity called Nixon who is salient enough to be the denotation of *Nixon*, and that is the man who, in actual fact, was the U.S. president in 1970, and there is no reason, in the absence of some convoluted context, why people should light upon different entities called Nixon when they attempt to consider different possible circumstances. In fact even if people did do this, the sentence would still be false, since for each circumstance *w* it would claim that the Nixon selected in *w* was not the Nixon selected in *w*. The only way to get the sentence to turn out true, then, would be to have the two occurrences of *Nixon* refer to different Nixons, and this, if it is possible at all, would require heroic efforts at constructing a suitable context. So even if we do not have a nontrivial index, but have the index 0, (20b) is still predicted to be judged false with respect to all possible circumstances of evaluation.

The above discussion has an obvious bearing on the distinction between de jure and de facto rigidity. A designator is de jure rigid if its reference is stipulated, in its semantics, to be a single object, whether we are talking about the actual world or other possible worlds. A designator is de facto rigid if it just happens to denote the same object in all possible worlds, by some other means. Kripke's (1972) thesis was that names are rigid de jure.[12] Now strictly speaking, in the view being advocated here, proper names are not rigid in any sense: they are predicates that could apply to different things in different possible worlds, since things could be named in different ways in different possible worlds. But we can also consider proper names within the structure of definite article plus index that is alleged to accompany them in apparently unmodified uses, and ask about the rigidity of this entire structure. If we consider a structure like [[THE 2] John] interpreted with respect to some variable assignment that gives a value for the index 2, we will have a rigid expression, since some particular John will be contributed; and the expression will in a way be de jure rigid, since the rigidity comes from the index, and indices are stipulated to contribute one entity to the truth conditions, and the system is not set up in such a way that the entity will change with respect to different circumstances of evaluation. It is evident, however, that this de jure rigidity for names comes about in a different way from that which Kripke originally envisaged: names bearing nontrivial indices are rigid (with respect to a variable assignment) in the same way that pronouns are, not in the way that Kripkean (directly referential) names are. If we now turn our attention to names with the index 0, it is evident that, if they do indeed occur, they will generally be rigid, as argued above, but only rigid de facto. There will be nothing in the semantics of any constituent of them that contributes de jure rigidity, but the pragmatic factors described above will generally ensure rigidity.

Overall, then, I believe that the modal considerations put forward by Kripke do not count against the current theory of proper names.

6.2.2 The Circularity Objection

Kripke's (1972) argument from circularity goes as follows.[13] A theory of the reference of some expression must not explicate its reference in terms that make crucial mention of its reference. Otherwise, the theory would be viciously circular. But the theory that *Socrates* means "the entity called 'Socrates'" does precisely this. We may as well say that the reference of the name *Socrates* is the entity that the name *Socrates* refers to.

I am in considerable sympathy with the answer to this objection already given by Loar (1980) and Recanati (1993, 158–161). They say that the "called" in the paraphrase does not mean "whom I am presently calling" (in which case the definition would indeed be circular). Instead it makes reference to the social and psychological practice of naming already mentioned in section 6.1.2. This is all one needs in order to forestall Kripke's objection.

One should also note, of course, that in the current view names contain a free variable which can be assigned a referent directly. So the descriptive content does not in any case bear the whole burden of getting reference off the ground.

6.2.3 The Generality Objection

Kripke's (1972) argument from generality goes as follows.[14] We can take any noun and construct a definition of it along the lines of Burge's explication of the meaning of proper names. "Since it's trifling to be told that sages are called 'sages', 'sages' just means 'the people called "sages."'" Now plainly this isn't really a very good argument, nor can it therefore be the only explanation of why it's trifling to be told that Socrates is called 'Socrates.'"

As I understand it, the argument here, which is rather compact, comes down to nothing more than an appeal to treat proper names on a par with other words, in particular nouns. Since "people called 'sages'" is not really the meaning of *sages*, "the entity called 'Socrates'" cannot really be the meaning of the word *Socrates*. As far as I can see, this argument completely fails to get off the ground. It is open to the rejoinder that perhaps proper names are different from other nouns in this respect. Kripke has really shown us no reason to think that they are not.

This concludes the examination of Kripke's arguments against descriptive theories of proper names. None of them have been very effective against the particular theory of proper names currently being advocated.

6.3 Further Evidence in Favor of Burge's Theory

6.3.1 N to D Raising in Italian

It is possible to show in some cases that names which have no overt determiner preceding them do nevertheless occupy a [D NP] structure, with the name a noun. Longobardi (1994) has put forward compelling arguments showing that proper names in Italian are nouns that raise to D. One of his arguments, for example, concerns the behavior of the adjective *solo*, which means "only" when it occurs prenominally and "alone" when it occurs postnominally, as shown in (21) and (22).

(21) a. La sola Maria si è presentata.
       the only Maria self is having-presented
       'Only Maria showed up.'
     b. La Maria sola si è presentata.
       the Maria alone self is having-presented
       'The Maria who is (notoriously) alone showed up.'

(22) a. La sola ragazza presente era antipatica.
       the only girl   present was dislikable
       'The only girl present was dislikable.'
     b. La ragazza sola   presente era antipatica.
       the girl   alone present was dislikable
       'The girl who was alone who was present was dislikable.'

However, if we use this adjective with an articleless proper name, the A-N order is impossible, and the N-A order produces the same meaning for *sola* as is normally present with the A-N order:

(23) a. *Sola Maria si è presentata.
             Maria self is having-presented
     b. Maria sola si è presentata.
        Maria only self is having-presented
        'Only Maria showed up.'

We can explain these facts, says Longobardi, if we suppose that articleless proper names in Italian obligatorily raise from N to D: *sola Maria* is impossible, because it has *Maria* to the right of an adjective and thus still inside NP; *Maria sola* can mean 'only Maria', a meaning that is generally produced by *sola* being prenominal, because it is derived from an underlying [D [sola Maria]]. (I assume there must be reconstruction of *Maria* at LF.) Note that this hypothesis, which is supported by many other arguments in Longobardi 1994, crucially relies on proper names being nouns, just as Burge says they are.[15]

6.3.2   An Argument from Distribution

While we are surveying syntactic facts, I think it worth while paying heed to the following suggestive consideration.

As mentioned in section 3.3.2, Chomsky (1986, 188) draws attention to the following paradigm in order to argue that phrases like *John's* in *John's book* originate within NP.

(24) a.   a book of John's
     b.   that book of John's
     c.   *the book of John's
     d.   the book of John's that you read
     e.   *John's book that you read
     f.   John's book

As Chomsky says, possessives like *of John's* cannot appear with the definite article, unless a further postnominal restrictor such as *that you read* is present also. Alongside this gap in the paradigm, there are phrases like *John's book*, which, furthermore, has exactly the same meaning as the missing option (24c). The data suggest, then, that (24f) might be derived from an underlying form like that in (24c).

It is striking that the data in (24) are closely paralleled by the data concerning proper names in English, as we see in (25).

(25) a.   an Alfred Russell
     b.   that Alfred
     c.   *the Alfred
     d.   the Alfred that I know
     e.   *Alfred that I know
     f.   Alfred

And again, the same considerations apply. There is an apparent gap in the paradigm, (25c). There is also a seemingly anomalous form (25f) that seems to have the meaning that would be expected for the missing option. Considerations of economy, then, dictate that we should see the anomalous form as spelling out the missing option, which is thus not really missing after all.

6.3.3 D-Type Proper Names

If proper names really do have the same structure as definite descriptions when they appear to occur unmodified, it is natural to wonder if they can have bound and D-type readings, since we know that we can have bound and D-type definite descriptions, as in (26). (See sections 3.3.2 and 2.1.1 for discussion.)

(26) a. Mary talked to no senator before the senator was lobbied.
     b. Every man who owns a donkey beats the donkey.

Initial results when we try to construct examples of bound and D-type proper names are not encouraging, as we see in (27).

(27) a. ??Mary talked to no-one called Alfred before Alfred was lobbied.
     b. ??Every man who owns a donkey called Flossy beats Flossy.

This is not a point against the current theory, of course: it is quite open to us to say that, while they have the structure of definite descriptions, proper names also have some additional features that prevent their occurrence in sentences like those in (27).

There is in fact independent evidence that proper names are subject to severe collocational constraints. The traditional Condition C of the Binding Theory is one proposal for constraining their distribution. But actually, the restrictions are more severe than are predicted by Condition C alone, as we see in (28).

(28) a. John came home. He turned on the TV.
     b. John came home. ?*John turned on the TV.

There seems to be a moderately strong constraint (in English at least) against repeating proper names in close proximity to each other.[16] Interestingly, though, the constraint does not hold when use of the proper name serves to make a contrast. Thus, while (28b) is awkward, (29) is fine.

(29) Mary and John came home. John turned on the TV.

I will not attempt to work out exactly what is going on here. For our present purposes, we can just note that the awkwardness of the sentences in (27) can plausibly be ascribed to a special feature of proper names, which is not, however, inconsistent with proper names having basically the structure of definite descriptions.

In fact (29) suggests a strategy that might lead to grammatical examples of bound and D-type proper names. If we could construct examples in which proper names were in a position to be bound or D-type and also contrasted appropriately with some other constituent of the sentence, we might get better results. The results are shown in (30).

(30) a. ??I introduced no one called Seamus to anyone called Romano before Seamus had told me what he thought of the Treaty of Nice.

    b. Every woman who has a husband called John and a lover called Gerontius takes only Gerontius to the Rare Names Convention.

(30a) is still quite bad, which is not to be wondered at, given that for the second occurrence of *Seamus* to be bound it would have to be c-commanded by its potential binder. However, quite strikingly, (30b) is fine. The *Gerontius* in *only Gerontius* is not c-commanded and there is now the necessary element of contrast in the sentence. Presumably this D-type proper name will have index 0 (since it cannot be bound or referential) and will behave like any other D-type definite description.

The existence of grammatical D-type proper names is a very strong argument against the direct reference view of proper names and in favor of the theory currently being advocated. Since the direct reference view holds that the contribution of a proper name to the truth conditions of a sentence in which it appears is always just one individual, it cannot deal with covarying proper names. Note also that on the view of D-type anaphora advocated in this book the descriptive content of *Gerontius* must enter into the proposition in (30b), since we need to find the person with the property of being called Gerontius in each of a set of previously defined situations; this argues against Recanati's (1993) view that proper names have senses or characters of the type that Burge would give them, but that these senses do not enter the proposition expressed.

6.3.4 Naming Hypothetical Entities

Let us consider the following example, which is due to Irene Heim (personal communication).[17] John has four sons: Primus, Secundus, Tertius, and Quartus. Detecting a pattern here, and knowing that the four sons are very overbearing, we say (31).

(31) If John had had five sons, Quintus would have been bullied by the others.

This sentence is perfectly grammatical under the interpretation whereby it claims that John's fifth son would have been bullied by the others. Note, however, that we do not have to interpret *Quintus* (with the help of whatever knowledge of Latin we have) as actually having semantic content equivalent to "the fifth one." *Quintus* in English is just a name, and all we need to do in order to find (31) grammatical is accommodate the presupposition that John's fifth son would have had this name. Other examples with names that have even less claim to present descriptive content also work, if the context is set up so as to make the relevant accommodation easy. For example, (32) seems perfectly unexceptionable.

(32) If John insists on calling his next son Gerontius, then his wife will be annoyed and Gerontius will get made fun of because of his name.

No special semantic content not typical of names in general, then, is required in order to obtain the relevant reading of (31).

Given this, the theory of proper names currently being advocated can explain the behavior of *Quintus* in (31) by saying that it incorporates the index 0 and a bound world variable attached to the descriptive content. Assuming some version of the semantics for counterfactual conditionals worked out by Stalnaker (1968) and Lewis (1973), the truth conditions for (31) on the current theory are roughly those in (33).

(33) For all worlds *w*, if *w* is a member of the set of worlds in which John has five sons but which are otherwise as similar as possible to the actual world, then the unique entity called Quintus in *w* is bullied in *w*.

We are talking about John's sons and the possibility of him having a fifth son, so the maximally salient entity called Quintus in each of the worlds where John has five sons is of course John's fifth son. So we can make sense of the definite description "the unique entity called Quintus in *w*." It seems, then, that Burge's view of proper names correctly predicts that (31) has the reading it does.

Consider now the consequences of trying to deal with this type of sentence on the direct reference view of proper names. Since there is no such person as Quintus, we are immediately in the realm of the problem of how direct reference theories deal with nondenoting proper names. It is not clear to me that any satisfactory solution can be given to this problem, but for the sake of argument (since my main point is actually orthogonal) let us suppose that we can in fact say something coherent on this point. Kaplan himself (1989a, 609–610, note 107) has endorsed a suggestion made in a lecture by Kripke, to the effect that "there are abstract but actual (not merely possible) *fictional individuals* that serve as the referents of names like *Sherlock Holmes*," and I suspect that any solution to the problem would have to be along these lines.[18] We may be worried by the metaphysical extravagance involved in such a theory, but let us countenance it for the moment.

The problem is that a theory about abstract fictional individuals of this kind will not enable the direct reference theorist to analyze (31). The reason is that the relevant person called Quintus could be a different person in different possible worlds. To see this clearly, imagine that John's four sons have been with Mary, and that he had gone on to have a fifth son with Mary. There are many possible worlds that include this train of events. But consider that John could also have had his fifth son with someone else, say Sue. I think that it is clear to our intuitions that this fifth son would not be the same person as any fifth son that John might have had with Mary. But, according to our hypothesis, he would still have been called Quintus and he is still covered by the generalization in (31). There are, then, at least as many different possible Quintuses as there are possible women that John might have had children with. Presumably, then, there are infinitely many possible Quintuses, each of whom falls under the claim in (31).

Things are similar with (32). We can imagine a scenario in which John's next son is not with his wife: she still gets annoyed (and not just about the name!) and Gerontius is still made fun of, and there are at least as many different possible Gerontii as there are women that John could have them with. But suppose that Gerontius is the product of a nonadulterous union. I think it is still clear to our intuitions that John and his wife could have various people as their next son. We might differentiate them by gametes: spermatozoon 1 and ovum 1 would produce one person, spermatozoon 2 and ovum 2 would produce a different one, and so on. Or we might differentiate them by other characteristics.

In other words, *Quintus* in (31) and the second occurrence of *Gerontius* in (32) denote different people in different possible worlds. They therefore do not seem to be directly referential or rigid designators, and the widespread position that claims that proper names have these qualities as an essential part of their semantics has encountered a serious problem.

6.4   Conclusion

We have seen that Burge's theory of proper names is empirically superior
to its main rival, the direct reference theory, across a broad range of facts,
ranging from N to D raising in Italian to counterexamples in English to
Kripke's claim that proper names are rigid designators. The most natural
way of spelling out Burge's semantic analysis in a syntactically explicit
way involved the [[THE i] NP] structure that has already been argued to
be the one present in pronouns and normal definite descriptions.

Chapter 7
Conclusion

7.1 Expressions of Type e

In what has preceded, we have seen that pronouns, definite descriptions, and proper names can profitably be viewed as having a common syntactic structure [[THE i] NP], and, to a large extent, a common semantics derived from this. This does not imply that these items will behave the same under all circumstances, of course, since there remains scope for differences to emerge between the different definite articles that are possible (pronouns, normal *the*, and the null THE used with proper names in English) and the different NPs that are possible (normal ones, the null ONE, ones projected from proper names). It is essential that we allow for differences given the different behavior that pronouns, definite descriptions, and proper names display with respect to Condition C effects, for example. But we are still left with a common syntactic structure for these items and a common basis for their semantics.

If we make the further assumption, natural in contemporary generative grammar, that much of this information is encoded in Universal Grammar, this means that a child learning their first language need only work out that an expression refers to an individual in order to have access to its syntactic structure and an outline of its semantics. The language-learning task is thus facilitated.

7.2 Accounting for Donkey Anaphora

Another major theme of the preceding chapters has been the rivalry between three different approaches to donkey anaphora and related phenomena, the description-theoretic, dynamic, and variable-free approaches introduced in chapter 1. We saw in section 1.3.2 that the description-theoretic approach faced three main problems, those of indistinguishable participants, the formal link, and pronominal ambiguity. However, we have seen since that the revised version of the D-type analysis advocated here offered solutions for all these problems: indistinguishable participants were discussed in chapter 4, the formal link in section 2.4, and pronominal ambiguity in sections 3.2.2 and 3.5.

Dynamic semantics also faced three problems in chapter 1, as we saw in section 1.4.2: these were disjunctive antecedents, deep anaphora, and what I called neontological pronouns. I cannot at the moment see how to solve these problems. Furthermore, we saw three new problems arise for dynamic semantics during the course of the discussion: these were the problem of pronouns plus relative clause in section 3.4, the problem of coordinate subjects (indistinguishable participants) in section 4.3, and the behavior of Japanese *kare* and *kanozyo* in section 5.5.1.

Variable-free semantics faced two problems in chapter 1: the problems of the formal link and indistinguishable participants (section 1.5.2). We also saw later that it faced problems with strict and sloppy readings of elliptical continuations of donkey sentences (section 2.5.2), pronouns plus relative clause (section 3.4), and Japanese *kare* and *kanozyo* (section 5.5.2).

I tentatively conclude, then, that the revised version of the D-type analysis suggested here is empirically superior to both dynamic and variable-free theories of donkey anaphora and related phenomena.

7.3 Situations

Crucial use was made of situations in the analysis of donkey anaphora in chapters 2, 4, and 5. Only with situations could we neutralize the unwelcome uniqueness presuppositions that arise when we analyze donkey pronouns as definite descriptions, and situations were crucial in providing the basis for differentiating exactly those bishops that had to be differentiated in chapter 4. If I am correct in arguing that the resulting theory is empirically superior to the alternatives, then it might seem that we have gained some evidence that situations must be part of our linguistic ontology.[1]

This conclusion might be discomforting, in that we end up with a rather rich ontology. In fact, I have some sympathy with those who are unwilling to countenance situations. But I suspect that it will be possible to reduce them to other things that are already needed, namely, complex (plural) events. In the wake of the original proposal by Pāṇini and its reintroduction by Davidson (1967), a rich tradition has grown up of using event variables for the semantic analysis of adverbial modification, verbal argument structure, and various other things—see Parsons 1990 for an influential introduction, and Tenny and Pustejovsky 2000 for a collection of recent articles. It is also commonly assumed that events can be complex and have other events as parts; indeed, it has been argued by Hinrichs (1985), Bach (1986), Krifka (1986), and Link (1998, 269–310), among others, that the lattice-theoretic structure proposed by Link (1983) to model plural individuals should also be used to model the structure of events.[2] Crucially, there is good evidence that the eventualities quantified over by grammatical event variables can be stative as well as punctual (Pylkkänen 2000); there is reason to believe that nouns as well as verbs and adverbs must have denotations that make reference to events (Larson and Segal 1995, 496–501; Pustejovsky 2000, 461–462); and it has been convincingly argued that events must be individuated very finely, so that, for example, there are separate events of signaling and raising my hand if I signal by raising my hand (Parsons 1990, 157–159).

Given this picture of grammatical events, we can make the following comparison. In the situation-semantics analysis of donkey anaphora suggested by Heim (1990) and used in this book, we need to identify and quantify over the minimal situations s with the following characteristics:

1. There is a situation s' and an individual x such that s' is part of s and x is a man in s', and

2. There is a situation s'' and an individual y such that s'' is part of s and y is a donkey in s'', and

3. There is a situation s''' such that s''' is part of s and x owns y in s'''.

These situations s seem to contain exactly the same properties, relations, and individuals as the smallest plural events e with the following characteristics:

1. There is an event e' and an individual x such that e' is part of e and e' is an event of being a man, and x is the Theme of e', and

2. There is an event e'' and an individual y such that e'' is part of e and e'' is an event of being a donkey, and y is the Theme of e'', and

3. There is an event e''' such that e''' is part of e and e''' is an event of owning, and x is the Beneficiary of e''' and y is the Theme of e'''.

It is plausible, then, that we would achieve the same results whether we quantified over situations or events.

So it seems that the groundwork is already in place for the reduction of situations to plural events, which would exonerate the analysis of donkey anaphora given in this work of the charge of ontological extravagance. I will not undertake this project here, however, but will leave it for future research.

Appendix A

DPL Calculations

A.1 A Conditional Donkey Sentence in DPL

There follows a detailed calculation establishing that *If a man owns a donkey, he beats it* ((32) in section 1.4) does indeed have the semantic value in (34) in section 1.4, according to DPL. Numbers in statements like "by 30" refer to example numbers in section 1.4.

$\llbracket \exists x(Mx \wedge \exists y(Dy \wedge Oxy)) \rightarrow Bxy \rrbracket$

$= \{\langle g,h \rangle \mid h = g \ \& \ \forall k : \langle h,k \rangle \in \llbracket \exists x(Mx \wedge \exists y(Dy \wedge Oxy)) \rrbracket$
$\Rightarrow \exists j : \langle k,j \rangle \in \llbracket Bxy \rrbracket \}$ (by 30)

$= \{\langle g,h \rangle \mid h = g \ \& \ \forall k : \langle h,k \rangle \in \{\langle g,h \rangle \mid \exists k' : k'[x]g \ \& \ \langle k',h \rangle$
$\in \llbracket (Mx \wedge \exists y(Dy \wedge Oxy)) \rrbracket \} \Rightarrow \exists j : \langle k,j \rangle \in \llbracket Bxy \rrbracket \}$ (by 21)

$= \{\langle g,h \rangle \mid h = g \ \& \ \forall k : \exists k' : (k'[x]h \ \& \ \langle k',k \rangle \in \llbracket (Mx \wedge \exists y(Dy \wedge Oxy)) \rrbracket)$
$\Rightarrow \exists j : \langle k,j \rangle \in \llbracket Bxy \rrbracket \}$ (by reduction)

$= \{\langle g,h \rangle \mid h = g \ \& \ \forall k : \exists k' : (k'[x]h \ \& \ \langle k',k \rangle \in \{\langle g,h \rangle \mid \exists k'' : \langle g,k'' \rangle$
$\in \llbracket Mx \rrbracket \ \& \ \langle k'',h \rangle \in \llbracket \exists y(Dy \wedge Oxy) \rrbracket \}) \Rightarrow \exists j : \langle k,j \rangle \in \llbracket Bxy \rrbracket \}$ (by 23)

$= \{\langle g,h \rangle \mid h = g \ \& \ \forall k : \exists k' : (k'[x]h \ \& \ \exists k'' : \langle k',k'' \rangle \in \llbracket Mx \rrbracket \ \& \ \langle k'',k \rangle$
$\in \llbracket \exists y(Dy \wedge Oxy) \rrbracket) \Rightarrow \exists j : \langle k,j \rangle \in \llbracket Bxy \rrbracket \}$ (by reduction)

$= \{\langle g,h \rangle \mid h = g \ \& \ \forall k : \exists k' : (k'[x]h \ \& \ \exists k'' : \langle k',k'' \rangle \in \llbracket Mx \rrbracket \ \& \ \langle k'',k \rangle$
$\in \{\langle g,h \rangle \mid \exists k''' : k'''[y]g \ \& \ \langle k''',h \rangle \in \llbracket Dy \wedge Oxy \rrbracket \})$
$\Rightarrow \exists j : \langle k,j \rangle \in \llbracket Bxy \rrbracket \}$ (by 21)

$= \{\langle g,h \rangle \mid h = g \ \& \ \forall k : \exists k' : (k'[x]h \ \& \ \exists k'' : \langle k',k'' \rangle \in \llbracket Mx \rrbracket$
$\& \ \exists k''' : k'''[y]k'' \ \& \ \langle k''',k \rangle \in \llbracket Dy \wedge Oxy \rrbracket \}) \Rightarrow \exists j : \langle k,j \rangle \in \llbracket Bxy \rrbracket \}$
(by reduction)

$= \{\langle g,h \rangle \mid h = g \ \& \ \forall k : \exists k' : (k'[x]h \ \& \ \exists k'' : \langle k',k'' \rangle \in \llbracket Mx \rrbracket$
$\& \ \exists k''' : k'''[y]k'' \ \& \ \exists k'''' : \langle k''',k'''' \rangle \in \llbracket Dy \rrbracket$
$\& \ \langle k'''',h \rangle \in \llbracket Oxy \rrbracket \}) \Rightarrow \exists j : \langle k,j \rangle \in \llbracket Bxy \rrbracket \}$ (by 23)

$= \{\langle g,h \rangle \mid h = g \ \& \ \forall k : \exists k' : (k'[x]h \ \& \ \exists k'' : \langle k',k'' \rangle \in \llbracket Mx \rrbracket$
$\& \ \exists k''' : k'''[y]k'' \ \& \ \exists k'''' : \langle k''',k'''' \rangle \in \llbracket Dy \rrbracket \ \& \ \langle k'''',k \rangle \in \llbracket Oxy \rrbracket)$
$\Rightarrow \exists j : \langle k,j \rangle \in \llbracket Bxy \rrbracket \}$ (by reduction)

$$= \{\langle g,h\rangle \mid h = g \ \& \ \forall k : \exists k' : (k'[x]h \ \& \ \exists k'' : \langle k',k''\rangle \in \{\langle g,h\rangle \mid h = g$$
$$\& \ h(x) \in F(M)\} \ \& \ \exists k''' : k'''[y]k'' \ \& \ \exists k'''' : \langle k''',k''''\rangle \in \{\langle g,h\rangle \mid h = g$$
$$\& \ h(y) \in F(D)\} \ \& \ \langle k'''',k\rangle \in \{\langle g,h\rangle \mid h = g \ \& \ \langle h(x),h(y)\rangle \in F(O)\})$$
$$\Rightarrow \exists j : \langle k,j\rangle \in \{\langle g,h\rangle \mid h = g \ \& \ \langle h(x),h(y)\rangle \in F(B)\}\}\} \qquad \text{(by 22)}$$

$$= \{\langle g,h\rangle \mid h = g \ \& \ \forall k : \exists k' : (k'[x]h \ \& \ \exists k'' : k'' = k' \ \& \ k''(x) \in F(M)$$
$$\& \ \exists k''' : k'''[y]k'' \ \& \ \exists k'''' : k'''' = k''' \ \& \ k''''(y) \in F(D) \ \& \ k = k''''$$
$$\& \ \langle k(x),k(y)\rangle \in F(O)) \Rightarrow \exists j : j = k \ \& \ \langle j(x),j(y)\rangle \in F(B)\}$$
$$\text{(by reduction)}$$

$$= \{\langle g,h\rangle \mid h = g \ \& \ \forall k : \exists k' : (k'[x]h \ \& \ k'(x) \in F(M) \ \& \ k[y]k' \ \& \ k(y)$$
$$\in F(D) \ \& \ \langle k(x),k(y)\rangle \in F(O)) \Rightarrow \langle k(x),k(y)\rangle \in F(B)\} \qquad \text{(by =)}$$

$$= \{\langle g,h\rangle \mid h = g \ \& \ \forall k : (k[xy]h \ \& \ k(x) \in F(M) \ \& \ k(y) \in F(D)$$
$$\& \ \langle k(x),k(y)\rangle \in F(O)) \Rightarrow \langle k(x),k(y)\rangle \in F(B)\} \qquad \text{(by def.}[x])$$

A.2   A Relative-Clause Donkey Sentence in DPL

Again, numbers in statements like "by 30" refer to example numbers in section 1.4.

$$[\![\forall x((Mx \wedge \exists y(Dy \wedge Oxy)) \rightarrow Bxy)]\!]$$
$$= \{\langle g,h\rangle \mid h = g \ \& \ \forall k : k[x]h \Rightarrow \exists m : \langle k,m\rangle \in [\![((Mx \wedge \exists y(Dy \wedge Oxy))$$
$$\rightarrow Bxy)]\!]\} \qquad \text{(by 35)}$$

$$= \{\langle g,h\rangle \mid h = g \ \& \ \forall k : k[x]h \Rightarrow \exists m : \langle k,m\rangle \in \{\langle g,h\rangle \mid h = g$$
$$\& \ \forall k' : \langle h,k'\rangle \in [\![(Mx \wedge \exists y(Dy \wedge Oxy))]\!] \Rightarrow \exists j : \langle k',j\rangle \in [\![Bxy]\!]\}\}$$
$$\text{(by 30)}$$

$$= \{\langle g,h\rangle \mid h = g \ \& \ \forall k : k[x]h \Rightarrow (\exists m : m = k \ \& \ \forall k' : \langle m,k'\rangle$$
$$\in [\![(Mx \wedge \exists y(Dy \wedge Oxy))]\!] \Rightarrow \exists j : \langle k',j\rangle \in [\![Bxy]\!])\} \qquad \text{(by reduction)}$$

$$= \{\langle g,h\rangle \mid h = g \ \& \ \forall k : k[x]h \Rightarrow (\forall k' : \langle k,k'\rangle \in [\![(Mx \wedge \exists y(Dy \wedge Oxy))]\!]$$
$$\Rightarrow \exists j : \langle k',j\rangle \in [\![Bxy]\!])\} \qquad \text{(by =)}$$

$$= \{\langle g,h\rangle \mid h = g \ \& \ \forall k : k[x]h \Rightarrow (\forall k' : \langle k,k'\rangle \in \{\langle g,h\rangle \mid \exists k'' : \langle g,k''\rangle$$
$$\in [\![Mx]\!] \ \& \ \langle k'',h\rangle \in [\![\exists y(Dy \wedge Oxy)]\!]\} \Rightarrow \exists j : \langle k',j\rangle \in [\![Bxy]\!])\} \quad \text{(by 23)}$$

$$= \{\langle g,h\rangle \mid h = g \ \& \ \forall k : k[x]h \Rightarrow (\forall k' : \exists k'' : (\langle k,k''\rangle \in [\![Mx]\!]$$
$$\& \ \langle k'',k'\rangle \in [\![\exists y(Dy \wedge Oxy)]\!]) \Rightarrow \exists j : \langle k',j\rangle \in [\![Bxy]\!])\} \quad \text{(by reduction)}$$

$$= \{\langle g,h\rangle \mid h = g \ \& \ \forall k : k[x]h \Rightarrow (\forall k' : \exists k'' : (\langle k,k''\rangle \in [\![Mx]\!]$$
$$\& \ \langle k'',k'\rangle \in \{\langle g,h\rangle \mid \exists k''' : k'''[y]g \ \& \ \langle k''',h\rangle \in [\![Dy \wedge Oxy]\!]\})$$
$$\Rightarrow \exists j : \langle k',j\rangle \in [\![Bxy]\!])\} \qquad \text{(by 21)}$$

$$= \{\langle g,h\rangle \mid h = g \ \& \ \forall k : k[x]h \Rightarrow (\forall k' : \exists k'' : (\langle k,k''\rangle \in [\![Mx]\!]$$
$$\& \ \exists k''' : k'''[y]k'' \ \& \ \langle k''',k'\rangle \in [\![Dy \wedge Oxy]\!]) \Rightarrow \exists j : \langle k',j\rangle \in [\![Bxy]\!])\}$$
$$\text{(by reduction)}$$

$$= \{\langle g,h\rangle \mid h = g \ \& \ \forall k : k[x]h \Rightarrow (\forall k' : \exists k'' : (\langle k,k''\rangle \in [\![Mx]\!]$$
$$\& \ \exists k''' : k'''[y]k'' \ \& \ \langle k''',k'\rangle \in \{\langle g,h\rangle \mid \exists k'''' : \langle g,k''''\rangle \in [\![Dy]\!]$$
$$\& \ \langle k'''',h\rangle \in [\![Oxy]\!]\}) \Rightarrow \exists j : \langle k',j\rangle \in [\![Bxy]\!])\} \qquad \text{(by 23)}$$

$$= \{\langle g,h \rangle \,|\, h = g \ \& \ \forall k : k[x]h \Rightarrow (\forall k' : \exists k'' : (\langle k,k'' \rangle \in [\![Mx]\!]$$
$$\& \ \exists k''' : k'''[y]k'' \ \& \ \exists k'''' : \langle k''',k'''' \rangle \in [\![Dy]\!] \ \& \ \langle k'''',k' \rangle \in [\![Oxy]\!])$$
$$\Rightarrow \exists j : \langle k',j \rangle \in [\![Bxy]\!])\} \hspace{3cm} \text{(by reduction)}$$

$$= \{\langle g,h \rangle \,|\, h = g \ \& \ \forall k : k[x]h \Rightarrow (\forall k' : \exists k'' : (\langle k,k'' \rangle \in \{\langle g,h \rangle \,|\, h = g$$
$$\& \ h(x) \in F(M)\} \ \& \ \exists k''' : k'''[y]k'' \ \& \ \exists k'''' : \langle k''',k'''' \rangle \in \{\langle g,h \rangle \,|\, h = g$$
$$\& \ h(y) \in F(D)\} \ \& \ \langle k'''',k' \rangle \in \{\langle g,h \rangle \,|\, h = g \ \& \ \langle h(x),h(y) \rangle \in F(O)\})$$
$$\Rightarrow \exists j : \langle k',j \rangle \in \{\langle g,h \rangle \,|\, h = g \ \& \ \langle h(x),h(y) \rangle \in F(B)\})\} \hspace{1cm} \text{(by 22)}$$

$$= \{\langle g,h \rangle \,|\, h = g \ \& \ \forall k : k[x]h \Rightarrow (\forall k' : \exists k'' : (k'' = k \ \& \ k''(x) \in F(M)$$
$$\& \ \exists k''' : k'''[y]k'' \ \& \ \exists k'''' : k'''' = k''' \ \& \ k''''(y) \in F(D) \ \& \ k' = k''''$$
$$\& \ \langle k'(x),k'(y) \rangle \in F(O)) \Rightarrow \exists j : j = k' \ \& \ \langle j(x),j(y) \rangle \in F(B))\}$$
$$\hspace{7cm} \text{(by reduction)}$$

$$= \{\langle g,h \rangle \,|\, h = g \ \& \ \forall k : k[x]h \Rightarrow (\forall k' : (k'[y]k \ \& \ k(x) \in F(M) \ \& \ k'(y)$$
$$\in F(D) \ \& \ \langle k'(x),k'(y) \rangle \in F(O)) \Rightarrow \langle k'(x),k'(y) \rangle \in F(B))\} \hspace{0.6cm} \text{(by =)}$$

$$= \{\langle g,h \rangle \,|\, h = g \ \& \ \forall k : (k[xy]h \ \& \ k(x) \in F(M) \ \& \ k(y) \in F(D)$$
$$\& \ \langle k(x),k(y) \rangle \in F(O)) \Rightarrow \langle k(x),k(y) \rangle \in F(B)\} \hspace{1.5cm} \text{(by def.}[x]\text{)}$$

Appendix B

Situation Semantics Calculations

B.1 A Conditional Donkey Sentence

There follows a calculation establishing the truth conditions for a donkey sentence containing a quantificational adverb and an *if*-clause. See section 2.3.1.

$[\![[[\text{always } [\text{if } [\text{a man}] \, [\lambda_6 \, [[\text{a donkey}] \, [\lambda_2 \, [t_6 \text{ owns } t_2]]]]]]$
$[[\text{he man}] \text{ beats } [\text{it donkey}]]]]\!]^0$

$= [\![\text{always}]\!]^0([\![[\text{if } [\text{a man}] \, [\lambda_6 \, [[\text{a donkey}] \, [\lambda_2 \, [t_6 \text{ owns } t_2]]]]]\!]^0)$
$([\![[[\text{he man}] \text{ beats } [\text{it donkey}]]]\!]^0)$ \hfill (by FA)

$= [\![\text{always}]\!]^0([\![[\text{if } [\text{a man}] \, [\lambda_6 \, [[\text{a donkey}] \, [\lambda_2 \, [t_6 \text{ owns } t_2]]]]]\!]^0)$
$([\![\text{beats}]\!]^0 \, ([\![\text{it}]\!]^0([\![\text{donkey}]\!]^0))([\![\text{he}]\!]^0 \, ([\![\text{man}]\!]^0)))$ \hfill (by FA)

$= [\![\text{always}]\!]^0([\![[\text{if } [\text{a man}] \, [\lambda_6 \, [[\text{a donkey}] \, [\lambda_2 \, [t_6 \text{ owns } t_2]]]]]\!]^0)$
$([\lambda u_1. \, \lambda u_2. \, \lambda s_8. \, u_2(s_8) \text{ beats in } s_8 \, u_1(s_8)]$
$([\lambda f_{\langle\langle s,e\rangle,\langle s,t\rangle\rangle}. \, \lambda s_7 : \exists! x \, f(\lambda s_9.x)(s_7) = 1. \, \iota x \, f(\lambda s_9.x)(s_7) = 1]$
$(\lambda u_3. \, \lambda s_6. \, u_3(s_6) \text{ is a donkey in } s_6))$
$([\lambda f_{\langle\langle s,e\rangle,\langle s,t\rangle\rangle}. \, \lambda s_1 : \exists! x \, f(\lambda s_9.x)(s_1) = 1. \, \iota x \, f(\lambda s_9.x)(s_1) = 1]$
$(\lambda u_4. \, \lambda s_3. u_4(s_3) \text{ is man in } s_3)))$ \hfill (by Lex)

$= [\![\text{always}]\!]^0([\![[\text{if } [\text{a man}] \, [\lambda_6 \, [[\text{a donkey}] \, [\lambda_2 \, [t_6 \text{ owns } t_2]]]]]\!]^0)$
$([\lambda u_1. \, \lambda u_2. \, \lambda s_8. \, u_2(s_8) \text{ beats in } s_8 \, u_1(s_8)]$
$(\lambda s_7 : \exists! x \, x \text{ is a donkey in } s_7. \, \iota x \, x \text{ is a donkey in } s_7)$
$(\lambda s_1 : \exists! x \, x \text{ is a man in } s_1. \, \iota x \, x \text{ is a man in } s_1))$ \hfill (by λC)

$= [\![\text{always}]\!]^0([\![[\text{if } [\text{a man}] \, [\lambda_6 \, [[\text{a donkey}] \, [\lambda_2 \, [t_6 \text{ owns } t_2]]]]]\!]^0)$
$(\lambda s_8. \, \iota x \, x \text{ is a man in } s_8 \text{ beats in } s_8 \, \iota x \, x \text{ is a donkey in } s_8)$ \hfill (by λC)

$= [\![\text{always}]\!]^0([\![\text{if}]\!]^0([\![a]\!]^0 \, ([\![\text{man}]\!]^0)([\![\lambda_6 \, [[\text{a donkey}] \, [\lambda_2 \, [t_6 \text{ owns } t_2]]]]\!]^0)))$
$(\lambda s_8. \, \iota x \, x \text{ is a man in } s_8 \text{ beats in } s_8 \, \iota x \, x \text{ is a donkey in } s_8)$ \hfill (by FA)

$= [\![\text{always}]\!]^0([\![\text{if}]\!]^0([\![a]\!]^0([\![\text{man}]\!]^0) \, (\lambda u_6. \, [[[\text{a donkey}] \, [\lambda_2 \, [t_6 \text{ owns }$
$t_2]]]]\!]^{[6 \to u_6]}))) \, (\lambda s_8. \, \iota x \, x \text{ is a man in } s_8 \text{ beats in } s_8 \, \iota x \, x \text{ is a donkey in } s_8)$
\hfill (by PA)

$= [\![\text{always}]\!]^\emptyset([\![\text{if}]\!]^\emptyset([\![\text{a}]\!]^\emptyset([\![\text{man}]\!]^\emptyset)$

$(\lambda u_6. [\![\text{a}]\!]^{[6\to u_6]}([\![\text{donkey}]\!]^{[6\to u_6]})([\![\lambda_2 \, [t_6 \text{ owns } t_2]]\!]^{[6\to u_6]}))))$

$(\lambda s_8. \iota x \; x$ is a man in s_8 beats in s_8 $\iota x \; x$ is a donkey in $s_8)$ $\qquad$ (by FA)

$= [\![\text{always}]\!]^\emptyset([\![\text{if}]\!]^\emptyset([\![\text{a}]\!]^\emptyset([\![\text{man}]\!]^\emptyset)$

$(\lambda u_6. [\![\text{a}]\!]^{[6\to u_6]}([\![\text{donkey}]\!]^{[6\to u_6]})(\lambda u_2. [\![t_6 \text{ owns } t_2]\!]^{\left[\begin{smallmatrix}6\to u_6\\2\to u_2\end{smallmatrix}\right]}))))$

$(\lambda s_8. \iota x \; x$ is a man in s_8 beats in s_8 $\iota x \; x$ is a donkey in $s_8)$ $\qquad$ (by PA)

$= [\![\text{always}]\!]^\emptyset([\![\text{if}]\!]^\emptyset([\![\text{a}]\!]^\emptyset([\![\text{man}]\!]^\emptyset)$

$(\lambda u_6. [\![\text{a}]\!]^{[6\to u_6]}([\![\text{donkey}]\!]^{[6\to u_6]})$

$(\lambda u_2. [\![\text{owns}]\!]^{\left[\begin{smallmatrix}6\to u_6\\2\to u_2\end{smallmatrix}\right]} ([\![t_2]\!]^{\left[\begin{smallmatrix}6\to u_6\\2\to u_2\end{smallmatrix}\right]}) ([\![t_6]\!]^{\left[\begin{smallmatrix}6\to u_6\\2\to u_2\end{smallmatrix}\right]}))))))$

$(\lambda s_8. \iota x \; x$ is a man in s_8 beats in s_8 $\iota x \; x$ is a donkey in $s_8)$ $\qquad$ (by FA)

$= [\![\text{always}]\!]^\emptyset([\![\text{if}]\!]^\emptyset([\![\text{a}]\!]^\emptyset([\![\text{man}]\!]^\emptyset)$

$(\lambda u_6. [\![\text{a}]\!]^{[6\to u_6]}([\![\text{donkey}]\!]^{[6\to u_6]})(\lambda u_2. [\![\text{owns}]\!]^{\left[\begin{smallmatrix}6\to u_6\\2\to u_2\end{smallmatrix}\right]}(u_2)(u_6)))))$

$(\lambda s_8. \iota x \; x$ is a man in s_8 beats in s_8 $\iota x \; x$ is a donkey in $s_8)$ $\qquad$ (by TR)

$= [\![\text{always}]\!]^\emptyset([\![\text{if}]\!]^\emptyset([\![\text{a}]\!]^\emptyset([\![\text{man}]\!]^\emptyset) \, (\lambda u_6. [\![\text{a}]\!]^{[6\to u_6]}([\![\text{donkey}]\!]^{[6\to u_6]})$

$(\lambda u_2. [\lambda u_3. \lambda u_4. \lambda s_9. u_4(s_9) \text{ owns } u_3(s_9) \text{ in } s_9](u_2)(u_6)))))$

$(\lambda s_8. \iota x \; x$ is a man in s_8 beats in s_8 $\iota x \; x$ is a donkey in $s_8)$ $\qquad$ (by Lex)

$= [\![\text{always}]\!]^\emptyset([\![\text{if}]\!]^\emptyset([\![\text{a}]\!]^\emptyset([\![\text{man}]\!]^\emptyset) \, (\lambda u_6. [\![\text{a}]\!]^{[6\to u_6]}([\![\text{donkey}]\!]^{[6\to u_6]})$

$(\lambda u_2. \lambda s_9. u_6(s_9) \text{ owns } u_2(s_9) \text{ in } s_9))))$

$(\lambda s_8. \iota x \; x$ is a man in s_8 beats in s_8 $\iota x \; x$ is a donkey in $s_8)$ $\qquad$ (by λC)

$= [\![\text{always}]\!]^\emptyset([\![\text{if}]\!]^\emptyset([\![\text{a}]\!]^\emptyset([\![\text{man}]\!]^\emptyset)$

$(\lambda u_6. [\lambda f_{\langle\langle s,e\rangle,\langle s,t\rangle\rangle}. \lambda g_{\langle\langle s,e\rangle,\langle s,t\rangle\rangle}. \lambda s_1.$ there is an individual x and a situation s_2 such that s_2 is a minimal situation such that $s_2 \leq s_1$ and $f(\lambda s_5.x)(s_2) = 1$, such that there is a situation s_3 such that $s_3 \leq s_1$ and s_3 is a minimal situation such that $s_2 \leq s_3$ and $g(\lambda s_5.x)(s_3) = 1]$
$(\lambda u_3. \lambda s_6. u_3(s_6)$ is a donkey in $s_6) \, (\lambda u_2. \lambda s_9. u_6(s_9) \text{ owns } u_2(s_9) \text{ in } s_9))))$

$(\lambda s_8. \iota x \; x$ is a man in s_8 beats in s_8 $\iota x \; x$ is a donkey in $s_8)$ $\qquad$ (by Lex)

$= [\![\text{always}]\!]^\emptyset([\![\text{if}]\!]^\emptyset([\![\text{a}]\!]^\emptyset([\![\text{man}]\!]^\emptyset) \, (\lambda u_6. \lambda s_1.$ there is an individual x and a situation s_2 such that s_2 is a minimal situation such that $s_2 \leq s_1$ and $[\lambda u_3. \lambda s_6. u_3(s_6)$ is a donkey in $s_6] \, (\lambda s_5.x)(s_2) = 1$, such that there is a situation s_3 such that $s_3 \leq s_1$ and s_3 is a minimal situation such that $s_2 \leq s_3$ and $[\lambda u_2. \lambda s_9. u_6(s_9) \text{ owns } u_2(s_9) \text{ in } s_9](\lambda s_5.x)(s_3) = 1)))$

$(\lambda s_8. \iota x \; x$ is a man in s_8 beats in s_8 $\iota x \; x$ is a donkey in $s_8)$ $\qquad$ (by λC)

$= [\![\text{always}]\!]^\emptyset([\![\text{if}]\!]^\emptyset([\![\text{a}]\!]^\emptyset([\![\text{man}]\!]^\emptyset) \, (\lambda u_6. \lambda s_1.$ there is an individual x and a situation s_2 such that s_2 is a minimal situation such that $s_2 \leq s_1$ and x is a donkey in s_2, such that there is a situation s_3 such that $s_3 \leq s_1$ and s_3 is a minimal situation such that $s_2 \leq s_3$ and $u_6(s_3)$ owns x in $s_3)))$

$(\lambda s_8. \iota x \; x$ is a man in s_8 beats in s_8 $\iota x \; x$ is a donkey in $s_8)$ $\qquad$ (by λC)

$= [\![\text{always}]\!]^0([\![\text{if}]\!]^0 ([\lambda f_{\langle\langle s,e\rangle,\langle s,t\rangle\rangle}.\,\lambda g_{\langle\langle s,e\rangle,\langle s,t\rangle\rangle}.\,\lambda s_6.$ there is an individual y and a situation s_7 such that s_7 is a minimal situation such that $s_7 \leq s_6$ and $f(\lambda s_5.y)(s_7) = 1$, such that there is a situation s_9 such that $s_9 \leq s_6$ and s_9 is a minimal situation such that $s_7 \leq s_9$ and $g(\lambda s_5.y)(s_9) = 1]$ $(\lambda u_3.\,\lambda s_4.u_3(s_4)$ is man in s_4) $(\lambda u_6.\,\lambda s_1.$ there is an individual x and a situation s_2 such that s_2 is a minimal situation such that $s_2 \leq s_1$ and x is a donkey in s_2, such that there is a situation s_3 such that $s_3 \leq s_1$ and s_3 is a minimal situation such that $s_2 \leq s_3$ and $u_6(s_3)$ owns x in s_3)))

$(\lambda s_8.\,\iota x\ x$ is a man in s_8 beats in $s_8\ \iota x\ x$ is a donkey in s_8)   (by Lex)

$= [\![\text{always}]\!]^0([\![\text{if}]\!]^0 (\lambda s_6.$ there is an individual y and a situation s_7 such that s_7 is a minimal situation such that $s_7 \leq s_6$ and $[\lambda u_3.\,\lambda s_4.u_3(s_4)$ is man in $s_4](\lambda s_5.y)(s_7) = 1$, such that there is a situation s_9 such that $s_9 \leq s_6$ and s_9 is a minimal situation such that $s_7 \leq s_9$ and $[\lambda u_6.\,\lambda s_1.$ there is an individual x and a situation s_2 such that s_2 is a minimal situation such that $s_2 \leq s_1$ and x is a donkey in s_2, such that there is a situation s_3 such that $s_3 \leq s_1$ and s_3 is a minimal situation such that $s_2 \leq s_3$ and $u_6(s_3)$ owns x in $s_3](\lambda s_5.y)(s_9) = 1))$

$(\lambda s_8.\,\iota x\ x$ is a man in s_8 beats in $s_8\ \iota x\ x$ is a donkey in s_8)   (by λC)

$= [\![\text{always}]\!]^0([\![\text{if}]\!]^0 (\lambda s_6.$ there is an individual y and a situation s_7 such that s_7 is a minimal situation such that $s_7 \leq s_6$ and y is man in s_7, such that there is a situation s_9 such that $s_9 \leq s_6$ and s_9 is a minimal situation such that $s_7 \leq s_9$ and there is an individual x and a situation s_2 such that s_2 is a minimal situation such that $s_2 \leq s_9$ and x is a donkey in s_2, such that there is a situation s_3 such that $s_3 \leq s_9$ and s_3 is a minimal situation such that $s_2 \leq s_3$ and y owns x in s_3))

$(\lambda s_8.\,\iota x\ x$ is a man in s_8 beats in $s_8\ \iota x\ x$ is a donkey in s_8)   (by λC)

$= [\![\text{always}]\!]^0([\lambda p_{\langle s,t\rangle}.\,p](\lambda s_6.$ there is an individual y and a situation s_7 such that s_7 is a minimal situation such that $s_7 \leq s_6$ and y is man in s_7, such that there is a situation s_9 such that $s_9 \leq s_6$ and s_9 is a minimal situation such that $s_7 \leq s_9$ and there is an individual x and a situation s_2 such that s_2 is a minimal situation such that $s_2 \leq s_9$ and x is a donkey in s_2, such that there is a situation s_3 such that $s_3 \leq s_9$ and s_3 is a minimal situation such that $s_2 \leq s_3$ and y owns x in s_3))

$(\lambda s_8.\,\iota x\ x$ is a man in s_8 beats in $s_8\ \iota x\ x$ is a donkey in s_8)   (by Lex)

$= [\![\text{always}]\!]^0(\lambda s_6.$ there is an individual y and a situation s_7 such that s_7 is a minimal situation such that $s_7 \leq s_6$ and y is man in s_7, such that there is a situation s_9 such that $s_9 \leq s_6$ and s_9 is a minimal situation such that $s_7 \leq s_9$ and there is an individual x and a situation s_2 such that s_2 is a minimal situation such that $s_2 \leq s_9$ and x is a donkey in s_2,

such that there is a situation s_3 such that $s_3 \leq s_9$ and s_3 is a minimal
situation such that $s_2 \leq s_3$ and y owns x in s_3)

$(\lambda s_8.\, \iota x\ x$ is a man in s_8 beats in $s_8\ \iota x\ x$ is a donkey in s_8)   (by λC)

$= [\lambda p_{\langle s,t \rangle}.\, \lambda q_{\langle s,t \rangle}.\, \lambda s_1.$ for every minimal situation s_4 such that $s_4 \leq s_1$
and $p(s_4) = 1$, there is a situation s_5 such that $s_5 \leq s_1$ and s_5 is a
minimal situation such that $s_4 \leq s_5$ and $q(s_5) = 1] (\lambda s_6.$ there is an
individual y and a situation s_7 such that s_7 is a minimal situation
such that $s_7 \leq s_6$ and y is man in s_7, such that there is a situation s_9
such that $s_9 \leq s_6$ and s_9 is a minimal situation such that $s_7 \leq s_9$ and
there is an individual x and a situation s_2 such that s_2 is a minimal
situation such that $s_2 \leq s_9$ and x is a donkey in s_2, such that there is a
situation s_3 such that $s_3 \leq s_9$ and s_3 is a minimal situation such that
$s_2 \leq s_3$ and y owns x in s_3)

$(\lambda s_8.\, \iota x\ x$ is a man in s_8 beats in $s_8\ \iota x\ x$ is a donkey in s_8)   (by Lex)

$= \lambda s_1.$ for every minimal situation s_4 such that

$s_4 \leq s_1$ and there is an individual y and a situation s_7 such
that s_7 is a minimal situation such that $s_7 \leq s_4$ and y is man
in s_7, such that there is a situation s_9 such that $s_9 \leq s_4$ and s_9
is a minimal situation such that $s_7 \leq s_9$ and there is an
individual x and a situation s_2 such that s_2 is a minimal
situation such that $s_2 \leq s_9$ and x is a donkey in s_2, such that
there is a situation s_3 such that $s_3 \leq s_9$ and s_3 is a minimal
situation such that $s_2 \leq s_3$ and y owns x in s_3,

there is a situation s_5 such that

$s_5 \leq s_1$ and s_5 is a minimal situation such that $s_4 \leq s_5$ and
$\iota x\ x$ is a man in s_5 beats in $s_5\ \iota x\ x$ is a donkey in s_5 (by λC)

B.2   A Relative-Clause Donkey Sentence

There follows a calculation establishing the truth conditions for a donkey
sentence containing a QP and relative clause. See section 2.3.2.

$[\![[[$every $[$man $[$who $[\lambda_6\ [[$a donkey$]\ [\lambda_2\ [t_6$ owns $t_2]]]]]]]\ [$beats $[$it
donkey$]]]]]^0$

$= [\![$every$]\!]^0\ ([\![[$man $[$who $[\lambda_6\ [[$a donkey$]\ [\lambda_2\ [t_6$ owns $t_2]]]]]]]]\!]^0)$
$\quad ([\![$beats$]\!]^0([\![$it$]\!]^0\ ([\![$donkey$]\!]^0)))$ (by FA)

$= [\![$every$]\!]^0\ ([\![[$man $[$who $[\lambda_6\ [[$a donkey$]\ [\lambda_2\ [t_6$ owns $t_2]]]]]]]]\!]^0)$
$\quad ([\lambda u_1.\, \lambda u_2.\, \lambda s_8.\, u_2(s_8)$ beats in $s_8\ u_1(s_8)]$
$\quad ([\lambda f_{\langle\langle s,e\rangle,\langle s,t\rangle\rangle}.\, \lambda s_7 : \exists! x\, f(\lambda s_9.x)(s_7) = 1.\, \iota x\, f(\lambda s_9.x)(s_7) = 1]$
$\quad (\lambda u_3.\, \lambda s_6.\, u_3(s_6)$ is a donkey in $s_6)))$ (by Lex)

$= [\![\text{every}]\!]^0 \, ([\![[\text{man } [\text{who } [\lambda_6 \, [[\text{a donkey}] \, [\lambda_2 \, [t_6 \text{ owns } t_2]]]]]]]\!]^0)$
$([\lambda u_1. \, \lambda u_2. \, \lambda s_8. \, u_2(s_8) \text{ beats in } s_8 \, u_1(s_8)]$
$(\lambda s_7 : \exists! x \, x \text{ is a donkey in } s_7. \, \iota x \, x \text{ is a donkey in } s_7))$ (by λC)

$= [\![\text{every}]\!]^0 \, ([\![[\text{man } [\text{who } [\lambda_6 \, [[\text{a donkey}] \, [\lambda_2 \, [t_6 \text{ owns } t_2]]]]]]]\!]^0)$
$(\lambda u_2. \, \lambda s_8. \, u_2(s_8) \text{ beats in } s_8 \, \iota x \, x \text{ is a donkey in } s_8)$ (by λC)

$= [\![\text{every}]\!]^0 \, (\lambda u_1. \, \lambda s_7. \, [\![\text{man}]\!]^0(u_1)(s_7) = 1 \text{ and}$
$[\![[\text{who } [\lambda_6 \, [[\text{a donkey}] \, [\lambda_2 \, [t_6 \text{ owns } t_2]]]]]]\!]^0(u_1)(s_7) = 1)$
$(\lambda u_2. \, \lambda s_8. \, u_2(s_8) \text{ beats in } s_8 \, \iota x \, x \text{ is a donkey in } s_8)$ (by PM)

$= [\![\text{every}]\!]^0 \, (\lambda u_1. \, \lambda s_7. \, [\lambda u_3. \, \lambda s_3. u_3(s_3) \text{ is man in } s_3](u_1)(s_7) = 1 \text{ and}$
$[\![[\text{who } [\lambda_6 \, [[\text{a donkey}] \, [\lambda_2 \, [t_6 \text{ owns } t_2]]]]]]\!]^0(u_1)(s_7) = 1)$
$(\lambda u_2. \, \lambda s_8. \, u_2(s_8) \text{ beats in } s_8 \, \iota x \, x \text{ is a donkey in } s_8)$ (by Lex)

$= [\![\text{every}]\!]^0 \, (\lambda u_1. \, \lambda s_7. \, u_1(s_7) \text{ is a man in } s_7 \text{ and}$
$[\![[\text{who } [\lambda_6 \, [[\text{a donkey}] \, [\lambda_2 \, [t_6 \text{ owns } t_2]]]]]]\!]^0(u_1)(s_7) = 1)$
$(\lambda u_2. \, \lambda s_8. \, u_2(s_8) \text{ beats in } s_8 \, \iota x \, x \text{ is a donkey in } s_8)$ (by λC)

$= [\![\text{every}]\!]^0 \, (\lambda u_1. \, \lambda s_7. \, u_1(s_7) \text{ is a man in } s_7 \text{ and}$
$[\![[\lambda_6 \, [[\text{a donkey}] \, [\lambda_2 \, [t_6 \text{ owns } t_2]]]]]\!]^0(u_1)(s_7) = 1)$
$(\lambda u_2. \, \lambda s_8. \, u_2(s_8) \text{ beats in } s_8 \, \iota x \, x \text{ is a donkey in } s_8)$ (by Lex)

$= [\![\text{every}]\!]^0 \, (\lambda u_1. \, \lambda s_7. \, u_1(s_7) \text{ is a man in } s_7 \text{ and}$
$\lambda u_6. [\![[[\text{a donkey}] \, [\lambda_2 \, [t_6 \text{ owns } t_2]]]]\!]^{[6 \to u_6]}(u_1)(s_7) = 1)$
$(\lambda u_2. \, \lambda s_8. \, u_2(s_8) \text{ beats in } s_8 \, \iota x \, x \text{ is a donkey in } s_8)$ (by PA)

$= [\![\text{every}]\!]^0 \, (\lambda u_1. \, \lambda s_7. \, u_1(s_7) \text{ is a man in } s_7 \text{ and}$
$[\![[[\text{a donkey}] \, [\lambda_2 \, [t_6 \text{ owns } t_2]]]]\!]^{[6 \to u_1]}(s_7) = 1)$
$(\lambda u_2. \, \lambda s_8. \, u_2(s_8) \text{ beats in } s_8 \, \iota x \, x \text{ is a donkey in } s_8)$ (by λC)

$= [\![\text{every}]\!]^0 \, (\lambda u_1. \, \lambda s_7. \, u_1(s_7) \text{ is a man in } s_7 \text{ and}$
$[\![[\text{a}]\!]^{[6 \to u_1]}([\![\text{donkey}]\!]^{[6 \to u_1]})([\![\lambda_2 \, [t_6 \text{ owns } t_2]]\!]^{[6 \to u_1]})](s_7) = 1)$
$(\lambda u_2. \, \lambda s_8. \, u_2(s_8) \text{ beats in } s_8 \, \iota x \, x \text{ is a donkey in } s_8)$ (by FA)

$= [\![\text{every}]\!]^0 \, (\lambda u_1. \, \lambda s_7. \, u_1(s_7) \text{ is a man in } s_7 \text{ and}$

$[\![[\text{a}]\!]^{[6 \to u_1]}([\![\text{donkey}]\!]^{[6 \to u_1]})(\lambda u_4. [\![t_6 \text{ owns } t_2]\!]^{\left[\begin{smallmatrix}6 \to u_1\\2 \to u_4\end{smallmatrix}\right]})](s_7) = 1)$
$(\lambda u_2. \, \lambda s_8. \, u_2(s_8) \text{ beats in } s_8 \, \iota x \, x \text{ is a donkey in } s_8)$ (by PA)

$= [\![\text{every}]\!]^0 \, (\lambda u_1. \, \lambda s_7. \, u_1(s_7) \text{ is a man in } s_7 \text{ and}$
$[\![[\text{a}]\!]^{[6 \to u_1]}([\![\text{donkey}]\!]^{[6 \to u_1]})$

$(\lambda u_4. [\![\text{owns}]\!]^{\left[\begin{smallmatrix}6 \to u_1\\2 \to u_4\end{smallmatrix}\right]}([\![t_2]\!]^{\left[\begin{smallmatrix}6 \to u_1\\2 \to u_4\end{smallmatrix}\right]})([\![t_6]\!]^{\left[\begin{smallmatrix}6 \to u_1\\2 \to u_4\end{smallmatrix}\right]})))](s_7) = 1)$
$(\lambda u_2. \, \lambda s_8. \, u_2(s_8) \text{ beats in } s_8 \, \iota x \, x \text{ is a donkey in } s_8)$ (by FA)

$= [\![\text{every}]\!]^0 \, (\lambda u_1. \, \lambda s_7. \, u_1(s_7) \text{ is a man in } s_7 \text{ and}$
$[\![[\text{a}]\!]^{[6 \to u_1]}([\![\text{donkey}]\!]^{[6 \to u_1]})$

$(\lambda u_4. [\![\text{owns}]\!]^{\left[\begin{smallmatrix}6 \to u_1\\2 \to u_4\end{smallmatrix}\right]}(u_4)(u_1)))](s_7) = 1)$
$(\lambda u_2. \, \lambda s_8. \, u_2(s_8) \text{ beats in } s_8 \, \iota x \, x \text{ is a donkey in } s_8)$ (by TR)

$= [\![\text{every}]\!]^{\emptyset} \, (\lambda u_1. \lambda s_7. u_1(s_7) \text{ is a man in } s_7 \text{ and}$
$[[\text{a}]\!]^{[6 \to u_1]} ([\![\text{donkey}]\!]^{[6 \to u_1]})$
$(\lambda u_4. [\lambda u_5. \lambda u_6. \lambda s_9. u_6(s_9) \text{ owns } u_5(s_9) \text{ in } s_9](u_4)(u_1))](s_7) = 1)$
$(\lambda u_2. \lambda s_8. u_2(s_8) \text{ beats in } s_8 \; \iota x \; x \text{ is a donkey in } s_8)$ (by Lex)
$= [\![\text{every}]\!]^{\emptyset} \, (\lambda u_1. \lambda s_7. u_1(s_7) \text{ is a man in } s_7 \text{ and}$
$[[\text{a}]\!]^{[6 \to u_1]} ([\![\text{donkey}]\!]^{[6 \to u_1]})$
$(\lambda u_4. \lambda s_9. u_1(s_9) \text{ owns } u_4(s_9) \text{ in } s_9)](s_7) = 1)$
$(\lambda u_2. \lambda s_8. u_2(s_8) \text{ beats in } s_8 \; \iota x \; x \text{ is a donkey in } s_8)$ (by λC)
$= [\![\text{every}]\!]^{\emptyset} \, (\lambda u_1. \lambda s_7. u_1(s_7) \text{ is a man in } s_7 \text{ and}$
$[[\lambda f_{\langle\langle s, e\rangle, \langle s, t\rangle\rangle}. \lambda g_{\langle\langle s, e\rangle, \langle s, t\rangle\rangle}. \lambda s_1. \text{ there is an individual } x \text{ and a}$
situation s_2 such that s_2 is a minimal situation such that $s_2 \le s_1$ and
$f(\lambda s_5.x)(s_2) = 1$, such that there is a situation s_3 such that $s_3 \le s_1$ and
s_3 is a minimal situation such that $s_2 \le s_3$ and $g(\lambda s_5.x)(s_3) = 1]$
$(\lambda u_3. \lambda s_6. u_3(s_6) \text{ is a donkey in } s_6) \, (\lambda u_4. \lambda s_9. u_1(s_9) \text{ owns } u_4(s_9) \text{ in } s_9)]$
$(s_7) = 1)$
$(\lambda u_2. \lambda s_8. u_2(s_8) \text{ beats in } s_8 \; \iota x \; x \text{ is a donkey in } s_8)$ (by Lex)
$= [\![\text{every}]\!]^{\emptyset} \, (\lambda u_1. \lambda s_7. u_1(s_7) \text{ is a man in } s_7 \text{ and } [\lambda s_1. \text{ there is an individual}$
x and a situation s_2 such that s_2 is a minimal situation such that
$s_2 \le s_1$ and x is a donkey in s_2, such that there is a situation s_3 such
that $s_3 \le s_1$ and s_3 is a minimal situation such that $s_2 \le s_3$ and $u_1(s_3)$
owns x in $s_3](s_7) = 1)$
$(\lambda u_2. \lambda s_8. u_2(s_8) \text{ beats in } s_8 \; \iota x \; x \text{ is a donkey in } s_8)$ (by λC)
$= [\![\text{every}]\!]^{\emptyset} \, (\lambda u_1. \lambda s_7. u_1(s_7) \text{ is a man in } s_7 \text{ and there is an individual } x$
and a situation s_2 such that s_2 is a minimal situation such that $s_2 \le s_7$
and x is a donkey in s_2, such that there is a situation s_3 such that
$s_3 \le s_7$ and s_3 is a minimal situation such that $s_2 \le s_3$ and $u_1(s_3)$ owns
x in $s_3) \, (\lambda u_2. \lambda s_8. u_2(s_8) \text{ beats in } s_8 \; \iota x \; x \text{ is a donkey in } s_8)$ (by λC)
$= [\lambda f_{\langle\langle s, e\rangle, \langle s, t\rangle\rangle}. \lambda g_{\langle\langle s, e\rangle, \langle s, t\rangle\rangle}. \lambda s_4. \text{ for every individual } y: \text{ for every}$
minimal situation s_5 such that $s_5 \le s_4$ and $f(\lambda s_1.y)(s_5) = 1$, there is a
situation s_6 such that $s_6 \le s_4$ and s_6 is a minimal situation such that
$s_5 \le s_6$ and $g(\lambda s_1.y)(s_6) = 1] \, (\lambda u_1. \lambda s_7. u_1(s_7) \text{ is a man in } s_7 \text{ and there}$
is an individual x and a situation s_2 such that s_2 is a minimal situation
such that $s_2 \le s_7$ and x is a donkey in s_2, such that there is a situation
s_3 such that $s_3 \le s_7$ and s_3 is a minimal situation such that $s_2 \le s_3$ and
$u_1(s_3)$ owns x in $s_3)$
$(\lambda u_2. \lambda s_8. u_2(s_8) \text{ beats in } s_8 \; \iota z \; z \text{ is a donkey in } s_8)$ (by Lex)
$= \lambda s_4. \text{ for every individual } y: \text{ for every minimal situation } s_5 \text{ such that}$
$s_5 \le s_4$ and $[\lambda u_1. \lambda s_7. u_1(s_7) \text{ is a man in } s_7 \text{ and there is an individual } x$
and x is a donkey in s_2, such that there is a situation s_3 such that

$s_3 \leq s_7$ and s_3 is a minimal situation such that $s_2 \leq s_3$ and $u_1(s_3)$ owns x in $s_3](\lambda s_1.y)(s_5) = 1$, there is a situation s_6 such that $s_6 \leq s_4$ and s_6 is a minimal situation such that $s_5 \leq s_6$ and $[\lambda u_2. \lambda s_8. u_2(s_8)$ beats in s_8 $\imath z$ z is a donkey in $s_8](\lambda s_1.y)(s_6) = 1$ (by λC)

$= \lambda s_4.$ for every individual y:

> for every minimal situation s_5 such that
>
> > $s_5 \leq s_4$ and y is a man in s_5 and there is an individual x and a situation s_2 such that s_2 is a minimal situation such that $s_2 \leq s_5$ and x is a donkey in s_2, such that there is a situation s_3 such that $s_3 \leq s_5$ and s_3 is a minimal situation such that $s_2 \leq s_3$ and y owns x in s_3,
>
> there is a situation s_6 such that
>
> > $s_6 \leq s_4$ and s_6 is a minimal situation such that $s_5 \leq s_6$ and y beats in s_6 $\imath z$ z is a donkey in s_6 (by λC)

Notes

Chapter 1

1. I suppose that simple and complex demonstratives are to be assimilated to definite descriptions. See Neale 1993 for this proposal with respect to complex demonstratives, and King 2001 for a treatment of simple and complex demonstratives that has them resemble Russellian definite descriptions. See also section 3.5.1 in the present work.

2. Variable binding is used for this purpose even for the so-called variable-free semantics explored in connection with Categorial Grammar. In this approach, it is true that what we call bound pronouns are not given the semantics of individual variables—rather, they are translated as the identity function over individuals. But the overall representation for such sentences still ends up modeling the covariation by variable binding. It just gets there by a more circuitous route, as it were. See section 1.5 for further discussion. A possible exception to the generalization is Steedman 2000, where a lot of semantic work is done by combinators, and it is claimed that lambda calculus is used only in the domain of the word, to ensure that arguments are inserted into predicate-argument structures (Steedman 2000, 38). But Steedman does not attempt to produce an explicit account of long-distance pronominal binding with his limited mechanisms (Steedman 2000, 75).

3. Actually, Geach's example was *Any man who owns a donkey beats* (1962, section 72), but this has been tacitly emended ever since, presumably because people working on donkey anaphora have enough on their minds already without adding free-choice *any* to their troubles.

4. There seems to be no good name that encompasses all the theories that fall under this heading, which is my own, hopefully bland and inoffensive, coinage. The term *E-type analysis* is sometimes used loosely to denote what I am calling the description-theoretic approach, but this can lead to confusion since this term is also used to refer to the particular version of the description-theoretic approach proposed by Evans (1977, 1980). I will follow the more restrictive usage and will reserve *E-type analysis* for Evans's theory.

5. This definition comes from a letter from Kripke to David Kaplan, cited on page 569 of Kaplan 1989a.

6. I am here indebted to the lucid discussion in Neale 1990, 185–191, which should be consulted for more details.

7. Why should (11) only have a *de re* reading? This presumably has something to do with the fact that the descriptive content *who murdered Smith* is omitted, and thus John is free to think of the man in other ways. But we need to find a way of preventing the incomplete definite description from being understood as "the man who murdered Smith," which will not be easy to come by on all contemporary theories of incompleteness. In particular, it looks as if what Neale (1990, 95) calls the *explicit approach*, whereby the overt descriptive content in a definite description is supplemented with more linguistic or quasi-linguistic descriptive content, might have trouble in ruling out a reading of (11) whereby it is straightforwardly equivalent to (7b) and thus predicted to be ambiguous. More work is needed here.

8. On the Fregean view, definite descriptions presuppose that exactly one thing satisfies their predicate. On the Russellian view, they assert this. See chapter 3 for an argument against the Russellian and in favor of the Fregean view.

9. Possibly the earliest example of this type is Barbara Partee's (i), cited as a personal communication by Heim (1982, 21).

(i) I dropped ten marbles and found only nine of them. ??It is probably under the sofa.

10. I am not including the problem of distinguishing and predicting so-called weak and strong readings among the problems facing the D-type analysis, since my major concern is to distinguish between description-theoretic and dynamic theories, and the problem of weak and strong readings affects both. For discussion from differing theoretical perspectives, see Heim 1990, 148–158; Chierchia 1995, 62–72, 110–120; Schein 2001.

11. I will consider the work of Kurafuji (1998, 1999), who might be read as alleging something of this type for Japanese, in section 1.4.2. I will argue that his results do not establish this.

12. My introductory exposition of DPL will naturally owe much to the corresponding sections (2.2–2.5) in Groenendijk and Stokhof's (1991) article.

13. Henceforth, such calculations will be banished to appendixes. By "by =", I mean "by the principle of the substitutability of identicals."

14. See further the discussion of example (120) in section 2.7.2.

15. These particular examples are both from Cooper 1979. An early version of (44) was given in Karttunen 1969.

16. This would also account for the problems of disjunctive antecedents and deep anaphora, as remarked above.

17. This was tacitly incorporated in the rule for universal quantification given in (35). The trick to making an operator externally static is to make its semantic value such that the output assignments in each ordered pair in the set are the same as the input assignments: $\{\langle g, h \rangle \mid h = g \ldots\}$. Thus no variables introduced by existential quantifiers within the scope of such an operator have a chance of being carried over into the evaluation of clauses outside its scope.

18. Working in a D-type framework, Heim had previously likened D-type anaphora to ellipsis in her 1990 article. I myself will make heavy use of a variant of this idea in chapter 2.

19. For expositions of the general approach, readers are referred not only to Jacobson 2000a, but also to Jacobson 1996 and 1999.

20. For brevity of exposition, I will abstract away from the syntactic framework, Combinatory Categorial Grammar, in which she embeds her account. All the semantic composition needed for the present discussion is compatible with various syntactic theories.

Chapter 2

1. This proposal is related to but distinct from that of von Fintel (1994), who suggests that at LF pronouns can be rewritten as $[_{DP}$ the $[f_i^n [v_1 \ldots v_n]]]$, where f_i^n is a variable of the type of an n-place function with range of type $\langle e, t \rangle$, and where $v_1 \ldots v_n$ are variables of the appropriate types (von Fintel 1994, 156). Von Fintel proposed in his dissertation that all quantifiers have a hidden "resource domain argument" that intersects with the overt restrictor, implementing the covert narrowing of the domain of quantification produced by pragmatic factors, so the LF-fragment above can naturally be regarded as the expected semantic representation of the definite article on his view. The crucial difference between his proposal and mine, then, is the origin of the function of type $\langle e, t \rangle$, which forms the sister to the definite article in the semantics: von Fintel has it be a contextually salient function assigned to the variable f in the normal way. See section 2.4 for an argument against this. The present proposal is also closely related to one made by Heim (1990): see section 2.4.2. Another precedent is Jacobson's 1977 dissertation, where she argued that one of the pronouns in Bach-Peters sentences derives from an underlying full DP by the old pronominalization transformation. (She does not have the contribution of the pronoun be a definite article alone, as I do, but both of us would analyze one of the pronouns in Bach-Peters sentences as being a full DP semantically.)

2. We can add that *me* could be used in the same way in Early Modern English. See the following line from Shakespeare, *Love's Labour's Lost*: "That you three fools lacked me fool to make up the mess" (act 4, scene 3, line 204).

3. In this paragraph I presuppose some familiarity with the lattice-theoretic analysis of plurality of Link 1983. Briefly, a sum of individuals is a plural individual, an individual that is still of type e but that has other individuals as its parts.

4. Prominent references include Stockwell, Schachter, and Partee 1973; Abney 1987; Longobardi 1994; Uriagereka 1995.

5. There are some further remarks on this topic in section 2.7.2.

6. Lasnik and Saito (1992, 160–161) claim that NP-deletion is like VP-ellipsis in that it always requires a linguistic antecedent. (The corresponding demonstration for VP-ellipsis was made by Hankamer and Sag (1976).) Lasnik and Saito reject the possibility of aid from the immediate physical environment of the sort that I allow. In their example, Lasnik and Saito are in a yard filled with barking

domestic canines. Neither has spoken. They claim that it is distinctly odd for Lasnik to begin a conversation at this point by saying, "Harry's is particularly noisy," meaning that Harry's dog is particularly noisy. On the other hand, they go on, it is perfectly felicitous for him to make that comment if Saito has just said something like, "These dogs keep me awake at night with all their barking." I fear I must dispute their data, however. In an informal poll of six native speakers of English, all six found the first, allegedly bad, conversational opener quite felicitous.

7. I am unconvinced by the theory of Lobeck (1995, 85–96). Her general claim is that ellipsis is licensed in a position if it is governed by a head that bears strong morphology, the latter being defined as "productive morphological realization of features from which a significant proportion of the referential content of non-arbitrary *pro* is recovered" (Lobeck 1995, 15). The behavior of *every* is explained by positing a "strong" feature [partitive], which indicates the ability of a determiner to take part in a partitive construction: determiners apart from *every* have it, and thus license ellipsis of their NP complements, while *every* does not. This is entirely ad hoc, however, and indeed self-contradictory: the new feature simply does not fit the definition of "strong" morphology used elsewhere in Lobeck's book.

8. I argued exactly this in Elbourne 2001a, an earlier version of this chapter, where I noted that Yang (1999) had already proposed the same thing for independent reasons.

9. I am grateful to Uli Sauerland for alerting me to this point.

10. Noam Chomsky (personal communication) maintains that this conception of a thin particular cannot be the appropriate one for linguistics, because we can talk about entities like numbers that do not seem to occupy any space-time area. I think this is correct. Armstrong's metaphysics is not thereby undermined, since Armstrong, as a materialist, will presumably wish to say that no individuals exist that do not occupy space-time areas. But as linguists we must recognize that, even if materialism is in fact the correct account of the world, speakers do entertain ideas and formulate sentences about entities that do not (according to their thoughts) have the normal kind of spatial and temporal properties. In discussing the quasi-ontological foundations of a semantic system, we are not engaged in metaphysics but in "natural language metaphysics" (Bach 1989, 98). For relevant discussion, see Barwise and Perry 1983, 58–60; Bach 1989; Gamut 1991, chap. 3. I leave it as an open question whether any further linguistic account can be given of a thin particular beyond "a particular taken in abstraction from all its properties."

11. I follow Heim and Kratzer 1998 in assuming that movement creates objects like λ_2 in the syntax, which will be interpreted by the predicate-abstraction rule given above.

12. I followed the Heim 1990 approach in my earlier published work on this subject: Elbourne 2000, 2001a, 2001b, 2001c, 2001d.

13. In her 1990 paper, Heim sometimes had pronouns be functions that took individuals as arguments too.

14. An alternative hypothesis is that the denotation of the nuclear scope is actually a so-called structured proposition, in which the denotations of the definites are genuinely isolable. A semantic rule could plausibly operate on something like that in order to change the situation variables on the definites. I will not investigate this hypothesis any further here.

15. I am grateful to Daniel Büring for pointing out this fact to me.

16. A nonmaximal quantifier is one whose semantics does not involve exhaustiveness by some definition. Examples of maximal quantifiers, according to Neale, are *all*, *every*, and *the*.

17. I do not examine the corresponding examples with a generalized quantifier as the subject of the ellipsis sentence (as in (i)), because it seems that there is no trouble on any theory in arriving at their attested sloppy readings.

(i) In this town, every farmer who owns a donkey beats it, and every priest who
    owns a donkey does too.   (sloppy, strict)

We need only suppose that *beats it* in the first sentence can serve as antecedent for ellipsis of *beats it* in the second, which is then interpreted normally. This extends to sentences like (ii).

(ii) In this town, every farmer who owns a donkey beats it, and every priest does
     too.   (sloppy, strict)

We need only suppose that *who owns a donkey* is understood (by ellipsis or accommodation) after *priest*, and this is reduced to the last case.

18. Note that in a simple example of a sloppy reading like *John talks to his dog and Bill does too*, we have no difficulty going along with the supposition that Bill owns a dog. Example (72a) behaves just the same as simpler examples.

19. The only difference here is that a minority of native speakers do report a sloppy reading in (73b). Most speakers I have obtained judgments from, however, find that the sloppy reading is impossible here. Given the fact that the judgment in (72b) is very sharp and is shared by all speakers, I think the best way to make sense out of the apparent dialect divergence over (73b) is to say that those who report a sloppy reading of this sentence are engaging in some extralinguistic reconstruction of what they think might be meant. (This kind of thing goes on all the time, of course, to a certain extent.) The process would be similar to the process that takes place when speakers are confronted with (i).

(i) Every farmer who owns a donkey beats it, and the same can be said of the
    priest.

Here there seems to be a process of working out what is meant by *the same* (beating the farmers' donkeys? beating the donkeys he owns?) that is rather conscious. I conjecture that some speakers engage in a similar process when confronted with the admittedly unlovely (73b). The judgment that reflects the nature of VP-ellipsis, then, is the judgment of the majority of speakers, namely, that a sloppy reading is not possible.

20. There is in fact one more complication in the data, which I will examine in section 2.5.3.

21. Alternatively, one could claim that this universal quantificational force is part of the semantics, or a consequence of the semantics, of certain tenses, such as the simple present tense in English. For present purposes the exact mechanism here does not matter.

22. Fox (2000, 49–53) also discusses this point. Sabine Iatridou (personal communication) has questioned this principle, pointing out that it is difficult if not impossible to have *him* bound by *every man* in (i).

(i) Every man kissed Mary and Mary kissed him.

I agree with the judgment, but I would point out that with more context, binding into the second conjunct becomes possible:

(ii) Every man who entered her office kissed Mary and then Mary kissed him
      before he left.

In constructing (ii), I strove to create a context that favored the interpretation that Mary's kissing was interspersed with the men's kissing. The difficulty in obtaining the bound interpretation in (i) seems to be connected to the difficulty of construing it this way.

23. I am grateful to Kai von Fintel for this example.

24. Danny Fox (personal communication) draws my attention to the following additional problem concerning strict and sloppy identity: according to the present theory, it seems as though (i) should have a sloppy reading, by means of the LF in (ii), but it does not.

(i) If a farmer owns a [donkey he hates], he beats it and the priest does too.

(ii) he beats [it [donkey he hates]] and the priest beats [it [donkey he hates]]

However, note that the following parallel sentence with overt NP-deletion also does not easily have a sloppy reading.

(iii) If a farmer owns some donkeys he hates, he beats some, and the priest does
       too.

There is no problem for the NP-deletion theory of donkey anaphora, then, since it just predicts that (i) will behave like (iii); it is puzzling, though, that (iii) should lack a sloppy reading.

25. Gawron (1996, 249) uses the term *quantificational subordination* to refer to an example in which a pronoun is in the scope of a quantificational adverb whose restrictor is understood from material in the previous sentence. But this in my view falls under what Roberts (1989, 1996) calls *modal subordination*, since I follow those who analyze quantificational adverbs as involving quantification over situations. Gawron ultimately analyzes his example by means of a dynamic logic.

26. Before I leave this topic, it is worth noting that forms like *a book of John's* and *that book of John's* pose a difficulty for one aspect of the specific proposal that Larson and Cho (1999) present. They have *John's car* derive from the underlying structure in (i).

(i) [$_{D'}$ THE [$_{PP}$ [$_{NP}$ car][$_{P'}$ TO [$_{DP}$ John]]]]

Here, TO is an abstract morpheme indicating possession, and THE is the (semantic features of the) definite article; *John* raises to [Spec, DP] and TO incorporates into THE, *'s* being the spell-out of TO + THE. We see, however, that *'s* is quite possible even when the determiner is *not* THE.

27. The same problem was presented by example (42) in section 1.4.2.

28. I am not sure of the origin of this idea. For theoretical discussion, see van Benthem (1995), who does not doubt the existence of the operation but finds it impossible to fit into his otherwise elegant theory of what type-shifting operations are available (given a Categorial Grammar framework that makes heavy use of such operations).

29. This example was brought to my attention by Alexander Williams at WCCFL XIX.

30. Generally speaking, Tomioka sentences are conjunctions of sentences characterized as follows: the first sentence has a VP that, first, contains a D-type pronoun anaphoric to a preceding indefinite, and, second, serves as antecedent for an elided VP in the following sentence in such a way that the descriptive content of the pronoun understood in the elided VP comes from the second sentence, not the first. I am grateful to Dan Hardt, Bernhard Schwarz, Satoshi Tomioka, and an anonymous *Natural Language Semantics* reviewer for independently advising me of the relevance of these sentences to my theory.

Chapter 3

1. It is seldom, if ever, made clear what the indices used for reference and binding are supposed to be in the context of linguistic theory. Are they pieces of lexical material of the normal kind? If so, why do we not assign them semantic types and worry about their compatibility with their sisters or other syntactic neighbors? If not, what are they? I think that people should either abolish indices altogether or be explicit about what they are. The present system is one way of biting the bullet and being fully explicit on this question.

2. This is a return to the notation of Heim 1993, which is the first place, as far as I know, where the basics of the system in Heim and Kratzer 1998 were introduced.

3. These combinatorially complex traces may appear to be a disadvantage of the current approach, but in fact the technology introduced here will offer a considerable simplification of the mechanisms for producing traces when we get to the copy theory. See section 3.5. Note also a typological convention: I will write the normal English definite article in lowercase, and other postulated definite articles with the same or similar semantics in small capitals. There will be two of these latter definite articles: the ones used in traces, and ones used in conjunction with proper names in chapter 6. This practice should be taken to be neutral with regard to the question of whether the pronounced and unpronounced definite articles are really different lexical items. In the case of traces, at least, there are presumably independent reasons why the normal *the*, if it was inserted in them, could not be pronounced.

4. There is a question as to whether all binding is done by movement—that is, by the introduction by movement of the lambda abstractors that feature in the predicate-abstraction rules. A strong, and still viable, hypothesis says that this is the case, and that apparent binding by relative pronouns, for example, arises by these items moving. I will tentatively assume this hypothesis to be correct, although it would be possible for me to retreat to a weaker one simply by allowing lambda abstractors to be introduced in other ways.

5. Excellent critical surveys of this literature and the major issues therein are available in Heim 1991 and Larson and Segal 1995 (chap. 9). For an anthology containing a good sampling, see Ostertag 1998.

6. In common with most discussions of the definite article, mine will not deal with plural NP complements. The lexical entries given here will ultimately have to be reformulated so as to deal with plurality. See Link 1983 for a first approach. Note also that (14) has to be complicated for use in intensional systems: see (37) below.

7. Note that the difference does not lie in whether or not the definite article is a quantifier. If by *quantifier* we just mean a word that takes as arguments two expressions denoting sets and contributes a relation between them, there is no difficulty in writing an entry for the Fregean definite article that is a quantifier: $\lambda f : f \in D_{\langle e,t \rangle} \,\&\, \exists ! x\, f(x) = 1 . \lambda g : g \in D_{\langle e,t \rangle} . g(\iota x\, f(x) = 1) = 1$. Note, however, that it is impossible for the combination of Russellian definite article plus NP to be of type e; see Heim 1991, section 3.

8. It should also be noted that progress has recently been made on the following controversy. One might attempt to argue that, since most people disagree with Russell's judgment that (i) is straightforwardly false, and evince instead a reaction more compatible with its failing to express a proposition at all, Russell's original motivation for his existential analysis is simply wrong.

(i) The King of France is bald.

However, it is known that if we change the example to one like (ii), people do judge it straightforwardly false, which seems to lend support to the Russellian analysis.

(ii) My friend went for a drive with the King of France last week.

But von Fintel (2004) has recently argued convincingly that a Fregean analysis can deal with (ii), meaning that Frege has an advantage here.

9. We could also obtain the *de re* reading by means of the following indexing:

(i) $[\lambda w_1$ Mary believes w_1 $[\lambda w_2[[\text{her [neighbor } w_1]] \text{ [is a spy } w_2]]]]$

It is unclear to me whether we should allow such long-distance binding of world variables in the syntax. It certainly makes some predictions that are incorrect. Take the following LF, which features binding of this kind:

(ii) $[\lambda w_1$ Mary thinks w_1 $[\lambda w_2$ John believes w_2 $[\lambda w_3$ [his neighbor w_2 is a spy $w_3]]]]$

A speaker uttering this LF would accurately describe the following scenario: Bill is not John's neighbor and everyone except Mary knows this; Mary thinks Bill is John's neighbor, but knows that John does not share this belief; John thinks Bill is a spy and tells Mary this; Mary forms a thought accordingly. It is not possible for me or the four other native speakers I have consulted to hear *Mary thinks John believes his neighbor is a spy* as accurately describing this scenario. (The fully *de re* and fully *de dicto* readings are available, however.) But see Neale 1990, 123, for a contrary claim about a similar example. If Neale is correct here, supporters of the Fregean definite article could accommodate the data by means of LFs like (ii). Of course further investigation would have to be undertaken as to why at least some examples like this are apparently ungrammatical on the relevant reading.

10. Note that the semantic value of a definite description turns out to be an individual concept—that is, a function from circumstances of evaluation to individuals. This will be important in connection with the discussion of (62).

11. Note, however, that I am not denying the existence of scope-shifting operations like QR. It could be that both these and the kind of indexing devices I have been talking about are needed.

12. I am grateful to Stephen Neale (personal communication) for pointing out to me the importance of examples like this.

13. This is arguably a fault, as stressed by Heim in her classic 1983 paper, since we would ideally want to derive the presupposition from the asserted content, or have a semantics like that in Heim 1983 in which they both fall out from something else. But this way of doing things does at least have the merit of simplicity and clarity. I do not have anything original to say on the complex problem of the correct way to represent and derive presuppositions.

14. See the lexical entry in (37).

15. Stephen Schiffer independently suggested that having the contribution of definite descriptions be individual concepts was a solution to the current problem in a seminar jointly conducted by him and Stephen Neale at New York University in spring 2004.

16. This was in fact suggested to me in conversation by Stephen Schiffer.

17. Some speakers find examples like (77) slightly awkward, and prefer *that senator* to *the senator* in the position of the covarying phrase. But binding of DPs with *the* is generally possible.

18. There is in fact a fourth possible account, which is that the covariation could take place entirely by means of situation variables in the definite descriptions being bound. See section 5.6 for an explanation of this approach, and an argument against it.

19. Something like this is suggested by Larson and Segal (1995, 339–340, 350), but they do not spell it out as suggested here. Instead they attach an optional subscript index to the definite article, with the proviso that a definite description introduced by such a definite article will have the interpretation of the index as its denotation.

20. Chomsky (1986, 188) claims that phrases like *the cat of Mary's* are ungrammatical in the absence of a postnominal modifier such as a relative clause, and that this gap in the paradigm shows that *Mary's cat* is derived from an underlying form like *the cat of Mary's*. This latter phrase seems quite grammatical in

(92a), however. Meanwhile, the difference in semantic properties between the two phrases illustrated here detracts from the attractiveness of the position that they must be derived from the same underlying form, although I would not want to say that this is impossible.

21. For a good discussion of this issue, see Heim and Kratzer 1998, 159–172.

22. Note that in order for my argument to go through, I have to assume hardly anything about the syntax and semantics of phrases like *Mary's cat*. All that is necessary is that they should not incorporate an argument position for an index. The analysis of these items is in fact highly complicated, and I do not have an original proposal.

23. But see Reimer 1998 for a dissenting voice.

24. It is perhaps worth noting that one of Donnellan's best-known examples, "Smith's murderer is insane," cannot achieve a referential interpretation by means of an index on the current view, because it involves a Saxon genitive.

25. In (97), I assume that variable assignments are still partial functions from the natural numbers to individuals, as suggested in (6) and the surrounding discussion.

26. The semantics of the no-uniqueness reading is actually very similar to the way Heim said definite descriptions worked in her dissertation. See Heim 1982, 230–236.

27. It is easy to pronounce (105) with focal stress on *Republican*, which would of course give an independent reason for the lack of the no uniqueness reading. But one can also pronounce it with an entirely level intonation on *Mississippi's Republican senator*, or with focal stress on *Mississippi's* or *senator*, and the judgment still holds.

28. I think that the present proposal also works well in the case of Donnellan's examples where the descriptive content is incorrect. For example, I point at a man drinking water from a champagne flute and refer to him as "the man drinking champagne." In cases like this, I think we have the intuition that reference has been established successfully, even though the inaccurate description still makes the utterance deviant. This is entirely what we would expect in the present system, where the index can successfully be mapped to the man in question.

29. An analysis of the genericity of (113) is not relevant to our concerns here. One might explore the option of using the phonologically null quantificational adverb, introduced in sections 2.3.1 and 2.5.3, which brings about universal quantification over situations. The nature of the situations must be recovered without much help from linguistic material.

30. If the proposal to be made in section 3.5 is correct, the structure of these examples will be: [[he 0] [ONE [who hesitates]]]. See (128b).

31. English *this* and *that* seem to be restricted to applying to nonpersons when they are used "bare":

(i)   This woman looks happy.

(ii) *This looks happy.

This arbitrary-seeming restriction does not apply to the parallel alternations in other languages I have examined (e.g., Latin, ancient Greek, Sanskrit) and I will not attempt to account for it here.

32. It is notable, however, that the philosophical literature on demonstratives rarely considers Fregean accounts of demonstratives along the lines just suggested. For example, King (2001, chap. 1) argues compellingly that a direct-reference view of demonstratives is not adequate, but then concludes with no further argumentation that they must therefore be treated as quantifiers. But in fact none of King's arguments favors a quantificational over a Fregean view—they merely militate against direct-reference views. It seems to me that the null hypothesis on this matter is the one that accords with our intuition, namely, that demonstrative phrases are used to pick out individuals and are therefore of type e. The present, Fregean, view also generalizes very easily to those cases where demonstratives are bound:

(i) Mary talked to no senator before that senator was lobbied.

(ii) Mary talked to no senator without declaring that this was the one who would cosponsor her bill.

33. Despite Frege's analysis of the natural numbers as properties of properties of individuals, and other such logical wizardry, it seems likely to me that the natural numbers should be considered to be of type e for linguistic purposes, since they can be referred to by pronouns and their names can bind large PRO, and so on. This is one easy way of arguing that the domain of entities of type e is (for linguistic purposes) infinite.

34. One might think that this latter assumption would also be unnecessary. We could propose the following semantics for the definite article and pronouns and have indices be of type e:

(i) $\lambda x_e . \lambda g : g \in D_{\langle e, t \rangle}$ & $\exists! y(y = x$ & $g(y) = 1) . \iota y(y = x$ & $g(x) = 1)$.

However, this scheme leaves it unclear how to do the work of the index 0—that is, how to have an index be semantically vacuous when necessary.

35. The version in Sauerland 2002, 22, does not have focus on any element in the first sentence. I have added this in order to reduce to a minimum the ways the VPs of the two sentences could be claimed to differ in meaning.

36. I will be arguing in chapter 6 that proper names have indices, too, just like pronouns. This would make the current example even more like the previous case where two pronouns were argued to differ in meaning.

37. See Doron 1982, Sells 1984, and Sharvit 1999 for further discussion of the semantics of resumptive pronouns.

38. Sometimes it will be necessary to have the pronoun bound by the NP, since wh-phrases and QPs can be clitic left-dislocated. This might appear to pose a problem for an assumption made in this book, that binding is effected only by λ-operators, and that λ-operators are inserted only by movement (Heim and Kratzer 1998). But there could presumably be short-distance movement of the NP in cases like this, creating a trace and a λ-operator that could be coindexed with the lower clitic pronoun.

39. In an alternative analysis, Aoun, Choueiri, and Hornstein (2001, 397) basically follow Aoun and Benmamoun 1998 on this matter but claim that the resumptive pronoun ends up taking the trace as its complement. I can see no way of arriving at the right interpretation on the basis of this proposal.

40. It is impossible in Hebrew too to have weak pronouns in apposition to DPs (Yael Sharvit, personal communication), meaning that the apposition explanation would also fail for the Hebrew data in (146).

Chapter 4

1. A note on terminology. A symmetrical relation, of course, is defined in the textbooks as being a relation R such that, if aRb, then bRa, for arbitrary a and b. (Equivalently, R is symmetrical if and only if it is identical with its converse.) Now some relations are symmetrical in some domains but not others: if our domain consists only of a and b, and a sees b and b sees a, then seeing is a symmetrical relation (within this domain). But we know that seeing is not in general a symmetrical relation. In the literature on the problem of indistinguishable participants, *symmetrical* is used in a strong sense to pick out relations that are necessarily symmetrical: we might say that a relation R is symmetrical in this strong sense if and only if for all possible worlds w, if aRb in w, then bRa in w, for arbitrary a and b. This is how I too will use the term from now on.

2. This means a quantifier whose semantics does not involve exhaustiveness on some definition. Examples of maximal quantifiers, according to Neale, are *all*, *every*, and *the*; see Neale 1990, 180.

3. After arriving at this conclusion, I was pleased to see that Kanazawa (2001) had come up with a very similar criticism. Readers are referred to Kanazawa 2001 for more discussion of this issue.

4. This is known in some guises as the *proportion problem*. See section 2.7.1 for related discussion.

5. Note that Heim's (1990) framework had situation variables be part of the object language. Object-language situation variables are printed in normal italics, and metalanguage situation variables are printed in boldface. $g^{s/s}$ means g so altered as to map object-language variables s to the corresponding metalanguage variables **s**.

6. Parsons (1990, 74) maintains that no two arguments of the same event can have the same thematic role, but he does not consider symmetrical relations. The only reasoning he gives in support of his hypothesis concerns the avoidance of rather obvious errors—for example, he points out that if we consider both direct and indirect objects Themes, we would predict that if we give a fish to Mary we thereby give Mary to a fish (Parsons 1990, 293, note 5).

7. An ancestor of Ludlow 1994 is cited as Ludlow 1987 in Schein 1993. Schein explicitly endorses Ludlow's proposal.

8. Thanks to Kai von Fintel for suggesting these particular sentences. I had previously been trying to make the point of this section with *If two bishops meet, he blesses him, which would have been much more complicated, if not impossible.

9. Syntactic-category labels and nonbranching nodes are omitted for the sake of simplicity and generality. The representation, then, is actually ambiguous between at least two full syntactic representations: t_6 could be either in the Spec of V or v, or in the overt subject position. So the QP just above λ_2 must have QR'd from object position (unless there is overt object shift in English), but the higher one could be where it is either as a result of QR from the surface subject position or after overt movement from a VP-internal subject position. The semantics, of course, applies irrespective of which of these syntactic options is correct.

10. See appendix B.1.

11. Barwise and Perry (1983, 81–82) have already remarked that within a situation containing two individuals playing the same roles, in their terminology, it is possible to find smaller situations in which one of the said roles has only one individual playing it.

12. The possibility of the arguments in transitive cases being perceived differently simply on the basis of their syntactic position is confirmed by Gleitman et al. (1996, 347–352), who report, among other experimental results, that subjects given sentences with nonsense syllables in the subject and object positions of symmetrical predicates—for example, *The zum met the gax*—consistently judge the entity figuring in object position to be "more famous," "older," "bigger," "less mobile," and "more important" than the entity figuring in subject position. They suggest (Gleitman et al. 1996, 358) that this is to be explained by the two entities figuring in such predications being perceived as Figure (subject) and Ground (object). They do not, however, have any account of why the subject should be the Figure and the object the Ground (Gleitman et al. 1996, 360, note 23). In the case of (33), on the other hand, these assignments would make intuitive sense, since the subject situation s_2 is smaller than the extended situation s_3. The Figure is what I call "distinguished" here. Thanks to Irene Heim for drawing my attention to this work, and to Lila Gleitman for valuable discussion.

13. Irene Heim (personal communication) observes that a close parallel to these considerations can be found in the literature on plurality, in connection with sentences such as (i).

(i) The cards below seven and the cards from seven up were separated.

The most natural reading of this sentence claims that the deck was separated into two half decks, with the cards from 2 to 6 in one and those from 7 to ace in the other. But the simplest ways of theorizing about plurality would have the subject DP just denote the unstructured sum of all the cards in the deck, which would seem to give no basis for the right separation to be predicted to take place. So it is necessary to say either that the subject DP denotes an object composed of the cards, but which has complex internal structure (Landman 1989), or that, while the denotation does not strictly speaking have this kind of structure, the two groups mentioned in the subject DP are made salient and are thus still available to aid in the interpretation of *were separated* (Schwarzschild 1992; Link 1997).

14. Note that we can now go back and analyze Heim's (i), example (42) in chapter 2, by the same mechanisms.

(i) If a donkey is lonely, it talks to another donkey.

If the approach to indistinguishable participants suggested in this chapter is on the right track, there is no need for the kind of syncategorematic rule to bind situation variables described in connection with this example.

15. This kind of LF is assumed for these examples by Winter (2001, 237).

16. Kai von Fintel (personal communication) asks whether the denotations in (45) make the right prediction for a sentence like (i).

(i) No boy and no girl met in the lobby.

Example (45) predicts that (i) asserts that some group exists that met in the lobby, and that no boy or girl was part of it. Judgments are actually confused on (i), and it is unclear to me at the moment whether the prediction is correct or not. I leave this issue for further research. I suspect that any necessary adjustment to (45) would not change the fact that it makes the participants indistinguishable in the relevant kind of bishop sentence.

17. Irene Heim (personal communication) points out that, since the situations s_8 are defined as the minimal situations with the properties that follow, it may even be the case that they each contain only *one* bishop, since in the truth conditions in (48) it is possible to identify x with y, s_3 with s_6, and s_2 with s_5. This, of course, would mean that the sentence was ruled out for a different reason than that given in the main text. But it is conceivable, also, that the fact that *meet* is a plural predicate forces us to refrain from making these identifications, so as to have two bishops in the situations s_8. I will not attempt to resolve this issue here, since the sentence is plausibly ruled out either way.

Chapter 5

1. Sentences in which *kare* would be bound by a *wh*-phrase are generally also bad. Hoji (1991) reports that straightforward sentences like "Who said that Mary hit *kare*?" are ungrammatical on the reading where *kare* is bound by *who*. Interestingly, he reports that these sentences improve markedly when the restrictor on the *wh*-phrase is made to denote smaller and smaller sets: "Which writer said that Mary hit *kare*?" is better than "Who said that Mary hit *kare*?", and "Which Nobel Prize–winning writer said that Mary hit *kare*?" is pretty much fine. I do not have an explanation for this effect. I am uncertain how to interpret Hoji's own account: he says that the pronoun in these cases can be "coreferential" with the *wh*-phrase.

2. One could also suggest that there is competition between *kare/kanozyo* and *pro*, so that *kare* and *kanozyo* would not be possible when the null pronoun was possible. But this would predict that (1b) would be bad, given the possibility of (1c). See Noguchi's article (1997, 774) for another argument against this hypothesis.

3. Although it is not essential for the current argument, it may be interesting to note at this juncture that even *this*, which is a demonstrative that is sometimes claimed to be unbindable, can in fact be bound if one takes the trouble to construct an example in which its proximal semantics is not inappropriate. Sentence (i) seems to work pretty well.

(i) Mary talked to no senator without declaring that this was the one who would cosponsor her bill.

It was suggested to me at SALT XI that if *kare* is a demonstrative, then perhaps the distal/proximal aspect to its semantics might explain its inability to be bound. But this does not explain the contrasts attested—for example, there is no difference between the relationship that holds between John and himself in (1a), "John thinks that he's intelligent," and the relationship that holds between each male person and himself in (2a), "Everyone thinks he's intelligent." But (1a) is good (in the relevant dialect) and (2a) is bad.

4. I do not mean to imply that the predicates in *tiisai kare* and so on actually are nonrestrictive relative clauses. They could just be similar uses of adjectives. Irene Heim (personal communication) alerts me to the possible parallel of English expressions like *poor me, poor John.*

5. Actually things are not quite this simple, since these pronouns are also subject to constraints based on social standing. Noguchi (1997, 778) reports that one does not use them to refer to young children or to adults of higher social status. I abstract away from this here. We must also suppose that these expressions are like ordinary pronouns, and unlike some other definite descriptions, in that they are not subject to Condition C of the binding theory. This poses no problems, if only because no one knows why anything *should* be subject to Condition C of the binding theory.

6. To maintain the uniform schema proposed in section 3.5, we might propose [[the 0] male-person] and [[the 0] female-person]. These items would be frozen forms, with the index 0 obligatory. Richard Kayne (personal communication) points out that there may be a problem in explaining how children would ever learn that only the index 0 was available in these forms. I have nothing to say on this matter at present.

7. The most important emendation to Grodzinsky and Reinhart's original version is that their "corefer with" has been changed to "be covalued with"; this follows Heim's (1993) demonstration that Rule I needed to affect not only coreference but also cobinding, cases where two items are bound by the same binder. I see the present data from Japanese as indicating that the coverage of the rule needs to be extended yet again. The term *covalued* is from Reinhart 1997.

8. This is not to say that Rule I does not still face problems. Indeed the present data from Japanese give a new twist to an old conundrum concerning sentences like (i).

(i) Alfred thinks he is a great cook.

Grodzinsky and Reinhart (1993, 81, note 13) and Heim (1993, 211, 240–241) note that straightforward versions of Rule I predict that only a bound reading will be available for *he* in this sentence, and that this is undesirable: a continuation with VP-ellipsis would allow both sloppy and strict readings, among other factors. The same problem is posed by the isomorphic (1a) and (1b) above, in an even starker form, since we know on independent grounds that the pronouns in these examples cannot be bound. Without going through them in detail, let me just state here that the (mutually incompatible) solutions proposed by Grodzinsky and Reinhart, on the one hand, and Heim, on the other, do not extend to the present data. More work is needed on this.

Chapter 6

1. I will write THE in capitals in schemata illustrating the general structure postulated for type e items. Such occurrences are meant to be placeholders where any particular hypothesized definite article could be inserted.

2. The philosophical literature contains illuminating attempts to spell out the basic features of such an account. See especially Kripke 1972 and Evans 1973, 1982 (chap. 11). I would add, however, that an account of naming should not be thought of in purely sociological terms. It is quite possible to introduce names for one's own use in private thoughts, for such thinking as is done in words, without anyone else ever knowing of them. Nor should the fact that a sociological account would be relevant if we wanted to learn all about naming mislead us into acceding to what Chomsky calls the externalist view of language—that is, the view that languages like English somehow exist outside or independently of the internal mental states of people who speak in certain ways. See Chomsky 1995 and much other literature.

3. Larson and Segal (1995, 354–355) use another argument too, which seems to me to be open to challenge. It comes from Higginbotham 1988. Suppose I know a person called Mary, and see someone that I think is her coming out of a seafood restaurant at lunchtime. I then might say (i).

(i) Mary had fish for lunch.

The woman I see is not, in fact, my friend Mary; by coincidence, though, she is called Mary. Example (i) then seems to be false on its most natural reading, since the content of the utterance seems, intuitively, to be that my friend Mary had fish for lunch. On the other hand, if I had used (ii), I would have spoken truly.

(ii) That Mary had fish for lunch.

This is supposed to show that the determiner before *Mary* in (i) cannot be *that*, or an equivalent. It seems to me, however, that if one imagines (i) being accompanied with the kind of physical demonstration of the woman that naturally accompanies (ii), a reading on which it is true is brought out. I am not convinced, then, by this attempt to put distance between *Mary* and *that Mary*, although I do in fact agree with the conclusion.

4. Regular proper names are thus what Soames (2002, 51, 110–130) calls *partially descriptive names*, combining direct reference and descriptive content. Soames assumes that names with uncontested descriptive content like *Princeton University* are partially descriptive names, but as far as I can see he presents no considerations that show that regular names could not be too, provided the descriptive content is minimal and generally available, as on Burge's theory.

5. Michael Glanzberg (personal communication) asks about the status of the following sentences under this view of proper names.

(i) Mary is taller than Mary [WITH GESTURES AT DIFFERENT MARYS].

(ii) *The car is shorter than the car [WITH GESTURES AT DIFFERENT CARS].

Why should there be a contrast if both DPs have the determiner *the*? I do not know why there should be such a difference, but I would reply that it is the overt definite descriptions that are behaving strangely in light of the proposed semantics for definite articles, not the proper names.

6. Recanati advocates a theory of proper names very like Burge's, the difference being that, while proper names have senses or characters "entity called NN" in Recanati's view, a special feature prevents this description from entering the proposition expressed; only the bearer of the name enters the proposition expressed. Recanati's view is thus a hybrid between a descriptive theory and a pure direct-reference theory. We have already seen an argument, however, that indicates that the descriptive content of proper names must, at least occasionally, enter the proposition expressed, and that is the existence of sentences like (i).

(i) Most Alfreds are crazy.

Further arguments for the descriptive content of names entering the proposition expressed are the possibility of D-type proper names (section 6.3.3) and the possibility of naming certain hypothetical entities (section 6.3.4).

7. In the 1980 edition of *Naming and Necessity*, versions of this argument are advanced on page 30 and on pages 60–63.

8. Nevertheless, it is possible to construct devious examples in which the index 0 has to be the one present. I give an example like this in section 6.3.4.

9. These considerations recall the position of Jason Stanley (1997), who argues, surely correctly, that the rigidity of names does not tell against the position that names are definite descriptions, since part of the descriptive content of names could be a restriction that the rest of the descriptive content is to be evaluated with respect to the actual world. For example, a traditional descriptive view of names might be modified so as to have *Aristotle* mean "the *actual* teacher of Alexander," or Burge's view might be modified so as to have *Socrates* mean "the person *actually* called Socrates." Stanley's view is attractive (although see Soames 2002, 43–44, for an attempted counterargument), but I do not adopt it, since the job of contributing an actual person or thing is done perfectly well by the index on the current view. This is not to say, however, that I do not need the index w_0, referring to the actual world, on descriptive content in my setup, even in the case of names. Kai von Fintel (personal communication) has drawn my attention to example (i).

(i) Socrates might not have been called Socrates.

If we did not have the index w_0, this would have to mean, "There exists a possible world w such that the unique entity called Socrates in w and identical with Socrates is not called Socrates in w." With the index w_0 on the descriptive content of the first *Socrates*, we can obtain the correct meaning: "There exists a possible world w such that the unique entity called Socrates in w_0 and identical with Socrates is not called Socrates in w." The difference between Stanley's view and mine, then, is that I allow the descriptive content on names to be evaluated with respect to non-actual worlds, which seems necessary in examples like (31) and (32) in section 6.3.4.

10. Contrast differences between what is said and what is conveyed like that which obtains when the question "Could you close the door?" is taken as a request. We take such questions to be requests very easily, without thinking about it much, but it still seems that we are aware on some level that we are not responding to the literal content of what is said when we close the door. If the addressee was in a particularly bad mood, they might even shoot back, "I *could* ...," and then go on their way without closing the door, perversely secure in the knowledge that they have not failed to fulfill any request that was literally made of them. I doubt that there would be any such conscious knowledge of this kind of distinction in the (possibly hypothetical) case under discussion, however.

11. This definition comes from a letter from Kripke to David Kaplan, cited on page 569 of Kaplan 1989a.

12. This is made explicit in note 21 on page 21 of the preface to the 1980 edition of *Naming and Necessity*.

13. It is to be found on pages 68–70 in the 1980 edition of *Naming and Necessity*.

14. See page 69 of the 1980 edition of *Naming and Necessity*.

15. This is only an argument for the syntax of the current view of proper names, of course, not the semantics. Michael Glanzberg (personal communication) raises the possibility that Kripke could adapt his semantics for proper names to the current syntax. The result would presumably give proper names meanings like $[\lambda x. \, x = \text{John}]$, which was in fact an option raised earlier in section 2.7.2. I would not wish to rule out such a possibility, but I prefer Burge's view because of its ability to deal with examples like (4) and (31).

16. Note that this constraint, however it works, is not based just on the form of the name but on the person referred to. So in the case of people who have more than one name, it not possible to improve examples with the structure of (28b) by using different names each time:

(i) Cicero came home. ?*Tully told his slave to start reciting Greek verse.

In what may be a related phenomenon, it is sometimes also the case that a proper name is very awkward when it follows hard on the heels of a demonstrative, as we see in (ii).

(ii) ?*If this man [GESTURE AT CICERO] denounces Catiline, Cicero will be in danger.

This is important in note 17.

17. The first example of this sort, according to Heim (personal communication), was invented by Hans Kamp for a lecture he gave during a seminar on reference cotaught by Heim and Kamp at the University of Texas at Austin in the fall of 1985. Kamp's original example was (i), where we are to imagine that John has two sons, Primus and Secundus.

(i) Even if this man [GESTURE AT SECUNDUS] had been born first, Primus would still have inherited everything.

Here, Kamp observed, *Primus* behaves rigidly—that is, it picks out the man actually called Primus. I suspect, however, that this is at least partly due to the pragmatics of introducing a name to refer to someone as opposed to, say, using a pronoun: using Gricean reasoning, we may speculate that the fact that the speaker has gone to the trouble of introducing this novel descriptive content is taken to indicate that another person is being introduced; if the person already mentioned had been meant, *he* would have sufficed. The mysterious constraint against the use of proper names mentioned in section 6.3.3, note 16, will also play a role, if, indeed, it is to be considered separately and is not reducible to Gricean reasoning of the sort just sketched.

18. See Soames 2002, 89–95, for discussion.

Chapter 7

1. We might already have thought this on the basis of certain foundational considerations. As Soames (1989) has pointed out, we cannot really say that a proposition is a set of possible worlds, even ignoring the problems caused by propositional attitude contexts, because then *Florence is a beautiful city* and *Florence is a beautiful city and arithmetic is incomplete* would express the same proposition. It is tempting, then, to have situations take over the role of truth-supporting circumstances, since the minimal situation in which Florence is a beautiful city does not contain the information that arithmetic is incomplete. Note that Soames's (1987) argument against this relies on the doctrine that proper names and demonstratives are directly referential, which I take to have been undermined by the considerations advanced in this book. But the issues here are very complex, and I will not attempt to investigate them further in the present work. See Higginbotham 1992 for another response to the problem posed by necessary truths to truth-conditional semantics.

2. See Schein 1993, 99–101, for a slightly different take on the mereology of events.

References

Abney, Steven. 1987. *The English Noun Phrase in Its Sentential Aspect.* Doctoral dissertation, MIT. Distributed by MITWPL.

Aoun, Joseph, and Elabbas Benmamoun. 1998. Minimality, reconstruction, and PF movement. *Linguistic Inquiry* 29, 569–597.

Aoun, Joseph, Lina Choueiri, and Norbert Hornstein. 2001. Resumption, movement, and derivational economy. *Linguistic Inquiry* 32, 371–403.

Aoun, Joseph, and Norbert Hornstein. 1992. Bound and referential pronouns. In C.-T. James Huang and Robert May, eds., *Logical Structure and Linguistic Structure*, 1–23. Dordrecht: Kluwer.

Armstrong, David. 1978. *Universals and Scientific Realism*, Volume 1: *Nominalism and Realism.* Cambridge: Cambridge University Press.

Armstrong, David. 1997. *A World of States of Affairs.* Cambridge: Cambridge University Press.

Bach, Emmon. 1970. Problominalization. *Linguistic Inquiry* 1, 121–122.

Bach, Emmon. 1986. The algebra of events. *Linguistics and Philosophy* 9, 5–16.

Bach, Emmon. 1989. *Informal Lectures on Formal Semantics.* Albany: State University of New York Press.

Barwise, Jon, and John Perry. 1983. *Situations and Attitudes.* Cambridge, MA: MIT Press.

Bäuerle, Rainer. 1983. Pragmatisch-semantische Aspekte der NP-Interpretation. In Manfred Faust, Roland Harweg, Werner Lehfeldt, and Götz Wienold, eds., *Allgemeine Sprachwissenschaft, Sprachtypologie und Textlinguistik. Festschrift für Peter Hartmann*, 121–131. Tübingen: Gunter Narr Verlag.

Beaver, David. 1997. Presupposition. In Johan van Benthem and Alice ter Meulen, eds., *Handbook of Logic and Language*, 939–1008. Amsterdam and Cambridge, MA: Elsevier and MIT Press.

Berman, Stephen. 1987. Situation-based semantics for adverbs of quantification. In James Blevins and Anne Vainikka, eds., *Studies in Semantics*, 46–68. University of Massachusetts Occasional Papers in Linguistics, vol. 12. GLSA, University of Massachusetts at Amherst.

Burge, Tyler. 1973. Reference and proper names. *Journal of Philosophy* 70, 425–439.

Chierchia, Gennaro. 1992. Anaphora and dynamic binding. *Linguistics and Philosophy* 15, 111–183.

Chierchia, Gennaro. 1995. *Dynamics of Meaning: Anaphora, Presupposition, and the Theory of Grammar.* Chicago: University of Chicago Press.

Chomsky, Noam. 1976. Conditions on rules of grammar. *Linguistic Analysis* 2, 303–351.

Chomsky, Noam. 1986. *Knowledge of Language: Its Nature, Origin, and Use.* Westport, CT: Praeger.

Chomsky, Noam. 1993. A minimalist program for linguistic theory. In Kenneth Hale and Samuel Jay Keyser, eds., *The View from Building 20: Essays in Linguistics in Honor of Sylvain Bromberger*, 1–52. Cambridge, MA: MIT Press.

Chomsky, Noam. 1995. Language and nature. *Mind* 104, 1–61.

Cooper, Robin. 1979. The interpretation of pronouns. In Frank Heny and Helmut Schnelle, eds., *Syntax and Semantics 10: Selections from the Third Groningen Round Table*, 61–92. New York: Academic Press.

Davidson, Donald. 1967. The logical form of action sentences. In Nicolas Rescher, ed., *The Logic of Decision and Action*, 81–95. Pittsburgh: University of Pittsburgh Press.

Davies, Martin. 1981. *Meaning, Quantification, Necessity.* London: Routledge and Kegan Paul.

Donnellan, Keith. 1966. Reference and definite descriptions. *Philosophical Review* 75, 281–304.

Doron, Edit. 1982. On the syntax and semantics of resumptive pronouns. *Texas Linguistics Forum* 19, 1–48.

Elbourne, Paul. 2000. Donkey anaphora as NP-deletion. In Rajesh Bhatt, Martin Hackl, Patrick Hawley, and Ishani Maitra, eds., *The Linguistics Philosophy Interface*, 111–134. Cambridge, MA: MITWPL.

Elbourne, Paul. 2001a. E-type anaphora as NP-deletion. *Natural Language Semantics* 9(3), 241–288.

Elbourne, Paul. 2001b. E-type pronouns as definite articles. In Roger Billerey and Brook Danielle Lillehaugen, eds., *WCCFL 19: Proceedings of the 19th West Coast Conference on Formal Linguistics*, 83–96. Somerville, MA: Cascadilla Press.

Elbourne, Paul. 2001c. On the semantics of pronouns and definite articles. In Leora Bar-el and Karine Megerdoomian, eds., *WCCFL 20: Proceedings of the 20th West Coast Conference on Formal Linguistics*, 164–177. Somerville, MA: Cascadilla Press.

Elbourne, Paul. 2001d. When is situation semantics allowed? In Rachel Hastings, Brendan Jackson, and Zsofia Zvolenszky, eds., *Proceedings of Semantics and Linguistic Theory XI*, 152–171. Ithaca, NY: CLC Publications.

Evans, Gareth. 1973. The causal theory of names. *Aristotelian Society Supplementary Volume* 47, 187–208.

Evans, Gareth. 1977. Pronouns, quantifiers and relative clauses (I). *Canadian Journal of Philosophy* 7, 467–536.

Evans, Gareth. 1980. Pronouns. *Linguistic Inquiry* 11, 337–362.

Evans, Gareth. 1982. *The Varieties of Reference.* Oxford: Clarendon Press.

Farkas, Donka. 1997. Evaluation indices and scope. In Anna Szabolcsi, ed., *Ways of Scope Taking*, 183–215. Dordrecht: Kluwer.

Fiengo, Robert, and Robert May. 1994. *Indices and Identity.* Cambridge, MA: MIT Press.

von Fintel, Kai. 1993. Exceptive constructions. *Natural Language Semantics* 1, 123–148.

von Fintel, Kai. 1994. Restrictions on Quantifier Domains. Doctoral dissertation, University of Massachusetts at Amherst.

von Fintel, Kai. 2004. Would you believe it? The King of France is back! (Presuppositions and truth-value intuitions.) In Anne Bezuidenhout and Marga Reimer, eds., *Descriptions and Beyond: An Interdisciplinary Collection of Essays on Definite and Indefinite Descriptions and Other Related Phenomena*, 315–341. Oxford: Oxford University Press.

Fox, Danny. 2000. *Economy and Semantic Interpretation.* Cambridge, MA: MIT Press.

Fox, Danny. 2002. Antecedent-contained deletion and the copy theory of movement. *Linguistic Inquiry* 33, 63–96.

Frege, Gottlob. 1893. Über Sinn und Bedeutung. *Zeitschrift für Philosophie und Philosophische Kritik* 100, 25–50. (Translated as "On sense and reference," in Peter Geach and Max Black, eds., *Translations from the Philosophical Writings of Gottlob Frege*, 56–78. Oxford: Blackwell.)

Gamut, L. T. F. 1991. *Logic, Language, and Meaning*, Volume 2: *Intensional Logic and Logical Grammar.* Chicago: University of Chicago Press.

Gardent, Claire. 1991. Dynamic semantics and VP-ellipsis. In Jan van Eijck, ed., *Logics in AI*, 251–266. Berlin: Springer-Verlag.

Gawron, Jean Mark. 1996. Quantification, quantificational domains, and dynamic logic. In Shalom Lappin, ed., *The Handbook of Contemporary Semantic Theory*, 247–267. Oxford: Blackwell.

Geach, Peter. 1962. *Reference and Generality.* Ithaca, NY: Cornell University Press.

Gleitman, Lila, Henry Gleitman, Carol Miller, and Ruth Ostrin. 1996. Similar, and similar concepts. *Cognition* 58, 321–376.

Grodzinsky, Yosef, and Tanya Reinhart. 1993. The innateness of binding and coreference. *Linguistic Inquiry* 24, 69–101.

Groenendijk, Jeroen, and Martin Stokhof. 1990. Dynamic Montague Grammar. In László Kálmán and László Pólos, eds., *Papers from the Second Symposium on Logic and Language*, 3–48. Budapest: Akadémiai Kiadó.

Groenendijk, Jeroen, and Martin Stokhof. 1991. Dynamic Predicate Logic. *Linguistics and Philosophy* 14, 39–100.

Grosz, Barbara, Aravind Joshi, and Scott Weinstein. 1995. Centering: A framework for modelling the local coherence of discourse. *Computational Linguistics* 21, 203–225.

Hankamer, Jorge, and Ivan Sag. 1976. Deep and surface anaphora. *Linguistic Inquiry* 7, 391–426.

Hardt, Dan. 1999. Dynamic interpretation of verb phrase ellipsis. *Linguistics and Philosophy* 22, 187–221.

Heim, Irene. 1982. The Semantics of Definite and Indefinite Noun Phrases. Doctoral dissertation, University of Massachusetts at Amherst.

Heim, Irene. 1983. On the projection problem for presuppositions. In Michael Barlow, Dan P. Flickinger, and Michael T. Wescoat, eds., *Proceedings of the 2nd West Coast Conference on Formal Linguistics*, 114–125. Stanford, CA: Department of Linguistics, Stanford University.

Heim, Irene. 1990. E-type pronouns and donkey anaphora. *Linguistics and Philosophy* 13, 137–177.

Heim, Irene. 1991. Artikel und Definitheit. In Arnim von Stechow and Dieter Wunderlich, eds., *Semantik. Ein internationales Handbuch der zeitgenössischen Forschung*, 487–535. Berlin: Walter de Gruyter.

Heim, Irene. 1993. Anaphora and semantic interpretation: A reinterpretation of Reinhart's approach. University of Tübingen Seminar für Sprachwissenschaft working paper series (SfS-Report-07-93). (Also published in Uli Sauerland and Orin Percus, eds., *The Interpretive Tract*, 205–246. MIT Working Papers in Linguistics 25. Cambridge, MA: MIT Working Papers in Linguistics, 1998.)

Heim, Irene, and Angelika Kratzer. 1998. *Semantics in Generative Grammar*. Oxford: Blackwell.

Heim, Irene, Angelika Kratzer, and Kai von Fintel. 1998. Introduction to intensional semantics. Class notes, MIT.

Higginbotham, James. 1988. Contexts, models, and meaning: A note on the data of semantics. In Ruth Kempson, ed., *Mental Representations: The Interface between Language and Reality*, 29–48. Cambridge: Cambridge University Press.

Higginbotham, James. 1992. Truth and understanding. *Philosophical Studies* 65, 3–16.

Hinrichs, Erhard. 1985. A Compositional Semantics for Aktionsarten and NP Reference in English. Doctoral dissertation, Ohio State University.

Hoji, Hajime. 1991. *Kare*. In Carol Georgopoulos and Robert Ishihara, eds., *Interdisciplinary Approaches to Language: Essays in honor of S.-Y. Kuroda*, 287–304. Dordrecht: Kluwer.

Huang, C.-T. James. 1991. Remarks on the status of the null subject. In Robert Freidin, ed., *Principles and Parameters in Comparative Grammar*, 56–76. Cambridge, MA: MIT Press.

Jackendoff, Ray. 1968. Quantifiers in English. *Foundations of Language* 4, 422–442.

Jackendoff, Ray. 1971. Gapping and related rules. *Linguistic Inquiry* 2, 21–35.

Jacobson, Pauline. 1977. The Syntax of Crossing Coreference Sentences. Doctoral dissertation, University of California at Berkeley.

Jacobson, Pauline. 1996. The syntax/semantics interface in Categorial Grammar. In Shalom Lappin, ed., *The Handbook of Contemporary Semantic Theory*, 89–116. Oxford: Blackwell.

Jacobson, Pauline. 1999. Towards a variable-free semantics. *Linguistics and Philosophy* 22, 117–184.

Jacobson, Pauline. 2000a. Paycheck pronouns, Bach-Peters sentences, and variable-free semantics. *Natural Language Semantics* 8, 77–155.

Jacobson, Pauline. 2000b. Paychecks, stress, and variable-free semantics. In Brendan Jackson and Tanya Matthews, eds., *Proceedings from Semantics and Linguistic Theory X*, 65–82. Ithaca, NY: CLC Publications.

Kadmon, Nirit. 1987. On Unique and Non-unique Reference and Asymmetric Quantification. Doctoral dissertation, University of Massachusetts at Amherst.

Kamp, Hans. 1981. A theory of truth and semantic representation. In Jeroen Groenendijk, Theo Janssen, and Martin Stokhof, eds., *Formal Methods in the Study of Languages*, 277–322. Tract 135. Amsterdam: Mathematical Centre.

Kanazawa, Makoto. 2001. Singular donkey pronouns are semantically singular. *Linguistics and Philosophy* 24, 383–403.

Kaplan, David. 1989a. Afterthoughts. In Joseph Almog, John Perry, and Howard Wettstein, eds., *Themes from Kaplan*, 565–614. Oxford: Oxford University Press.

Kaplan, David. 1989b. Demonstratives. In Joseph Almog, John Perry, and Howard Wettstein, eds., *Themes from Kaplan*, 481–563. Oxford: Oxford University Press.

Karttunen, Lauri. 1969. Pronouns and variables. In Robert Binnick, Alice Davison, Georgia Green, and Jerry Morgan, eds., *Papers from the Fifth Regional Meeting of the Chicago Linguistic Society*, 108–116. Chicago: Department of Linguistics, University of Chicago.

Karttunen, Lauri. 1973. Presuppositions of compound sentences. *Linguistic Inquiry* 4, 167–193.

Karttunen, Lauri. 1974. Presupposition and linguistic context. *Theoretical Linguistics* 1, 181–194.

Karttunen, Lauri. 1976. Discourse referents. In James McCawley, ed., *Syntax and Semantics* 7, 363–385. New York: Academic Press.

Karttunen, Lauri, and Stanley Peters. 1979. Conventional implicatures in Montague Grammar. In Choon-Kyu Oh and David A. Dineen, eds., *Syntax and Semantics 11: Presupposition*, 1–56. New York: Academic Press.

Katada, Fusa. 1991. The LF representation of anaphors. *Linguistic Inquiry* 22, 287–313.

King, Jeffrey. 2001. *Complex Demonstratives: A Quantificational Account.* Cambridge, MA: MIT Press.

Kratzer, Angelika. 1989. An investigation of the lumps of thought. *Linguistics and Philosophy* 12, 607–653.

Krifka, Manfred. 1986. Massennomina. Mit einem Exkurs zu Aktionsarten. *Berichte des Sonderforschungsbereichs 99 "Grammatik und sprachliche Prozess" der Universität Konstanz* 117, Mai 1986.

Kripke, Saul. 1972. Naming and necessity. In Donald Davidson and Gilbert Harman, eds., *Semantics of Natural Languages*, 253–355. Dordrecht: Reidel. (Also published as a separate volume with a new introduction, *Naming and Necessity*. Cambridge, MA: Harvard University Press, 1980.)

Kripke, Saul. 1979. Speaker's reference and semantic reference. In Peter A. French, Theodore Uehling Jr., and Howard Wettstein, eds., *Contemporary Perspectives in the Philosophy of Language*, 6–27. Minneapolis: University of Minnesota Press.

Kurafuji, Takeo. 1998. Dynamic binding and the E-type strategy: Evidence from Japanese. In Devon Strolovitch and Aaron Lawson, eds., *Proceedings of Semantics and Linguistic Theory VIII*, 129–144. Ithaca, NY: CLC Publications.

Kurafuji, Takeo. 1999. Japanese Pronouns in Dynamic Semantics: The Null/Overt Contrast. Doctoral dissertation, Rutgers University.

Lakoff, George. 1970. Repartee, or a reply to "Negation, conjunction, and quantifiers." *Foundations of Language* 6, 389–422.

Landman, Fred. 1989. Groups, I. *Linguistics and Philosophy* 12, 559–605.

Larson, Richard, and Sungeun Cho. 1999. Temporal adjectives and the structure of possessive DPs. In Sonya Bird, Andrew Carnie, Jason Haugen, and Peter Norquest, eds., *WCCFL 18 Proceedings*, 299–311. Somerville, MA: Cascadilla Press.

Larson, Richard, and Gabriel Segal. 1995. *Knowledge of Meaning: An Introduction to Semantic Theory.* Cambridge, MA: MIT Press.

Lasnik, Howard, and Mamoru Saito. 1992. *Move α.* Cambridge, MA: MIT Press.

Lewis, David. 1968. Counterpart theory and quantified modal logic. *Journal of Philosophy* 65, 113–126.

Lewis, David. 1973. *Counterfactuals.* Oxford: Blackwell.

Link, Godehard. 1983. The logical analysis of plurals and mass terms: A lattice-theoretical approach. In Rainer Bäuerle, Christoph Schwarze, and Arnim von Stechow, eds., *Meaning, Use and Interpretation of Language*, 302–323. Berlin: Walter de Gruyter. (Also published in Godehard Link, *Algebraic Semantics in Language and Philosophy*, 11–34. Stanford, CA: CSLI Publications, 1998.)

Link, Godehard. 1997. Ten years of research on plurals—where do we stand? In Fritz Hamm and Erhard Hinrichs, eds., *Plurality and Quantification*, 19–54. Dordrecht: Kluwer. (Also published in Godehard Link, *Algebraic Semantics in Language and Philosophy*, 163–187. Stanford: CSLI Publications, 1998.)

Link, Godehard. 1998. *Algebraic Semantics in Language and Philosophy.* Stanford, CA: CSLI Publications.

Loar, Brian. 1980. Names and descriptions: A reply to Michael Devitt. *Philosophical Studies* 38, 85–89.

Lobeck, Anne. 1995. *Ellipsis.* Oxford: Oxford University Press.

Longobardi, Giuseppe. 1994. Reference and proper names: A theory of N-movement in syntax and logical form. *Linguistic Inquiry* 25, 609–665.

Ludlow, Peter. 1994. Conditionals, events, and unbound pronouns. *Lingua e Stile* 29, 165–183.

May, Robert. 1977. The Grammar of Quantification. Doctoral dissertation, MIT.

May, Robert. 1985. *Logical Form: Its Structure and Derivation.* Cambridge, MA: MIT Press.

Merchant, Jason. 2001. *The Syntax of Silence: Sluicing, Islands, and the Theory of Ellipsis.* Oxford: Oxford University Press.

Montague, Richard. 1973. The proper treatment of quantification in ordinary English. In Jaakko Hintikka, Julius Moravcsik, and Patrick Suppes, eds., *Approaches to Natural Language: Proceedings of the 1970 Stanford Workshop on Grammar and Semantics,* 221–242. Dordrecht: Reidel.

Montalbetti, Mario. 1984. After Binding: On the Interpretation of Pronouns. Doctoral dissertation, MIT.

Neale, Stephen. 1990. *Descriptions.* Cambridge, MA: MIT Press.

Neale, Stephen. 1993. Term limits. In James E. Tomberlin, ed., *Philosophical Perspectives 7: Logic and language,* 89–123. Atascadero, CA: Ridgeview Publishing.

Noguchi, Tohru. 1997. Two types of pronouns and variable binding. *Language* 73, 770–797.

Ostertag, Gary, ed. 1998. *Definite Descriptions: A Reader.* Cambridge, MA: MIT Press.

Parsons, Terence. 1990. *Events in the Semantics of English: A study in Subatomic Semantics.* Cambridge, MA: MIT Press.

Partee, Barbara, and Mats Rooth. 1983. Generalized conjunction and type ambiguity. In Rainer Bäuerle, Christoph Schwarze, and Arnim von Stechow, eds., *Meaning, Use, and the Interpretation of Language,* 362–383. Berlin: Walter de Gruyter.

Peacocke, Christopher. 1975. Proper names, reference, and rigid designation. In Simon Blackburn, ed., *Meaning, Reference, Necessity,* 109–132. Cambridge: Cambridge University Press.

Pelletier, Jeffry, and Lenhart Schubert. 1989. Generically speaking. In Gennaro Chierchia, Barbara Partee, and Raymond Turner, eds., *Properties, Types and Meaning,* vol. 2, 193–268. Dordrecht: Kluwer.

Percus, Orin. 2000. Constraints on some other variables in syntax. *Natural Language Semantics* 8, 173–229.

Perlmutter, David. 1970. On the article in English. In Manfred Bierwisch and Karl Erich Heidolph, eds., *Progress in Linguistics*, 233–248. The Hague: Mouton.

Poesio, Massimo, and Alessandro Zucchi. 1992. On telescoping. In Chris Barker and David Dowty, eds., *SALT II: Proceedings from the Second Confeence on Semantics and Linguistic Theory*, 347–366. Columbus: Department of Linguistics, Ohio State University.

Postal, Paul. 1966. On so-called "pronouns" in English. In F. Dinneen, ed., *Report on the Seventeenth Annual Round Table Meeting on Linguistics and Language Studies*, 177–206. Washington, DC: Georgetown University Press.

Pustejovsky, James. 2000. Events and the semantics of opposition. In Carol Tenny and James Pustejovsky, eds., *Events as Grammatical Objects: The Converging Perspectives of Lexical Semantics and Syntax*, 445–482. Stanford, CA: CSLI Publications.

Pylkkänen, Liina. 2000. On stativity and causation. In Carol Tenny and James Pustejovsky, eds., *Events as Grammatical Objects: The Converging Perspectives of Lexical Semantics and Syntax*, 417–444. Stanford, CA: CSLI Publications.

Recanati, François. 1993. *Direct Reference: From Language to Thought.* Oxford: Blackwell.

Reimer, Marga. 1998. Donnellan's distinction/Kripke's test. *Analysis* 58, 89–100.

Reinhart, Tanya. 1983. *Anaphora and Semantic Interpretation.* London: Croom Helm.

Reinhart, Tanya. 1997. Strategies of anaphora resolution. Utrecht Institute of Linguistics OTS Working Paper TL97-007. Universiteit Utrecht.

Roberts, Craige. 1987. Modal Subordination, Anaphora, and Distributivity. Doctoral dissertation, University of Massachusetts at Amherst.

Roberts, Craige. 1989. Modal subordination and pronominal anaphora in discourse. *Linguistics and Philosophy* 12, 683–721.

Roberts, Craige. 1996. Anaphora in intensional contexts. In Shalom Lappin, ed., *The Handbook of Contemporary Semantic Theory*, 215–246. Oxford: Blackwell.

Rodman, Robert. 1976. Scope phenomena, "movement transformations," and relative clauses. In Barbara Partee, ed., *Montague Grammar*, 165–176. New York: Academic Press.

Rooth, Mats. 1992a. Ellipsis redundancy and reduction redundancy. In Stephen Berman and Arild Hestvik, eds., *Proceedings of the Stuttgart Ellipsis Workshop.* Arbeitspapiere des Sonderforschungsbereichs 340, Bericht Nr. 29. Heidelberg: IBM Germany.

Rooth, Mats. 1992b. A theory of focus interpretation. *Natural Language Semantics* 1, 75–116.

Ross, John. 1967. Constraints on Variables in Syntax. Doctoral dissertation, MIT.

Russell, Bertrand. 1903. *The Principles of Mathematics.* Cambridge: Cambridge University Press.

Russell, Bertrand. 1905. On denoting. *Mind* 14, 479–493.

Ruys, Eddy. 1993. *The Scope of Indefinites*. Utrecht: OTS Dissertation Series.

Saito, Mamoru, and Keiko Murasugi. 1989. N'-deletion in Japanese: A preliminary study. Paper presented at the 1989 Southern California Japanese/Korean Linguistics Conference.

Sauerland, Uli. 2000. The content of pronouns: Evidence from focus. In Brendan Jackson and Tanya Matthews, eds., *Proceedings from Semantics and Linguistic Theory X*, 167–184. Ithaca, NY: CLC Publications.

Sauerland, Uli. 2002. The silent content of bound variable pronouns. Unpublished manuscript, Universität Tübingen. Final version to appear in Kyle Johnson, ed., *Topics in Ellipsis*, Cambridge University Press.

Schein, Barry. 1993. *Plurals and Events*. Cambridge, MA: MIT Press.

Schein, Barry. 2001. Adverbial, descriptive reciprocals. In Rachel Hastings, Brendan Jackson, and Zsofia Zvolenszky, eds., *Proceedings of Semantics and Linguistic Theory XI*, 404–430. Ithaca, NY: CLC Publications.

Schwarz, Bernhard. 2000. Topics in Ellipsis. PhD dissertation, University of Massachusetts at Amherst.

Schwarzschild, Roger. 1992. Types of plural individuals. *Linguistics and Philosophy* 15, 641–675.

Schwarzschild, Roger. 1999. Givenness, AvoidF and other constraints on the placement of accent. *Natural Language Semantics* 7, 141–177.

Sells, Peter. 1984. Syntax and Semantics of Resumptive Pronouns. Doctoral dissertation, University of Massachusetts at Amherst.

Sharvit, Yael. 1999. Resumptive pronouns in relative clauses. *Natural Language and Linguistic Theory* 17, 587–612.

Smullyan, Arthur F. 1948. Modality and description. *Journal of Symbolic Logic* 13, 31–37.

Soames, Scott. 1987. Direct reference, propositional attitudes, and semantic content. *Philosophical Topics* 15, 47–87.

Soames, Scott. 1989. Semantics and semantic competence. *Philosophical Perspectives* 3, 575–596.

Soames, Scott. 2002. *Beyond Rigidity: The Unfinished Semantic Agenda of Naming and Necessity*. Oxford: Oxford University Press.

Sommers, Fred. 1982. *The Logic of Natural Language*. Oxford: Clarendon Press.

Stalnaker, Robert. 1968. A theory of conditionals. In Nicholas Rescher, ed., *Studies in Logical Theory*, 98–112. Oxford: Blackwell.

Stalnaker, Robert. 1979. Assertion. In Peter Cole, ed., *Syntax and Semantics 9: Pragmatics*, 315–332. New York: Academic Press.

Stanley, Jason. 1997. Names and rigid designation. In Bob Hale and Crispin Wright, eds., *A Companion to the Philosophy of Language*, 555–585. Oxford: Blackwell.

Steedman, Mark. 2000. *The Syntactic Process*. Cambridge, MA: MIT Press.

Stockwell, Robert, Paul Schachter, and Barbara Hall Partee. 1973. *The Major Syntactic Structures of English*. New York: Holt, Rinehart and Winston.

Stone, Matthew. 1992. *Or* and anaphora. In Chris Barker and David Dowty, eds., *SALT II: Proceedings from the Second Conference on Semantics and Linguistic Theory*, 367–385. Columbus: Department of Linguistics, Ohio State University.

Suñer, Margarita. 1998. Resumptive relative clauses: a cross-linguistic perspective. *Language* 74, 335–364.

Tenny, Carol, and James Pustejovsky. 2000. *Events as Grammatical Objects: The Converging Perspectives of Lexical Semantics and Syntax*. Stanford, CA: CSLI Publications.

Tomioka, Satoshi. 1997. Focusing Effects and NP Interpretation in VP Ellipsis. Doctoral dissertation, University of Massachusetts at Amherst.

Tomioka, Satoshi. 1999. A sloppy identity puzzle. *Natural Language Semantics* 7, 217–241.

Uriagereka, Juan. 1995. Aspects of the syntax of clitic placement in Western Romance. *Linguistic Inquiry* 26, 79–123.

van Benthem, Johan. 1995. *Language in Action: Categories, Lambdas, and Dynamic Logic*. Cambridge, MA: MIT Press.

van der Sandt, Rob. 1992. Presupposition projection as anaphora resolution. *Journal of Semantics* 9, 333–377.

van Eijck, Jan, and Hans Kamp. 1997. Representing discourse in context. In Johan van Benthem and Alice ter Meulen, eds., *Handbook of Logic and Language*, 179–237. Amsterdam and Cambridge, MA: Elsevier and MIT Press.

Webber, Bonnie. 1978. A Formal Approach to Discourse Anaphora. Doctoral dissertation, Harvard University.

Williams, Edwin. 1977. Discourse and logical form. *Linguistic Inquiry* 8, 101–139.

Winter, Yoad. 2001. *Flexibility Principles in Boolean Semantics: The Interpretation of Coordination, Plurality, and Scope in Natural Language*. Cambridge, MA: MIT Press.

Yang, Charles. 1999. Unordered merge and its linearization. *Syntax* 2, 38–64.

Zeevat, Henk. 1992. Presupposition and accommodation in update semantics. *Journal of Semantics* 9, 379–412.

Index

Abney, Steven, 81, 203
Antecedents for ellipsis, 44–45, 84–89, 203
Aoun, Joseph, 133–134, 161, 212
Apposition, 43, 134
Arabic, Lebanese, 133–135
Armstrong, David, 10, 48, 148, 204

Bach, Emmon, 79–80, 187, 203–204
Bach-Peters sentences, 79, 203
Barwise, Jon, 48, 54–55, 204, 213
Bäuerle, Rainer, 100, 104–105
Beaver, David, 61–62
Benmamoun, Elabbas, 133–135, 212
Berman, Stephen, 9–10, 48
Burge, Tyler, 88, 169–172, 177–179, 181–182, 184, 216–217
Büring, Daniel, 205

Categorial grammar, 4, 201, 203, 207
C-command, 3, 20, 34, 36, 39, 42, 134
Centering theory, 32
Chierchia, Gennaro, 22–24, 26–27, 30–31, 33, 65, 83–84, 202
Cho, Sungeun, 82–83, 206
Chomsky, Noam, 3, 66, 119, 179, 204, 209, 216
Chomsky-adjunction, 66
Choueiri, Lina, 135, 212
Clitic left-dislocation, 133–135, 211
Collective reading, 154
Common ground, 13
Compositionality, 13
Conditionals, 9–10, 17, 51–52, 57, 70–75, 146, 182
Condition C, 180, 185, 215
Conjunction, 76, 85, 111, 154–155
Context, 13
Cooper, Robin, 7–8, 11, 22, 28, 68, 81, 202
Coordinate Structure Constraint, 76, 105, 111, 153–154

Coordinate subjects, problem of, 145–146, 186
Copy theory of movement, 96, 113, 119

Davidson, Donald, 186
Davies, Martin, 6
Deep anaphora, problem of, 20, 39, 186, 202
Definite article, 1–2, 8, 41–44, 80, 84, 88, 93, 95–120, 122, 124, 130, 135, 170, 172, 176, 185, 207, 217. See also Definite descriptions
Definite descriptions, 1–2, 5, 11, 19, 23, 33, 39–40, 62, 81, 84, 93, 98–120, 123, 130, 136–137, 163–165, 169, 172, 174, 181, 184–185, 217
  attributive, 115–120, 135
  bound, 112–115, 117, 120, 135, 164, 180, 209
  de dicto readings of, 6–7, 99–100, 102–106, 111, 209
  de re readings of, 7, 99–100, 102–106, 111, 202, 208–209
  D-type, 42, 180
  Fregean analysis of, 93, 96–100, 102–112, 173, 202, 208–209
  genitival, 114–115, 118
  incomplete, 130–131, 151–152, 165
  nondenoting, 99, 106–109
  referential, 115–120, 135
  Russellian analysis of, 98–100, 104, 106, 109–112, 201–202, 208
  uniqueness presuppositions of, 9, 39, 61–64, 98–99, 110, 118, 120, 186
Demonstratives, 116, 121, 125, 162, 171, 173, 201, 210–211, 214–215, 218
Determiner Phrases (DPs), 8, 43–44, 65, 82, 84, 104, 131, 153, 167
  possessive 82–83, 179, 210
Direct reference, 1–2, 169, 171, 176, 181–182, 184, 211, 216, 217

Discourse Representation Theory (DRT), 13, 18
Disjunctive antecedents, problem of, 19–20, 39, 186, 202
Distributive reading, 154
Donkey anaphora, 1–2, 4–6, 164–165, 207
description-theoretic theories of, 3–11, 201–202
D-type theories of, 5, 7–12, 20, 22–28, 30–31, 33, 39–40, 41–92, 95, 137–157, 164, 180–181, 185–186, 202–203
dynamic theories of, 12–33, 92, 122, 138, 145–146, 156–157, 159, 165, 168, 185–186, 202
E-type theory of, 5–7
NP-deletion theory of, 42–92, 123, 139–140, 164–165, 206
Variable-free theory of, 34–39, 70–71, 122, 166, 168, 185–186
Donnellan, Keith, 116–117, 119, 210
Doron, Edit, 211
Dynamic Montague Grammar, 13
Dynamic Predicate Logic (DPL), 13–19, 25, 146, 202
Dynamic semantics, 3–5, 9, 12–33, 39, 92, 122, 145–146, 156–157, 165, 168, 202

Elbourne, Paul, 204
Ellipsis, 31, 45, 66, 68–79, 82, 84–91, 105, 130, 203–204. *See also* NP-deletion
Evans, Gareth, 5–7, 201, 216
Events, 25, 142–145, 186–187, 219

Farkas, Donka, 100
Fiengo, Robert, 85, 91
Focus, 126–131, 136
Formal link, problem of, 11, 38–40, 45, 64–68, 92, 137, 185–186
Fox, Danny, 68, 105, 119, 167, 206
Frege, Gottlob, 93, 96–97, 100, 104, 106–110, 112, 173, 202, 208, 211
Functional application, 50, 96

Gardent, Claire, 31, 33
Gawron, Jean Mark, 206
Geach, Peter, 4, 21, 201
German, 47, 87, 172
Glanzberg, Michael, 216, 218
Gleitman, Lila, 213
Greek, classical, 87, 172, 211
Grice, H. Paul, 126, 219
Gricean maxims, 126, 219
Grodzinsky, Yosef, 167, 215
Groenendijk, Jeroen, 13, 16–17, 19, 30, 84, 202
Grosz, Barbara, 32

Hankamer, Jorge, 20, 45, 203
Hardt, Dan, 31–33, 91, 207
Hebrew, 132, 212
Heim, Irene, 3–4, 7–12, 22–25, 41, 48, 50, 56, 58–59, 64–68, 80, 83, 94–98, 100–101, 109, 112–115, 137, 140–141, 151–152, 167, 181, 187, 202–204, 207–216, 218
Higginbotham, James, 161, 216, 219
Hinrichs, Erhard, 187
Hoji, Hajime, 162, 214
Hornstein, Norbert, 161, 212
Huang, C.-T. James, 161–162

Iatridou, Sabine, 206
Indices, 1, 4, 93–98, 113, 115–118, 120–123, 126, 128–129, 132, 135, 173–174, 176, 181, 207, 215, 217
Indistinguishable participants, problem of, 2, 11, 38–40, 59, 137–157, 185–186, 214
Individual concept, 108
Intensional abstraction, 101
Irish, 132
Islands for movement, 3–4, 76, 105, 133–134
Italian, 178

Jacobson, Pauline, 4, 20, 34–35, 39, 70–71, 79, 130, 166, 203
Jackendoff, Ray, 42, 44
Japanese, 2, 26–30, 159–168, 186, 202, 214–215
Joshi, Aravind, 32

Kadmon, Nirit, 11, 64, 140
Kamp, Hans, 11–12, 18–19, 137, 218
Kanazawa, Makoto, 212
Kaplan, David, 169, 183, 201, 218
Karttunen, Lauri, 12, 81, 107–108, 110, 202
Katada, Fusa, 161
Kayne, Richard, 215
King, Jeffrey, 201, 211
Kratzer, Angelika, 3–4, 7–10, 41, 48–49, 50, 54–56, 68, 94–98, 100–101, 113, 204, 207, 210–211
Krifka, Manfred, 187
Kripke, Saul, 1, 5, 61, 116, 169–170, 173–178, 183–184, 201, 216, 218
Kurafuji, Takeo, 22, 25–31, 202

Lakoff, George, 76
Lambda-conversion, 50
Lambda-operator, 3–4, 8, 70, 95, 97, 120, 132, 204, 208, 211, 213
Landman, Fred, 154, 213
Language acquisition, 1, 123, 185
Larson, Richard, 82–83, 88, 151, 169, 171–172, 187, 206, 208–209, 216

Lasnik, Howard, 44, 203
Latin, 182, 211
Lewis, David, 182
Link, Godehard, 43, 154–155, 187, 203, 208, 213
Loar, Brian, 177
Lobeck, Anne, 46, 204
Logical Form (LF), 3, 8, 34, 41–42, 48, 51–53, 68, 76, 80, 82, 89, 94, 101–103, 105, 111–112, 114, 129, 140, 146–147, 152–154, 203, 206, 208–209
Longobardi, Giuseppe, 178–179, 203
Ludlow, Peter, 142, 145, 212

May, Robert, 3, 76, 85, 91
Merchant, Jason, 68
Miyagawa, Shigeru, 29
Modal subordination, 79–81
Montague, Richard, 2, 8
Montalbetti, Mario, 161
Murasugi, Keiko, 44–45

Names. See Proper names
Neale, Stephen, 5, 7–9, 65–67, 99–100, 106, 138–140, 201–202, 205, 209, 212
Neontological pronouns, problem of, 20–33, 39, 186
Noguchi, Tohru, 159, 161–163, 214–215
Noun Phrases (NPs), 1–2, 43, 65–66, 82, 93, 95, 97, 103, 113, 115, 123–124, 130–132, 135
NP-deletion, 2, 42, 44–47, 80–81, 85–87, 98, 123–124, 130, 203. See also Donkey anaphora
NP-deletion theory of ONE, 124–126, 185

Ostertag, Gary, 208

Pāṇini, 186
Parsons, Terence, 186–187, 212
Partee, Barbara, 2, 20, 30, 46, 155, 202–203
Particulars
  thick, 48–49, 148–150, 204
  thin, 10, 48–49, 148–150
Partitive constructions, 46
Peacocke, Christopher, 116
Pelletier, Jeffry, 23, 83
Percus, Orin, 100–101
Perlmutter, David, 42, 44, 46
Perry, John, 48, 54–55, 204, 213
Persistence, 54–56
Peters, Stanley, 79–80, 108, 203
Plurality, 43, 154–155, 203, 208, 213–214
Poesio, Massimo, 31
Pollard, Carl, 91
Possessives, 82–83
Possible worlds, 10, 108, 183, 219

Postal, Paul, 41–43
Predicate abstraction, 50, 95, 97, 204, 208
Predicate Logic, first-order, 13, 17, 67, 138
Predicate modification, 50, 113, 115
Presupposition, 9, 39, 61–63, 69, 78–79, 82, 97, 107–110, 114, 118, 120
Principle C, 180, 185, 215
Pronominal ambiguity, problem of, 12, 39–40, 92, 137, 185–186
Pronouns, 1, 113, 176
  Arabic, 133–135
  argument structure of, 122–135, 169, 172, 184–185
  bound, 2–3, 18–19, 34–35, 38, 40, 93–98, 126–131, 134–136, 159–160
  clitic, 133–135, 211
  donkey, 2, 4–92
  dynamically bound, 12–33
  D-type, 7–11, 20, 22–28, 30, 33, 40, 41–92, 95, 135
  E-type, 5–7 focused, 126–131, 136
  Japanese, 2, 26–30, 159–168, 186, 214–215
  of laziness, 20–21
  neontological, 20–33, 39, 186
  number features of, 139–140
  paycheck, 20–21, 79, 81–83
  phonologically null, 26–27
  referential, 2, 19, 27, 34, 38, 40, 93–98, 135, 159–160
  reflexive, 161
  and relative clauses, 120–122, 186
  resumptive, 131–136, 211
Proper names, 1–2, 40, 87–88, 123, 169–185, 216–219
Proportion problem, 212
Propositional attitudes, 35, 102–105, 107–110
Pustejovsky, James, 187
Pylkkänen, Liina, 187

Quantificational adverbs, 10, 51–52, 57, 71–75, 78, 140, 206, 210
Quantificational subordination, 79–81
Quantifier domain restriction, 56, 202–203
Quantifier phrases (QPs), 53, 74–77, 105, 154, 161, 211, 213
Quantifier raising (QR), 3–4, 52–53, 56, 76, 94, 104–105, 147, 154, 161, 209, 213
Quantifiers, 112, 114
  generalized, 1–3, 6, 31, 33, 70, 125–126, 205, 208, 212
  phonologically null, 10, 73, 78, 210
  in situation semantics, 53–64

Recanati, François, 173, 177, 181, 217
Reconstruction, 133–134

Reimer, Marga, 210
Reinhart, Tanya, 2–3, 159, 167, 215
Relative clauses, 131–132, 163
 following demonstratives, 121
 following pronouns, 120–122
Rigid designators, 1–2, 5–7, 169, 175–177,
 183–184
Roberts, Craige, 30, 80, 206
Rodman, Robert, 76
Rooth, Mats, 2, 20, 68, 127, 155
Ross, John Robert, 3, 76
Ruys, Eddy, 76
Rule I, 2, 159, 167–168, 215
Russell, Bertrand, 98–100, 104, 106, 109–
 112, 201–202, 208

Sag, Ivan, 20, 45, 203
Saito, Mamoru, 4445, 203
Sanskrit, 211
Sauerland, Uli, 126–131, 204, 211
Schachter, Paul, 46, 203
Schein, Barry, 142–145, 202, 212, 219
Schiffer, Stephen, 209
Schubert, Lenhart, 23, 83
Schwarz, Bernhard, 84, 91, 207
Schwarzschild, Roger, 127, 129–130, 213
Scope freezing, 105
Segal, Gabriel, 88, 151, 169, 171–172, 187,
 208–209, 216
Sells, Peter, 211
Sharvit, Yael, 131–132, 211–212
Situations, 9–10, 39, 42, 48–49, 148–150,
 186–187. *See also* Situation semantics
 extensions of, 10, 49
 minimal, 10–11, 23, 25, 49, 147
Situation semantics, 48–51, 137, 186–187
 of quantifiers, 53–64, 147–150
Sloppy interpretation in ellipsis, 32, 68–79,
 89–90, 92, 205, 215
Smullyan, Arthur, 100
Soames, Scott, 216–217, 219
Sommers, Fred, 5
Spanish, 87, 132
Split antecedents, 84–89
Stalnaker, Robert, 12, 182
Stanley, Jason, 217
States of affairs, 48–49, 148
Steedman, Mark, 201
Stockwell, Robert, 46, 203
Stokhof, Martin, 13, 16–17, 19, 30, 84, 202
Stone, Matthew, 19–20, 84
Strict interpretation in ellipsis, 68–79, 89–
 90, 92, 205, 215
Strong readings of donkey sentences, 22–23,
 83–84, 202
Sub-categorization, 115
Suñer, Margarita, 131

Tarski, Alfred, 93, 116
Tenny, Carol, 187
Thematic roles, 142, 144
Tomioka, Satoshi, 68, 89–91, 207
Topic, 29–30, 32
Trace conversion, 119–120, 135
Traces, 4, 50, 94, 96–97, 113, 119–120, 131–
 135, 207, 212
Traces and pronouns rule, 94–97
Truth, 16
Truth conditions, 13
Type-shifting, 34–39, 70–71, 87, 166, 207

Universal Grammar, 1, 185
Universals, 48
Uriagereka, Juan, 203

van Benthem, Johan, 207
van der Sandt, Rob, 62
van Eijck, Jan, 13, 18–19
Variable assignments, 13–14, 18, 20, 31, 34–
 35, 50, 58, 93–97, 112–114, 116, 118, 145,
 202
Variable-free semantics, 4–5, 34–39, 70–71,
 122, 166, 168, 176, 201
von Fintel, Kai, 9, 48, 56, 87, 100–101, 131,
 203, 206, 208, 212, 214, 217

Weak readings of donkey sentences, 22–23,
 83–84, 202
Webber, Bonnie, 85
Weinstein, Scott, 32
Williams, Alexander, 207
Williams, Edwin, 66
Winter, Yoad, 214

Yang, Charles, 204

Zeevat, Henk, 62
Zucchi, Alessandro, 31

Current Studies in Linguistics
Samuel Jay Keyser, general editor

1. *A Reader on the Sanskrit Grammarians*, J. F. Staal, editor
2. *Semantic Interpretation in Generative Grammar*, Ray Jackendoff
3. *The Structure of the Japanese Language*, Susumu Kuno
4. *Speech Sounds and Features*, Gunnar Fant
5. *On Raising: One Rule of English Grammar and Its Theoretical Implications*, Paul M. Postal
6. *French Syntax: The Transformational Cycle*, Richard S. Kayne
7. *Panini as a Variationist*, Paul Kiparsky and S. D. Joshi, editors
8. *Semantics and Cognition*, Ray Jackendoff
9. *Modularity in Syntax: A Study of Japanese and English*, Ann Kathleen Farmer
10. *Phonology and Syntax: The Relation between Sound and Structure*, Elisabeth O. Selkirk
11. *The Grammatical Basis of Linguistic Performance: Language Use and Acquisition*, Robert C. Berwick and Amy S. Weinberg
12. *Introduction to the Theory of Grammar*, Henk van Riemsdijk and Edwin Williams
13. *Word and Sentence Prosody in Serbocroatian*, Ilse Lehiste and Pavle Ivic
14. *The Representation of (In)definiteness*, Eric J. Reuland and Alice G. B. ter Meulen, editors
15. *An Essay on Stress*, Morris Halle and Jean-Roger Vergnaud
16. *Language and Problems of Knowledge: The Managua Lectures*, Noam Chomsky
17. *A Course in GB Syntax: Lectures on Binding and Empty Categories*, Howard Lasnik and Juan Uriagereka
18. *Semantic Structures*, Ray Jackendoff
19. *Events in the Semantics of English: A Study in Subatomic Semantics*, Terence Parsons
20. *Principles and Parameters in Comparative Grammar*, Robert Freidin, editor
21. *Foundations of Generative Syntax*, Robert Freidin
22. *Move α: Conditions on Its Application and Output*, Howard Lasnik and Mamoru Saito
23. *Plurals and Events*, Barry Schein
24. *The View from Building 20: Essays in Linguistics in Honor of Sylvain Bromberger*, Kenneth Hale and Samuel Jay Keyser, editors
25. *Grounded Phonology*, Diana Archangeli and Douglas Pulleyblank
26. *The Magic of a Common Language: Jakobson, Mathesius, Trubetzkoy, and the Prague Linguistic Circle*, Jindrich Toman
27. *Zero Syntax: Experiencers and Cascades*, David Pesetsky
28. *The Minimalist Program*, Noam Chomsky
29. *Three Investigations of Extraction*, Paul M. Postal
30. *Acoustic Phonetics*, Kenneth N. Stevens
31. *Principle B, VP Ellipsis, and Interpretation in Child Grammar*, Rosalind Thornton and Kenneth Wexler

32. *Working Minimalism*, Samuel Epstein and Norbert Hornstein, editors
33. *Syntactic Structures Revisited: Contemporary Lectures on Classic Transformational Theory*, Howard Lasnik with Marcela Depiante and Arthur Stepanov
34. *Verbal Complexes*, Hilda Koopman and Anna Szabolcsi
35. *Parasitic Gaps*, Peter W. Culicover and Paul M. Postal
36. *Ken Hale: A Life in Language*, Michael Kenstowicz, editor
37. *Flexibility Principles in Boolean Semantics: The Interpretation of Coordination, Plurality, and Scope in Natural Language*, Yoad Winter
38. *Phrase Structure Composition and Syntactic Dependencies*, Robert Frank
39. *Representation Theory*, Edwin Williams
40. *The Syntax of Time*, Jacqueline Gueron and Jacqueline Lecarme, editors
41. *Situations and Individuals*, Paul D. Elbourne